TRACING YOUR
BIRMINGHAM
ANCESTORS

FAMILY HISTORY FROM PEN & SWORD BOOKS

For more details see www.pen-and-sword.co.uk.

TRACING YOUR BIRMINGHAM ANCESTORS

A Guide for Family Historians

MICHAEL SHARPE

Pen & Sword
FAMILY HISTORY

First published in Great Britain in 2015 by
Pen & Sword Family History
an imprint of
Pen & Sword Books Ltd
47 Church Street
Barnsley
South Yorkshire
S70 2AS

ISBN 978 1 47383 344 9

A CIP catalogue record for this book is
available from the British Library

Typeset in 10pt Palatino by Mac Style Ltd, Bridlington, East Yorkshire
Printed and bound in the UK by CPI Group (UK) Ltd, Croydon, CRO 4YY

Pen & Sword Books Ltd incorporates the imprints of Pen & Sword
Archaeology, Atlas, Aviation, Battleground, Discovery, Family History,
History, Maritime, Military, Naval, Politics, Railways, Select, Social
History, Transport, True Crime, and Claymore Press, Frontline Books,
Leo Cooper, Praetorian Press, Remember When, Seaforth Publishing
and Wharncliffe.

For a complete list of Pen & Sword titles please contact
PEN & SWORD BOOKS LIMITED
47 Church Street, Barnsley, South Yorkshire, S70 2AS, England
E-mail: enquiries@pen-and-sword.co.uk
Website: www.pen-and-sword.co.uk

CONTENTS

ACKNOWLEDGEMENTS

A book such as this requires research on a broad range of subjects and specialties. I have been aided in this task by family historians, archivists and researchers across Birmingham and the wider Midlands region. Their experience has been invaluable and I would like to thank them all.

Special thanks are due to friends and colleagues in the Birmingham & Midland Society for Genealogy and Heraldry for their support and advice, in particular Bernie and Mary McLean (Chairman and Reference Librarian respectively), Steve Freeman (Bookshop Manager), and Jackie Cotterill (General Secretary). Dr Anthony Joseph also kindly offered comments on parts of the text.

I am indebted to staff at the Library of Birmingham for their help and advice in verifying sources and references, and their general assistance in ensuring the text is accurate and up to date. Staff at Staffordshire & Stoke-on-Trent Archives, Warwickshire County Record Office, and Worcestershire Archives & Archaeology Service also gave generously of their time in responding to my enquiries.

The following kindly gave permission to use photographs from their own private collections: Mark Norton, custodian of the work of his father Dennis John Norton; Chris Myers, owner of the Staffs Home Guard website; and Roger Mace, a fellow researcher and correspondent. The use of the work of Birmingham photographers Keith Berry and Phyllis Nicklin, now in the public domain, is also acknowledged.

Any errors and omissions remain my own.

ABBREVIATIONS

AHP	Archives, Heritage & Photography (at the Library of Birmingham)
BAA	Birmingham Archdiocesan Archives
BCC	Birmingham City Council
BCol	Birmingham Collection, The (at the Library of Birmingham)
BMAG	Birmingham Museums & Art Gallery
BMDs	births, marriages and deaths
BMSGH	Birmingham & Midland Society for Genealogy and Heraldry
BSA	Birmingham Small Arms Company
CRO	county record office
FHS	family history society
GENUKI	Genealogy UK and Ireland (website)
GRO	General Register Office
LDS	Church of Jesus Christ of Latter Day Saints
LoB	Library of Birmingham
LRO	Lichfield Record Office
MDR	Manorial Documents Register
NRA	National Register of Archives
PCC	Prerogative Court of Canterbury
PS	Petty Sessions
QS	Quarter Sessions
SSA	Staffordshire & Stoke-on-Trent Archives
TNA	The National Archives
TYAIB	Tracing Your Ancestors in Birmingham (a BMSGH website)
TYAIW	Tracing Your Ancestors in Warwickshire (a BMSGH website)
UoB	University of Birmingham, Cadbury Research Library
WAAS	Worcestershire Archives & Archaeology Service
WCRO	Warwickshire County Record Office
WMRC	University of Warwick, Modern Records Centre

INTRODUCTION

The Workshop of the World

This book is about Birmingham: how it shaped the modern world and how you can find your ancestors there.

Birmingham's transformation from provincial backwater to the first manufacturing town in the world is one of the most remarkable stories in economic history. Over a period of around 150 years, between 1700 and 1850, this small town on the edge of Warwickshire became a microcosm for the Industrial Revolution. Driven by the values of the Midlands Enlightenment – a conviction that science and industry should be applied to improve the human condition – the townsfolk of Birmingham began not just to make things, but to continually improve what they made: in other words, to innovate.

They started small, with guns, jewellery, buttons and other portable items, and gradually moved into a panoply of industrial and domestic metal goods. Everything from brass bedsteads and cabinet fittings, to domestic utensils and silver teapots, to the first transatlantic telegraph cable issued from Birmingham's workshops and factories to be distributed far and wide by the networks of canals and railways put in place for exactly that purpose. More than any other city, Birmingham can claim to have, literally, made the modern world. London had the money; Manchester and Leeds had important commodities such as cotton and linen; Liverpool and Bristol had the ships. But only in the Midlands, and in Birmingham especially, was there such diverse abilities to make things. Through its innovation and ingenuity Birmingham became known as 'the workshop of the world'.

On the face of it, Birmingham's economic success was surprising. Located at the centre of an upland area in the English Midlands some distance from a navigable river, it was relatively inaccessible in geographical terms. It was not a port or on the coast. It had no natural resources to speak of: no coal, or timber or precious metals. Nor was the area particularly productive for agriculture or livestock. Birmingham was not a county town, and indeed before 1700 barely registered on the national scene at all.

Furthermore, in Birmingham the pattern of development differed to that in the northern cities in important ways. Economic activity was characterised by artisan craftsmen operating in small-scale workshops with diverse outputs, rather than unskilled operators working in large standardized factories dedicated to a single product or sector. And the town's landlocked location made it highly dependent on transport infrastructure, both to bring raw materials in and take finished goods out.

But there is more to Birmingham's story than simply geography and economics. It is a city with a resilient working class, industrious entrepreneurs, a strong reforming tradition, and a rich cultural heritage. For family historians, this means that we may find our ancestors in many settings and across all social classes and religious groups. While, in all likelihood, they will be living in a back-to-back in Aston, do not be surprised if your ancestor was a performer in one of the many theatres, a school teacher, or a doctor. Even working in the manufacturing trades they are likely to have been highly skilled.

Brum and Brummies

The name Birmingham probably dates from Anglo-Saxon times. It is believed to derive from: 'Beorma', an Anglo-Saxon name; 'ing', meaning tribe or people; and 'ham', meaning home. Thus, Beorma-ing-ham would have been a settlement founded either by a leader called Beorma, or by a people named after him.

Today, 'Brummagem' or 'Brum' are in common usage and the people are known as 'Brummies'. Although these terms may sound like nineteenth-century slang, in fact they have a long heritage. 'Brummagem' was one of many variations in place-names used over the years. It arose in the Middle Ages when the 'r' and the 'i' or 'e' in Birmingham or Bermingham were reversed. This was not an isolated occurrence: for example, the word bird was 'brid' in Old English. A document of 1189, for instance, spells the surname of the lord of the manor as 'de Brummingeham' and in 1200 a property transaction notes 'Brimingham'. This was a common spelling by the early fifteenth century and Morden's Map of Warwickshire in 1695 states 'Brimingham alias Birmingham'.

Other spelling variations contributed to the confusion. The variants 'Bir', 'Ber' and 'Bur' were all used, while a series of linguistic substitutions resulted in 'ingham' being replaced by forms such as 'incham', 'echam', 'egem' and eventually 'agem'. Historians have counted 144 different spellings within the documentary record, some examples being 'Bermincham' in a patent roll of 1245, 'Burmicham' in 1317, and Brymecham in 1402. By the 1600s Brummagem had become accepted widely, as evidenced in a pamphlet published during the Civil War which refers to 'Brumagem'.

The activities of forgers and counterfeiters, such as the notorious William Booth of Great Barr, gave the area a poor reputation, and Brummagem came to mean cheap, showy or counterfeit. In an attempt to counter prejudice against Brummagem goods, eighteenth-century industrialists appear to have encouraged the use of the name Birmingham. Brummagem came to be viewed as an inferior moniker, used in 'vulgar' or popular speech only. This was never true of 'Brummie', however, as no alternative term for the Birmingham townsfolk evolved.

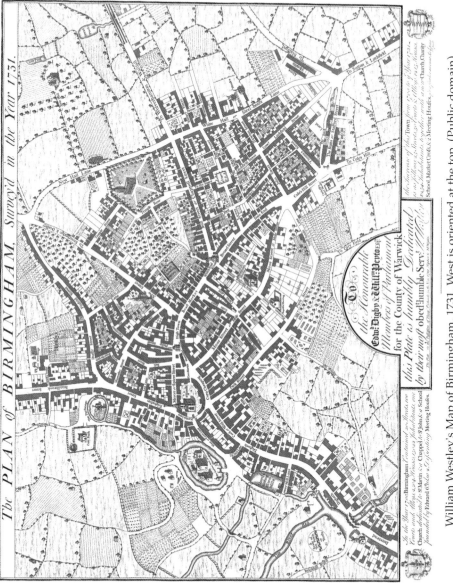

William Westley's Map of Birmingham, 1731. West is oriented at the top. (Public domain)

The Birmingham accent is often derided and frequently comes top in polls of the most annoying forms of English speech. Yet it, too, has a rich heritage and linguistically is thought to be the closest surviving form to the way Shakespeare spoke. Calls such as 'where yo' goin?', 'ee are ma wench', and 'tara a bit' resounded through the terraces of back-to-back houses that made up working-class Birmingham. The sharp-eared could even distinguish between the flatter tones of the northern districts, such as Aston, and the slightly softer speech of southern districts, such as Sparkbrook. When many of these folk were moved on during the post-war redevelopment of the city, they took the language with them to the suburbs and new estates. In places such as Acocks Green, Cotteridge and Shirley, the Brummie town speech has been tinged by more rural tones from areas that were once villages in Worcestershire and Warwickshire. The accent differs markedly from that of the adjacent Black Country, although outsiders often struggle to tell them apart. Like local dialects everywhere, Brummie continues to evolve, taking on words and speech patterns from the African Caribbean and South Asian communities, among others.

Researching in Birmingham

Birmingham's position as an economic hub and its proud manufacturing heritage make it an important focus for family historians. Many researchers will find that their trail leads through here in one way or another. Over the centuries, rural migrants, Quakers, Jews, Irish and Italians have all made Birmingham their home. In recent times they have been joined by people from the Caribbean, South-Asia and China. While not unique, the historical themes highlighted above bring particular interest to researching in the city.

Birmingham is, and always has been, a melting pot. The influxes of people that fuelled its rapid growth in population mean that most researchers will have to address the issue of migration at some point. Although you may think of yourself as a 'true Brummie', in all likelihood your Birmingham ancestry runs back only three or four generations. Most 'Birmingham people' in fact came from somewhere else and finding that your family has been in the town for centuries is unusual rather than the norm (though there are plenty of sources that will help you here too). So it is essential to determine exactly when your Birmingham ancestry starts and to be on the lookout for the all-important clues that may lead back elsewhere.

The second aspect is faith. The economic opportunities in Birmingham and its reputation for religious tolerance attracted people of all faiths and creeds. Quakers were just one of many dissenting protestant groups who settled in the town during the religious turbulence of the seventeenth and eighteenth centuries. Roman Catholics, too, were subject to persecution and saw the Midlands as one of their collective strongholds. In later years their numbers were swelled by Catholic migrants from Ireland, Italy and Central and Eastern Europe. So do not assume that your Birmingham ancestors were Anglican; you may also need to look at Roman Catholic, non-conformist and other faith records as well as those of the Church of England.

Administrative hurdles are another factor. Overlapping jurisdictions and constant boundary changes (see below) mean that as a researcher you need to keep a tight focus on locations and period to make sure you are researching in the right records and are in the right archive. The digitization of records and their release online mean this is less of an issue than it used to be. Even so, each website or database can have different datasets, so it is essential to know what is, and what is not, covered.

The dominance of small-scale manufacturing and retail businesses in the city's development is to the benefit of family historians. These types of businesses are likely to have left a significant documentary trail within business-related sources, such as apprenticeship records, trade directories, rate books, newspaper advertisements, solicitors' records, and licensing applications of various forms. Hence, we have a better chance of being able to find out more about our ancestors' lives and occupations than if they were working in a large factory or down a mine.

Researching in Birmingham has its challenges. Finding where people came from before they got to Birmingham can be difficult, especially in the pre-census period. Records may not be where we think they are for administrative or religious reasons. Birmingham's late arrival on the national scene means important sources – such as Quarter Sessions records and wills – are not located within the city (or at least they do not originate there; in some cases modern copies and transcriptions have been made).

The greatest challenge, perhaps, is simply being able to find our ancestors and then keep track of them within the mass of urban populace. People lived hand-to-mouth and moved frequently, especially in immigrant communities at the bottom of the social ladder. Often people could not read or write and had similar surnames (or foreign names become changed or corrupted from their original form). The issues here are no different to researching in London or any other urban centre, but the researcher should be aware of them nonetheless.

Scope: The City in Three Counties

Where is Birmingham? You may think this a trite question to ask of a city of one million people. As any schoolchild knows, Birmingham is Britain's second city and lies at the centre of the country more or less (at the centre of England, at any rate). Follow virtually any canal, railway line or motorway and you will get there. But for the family historian the answer is not quite so straightforward. As Birmingham was little more than a hamlet in medieval times, it was of little consequence when it came to drawing up administrative and ecclesiastical boundaries. In later years, of course, the town became much more significant economically and politically, meaning that Birmingham itself made a natural administrative unit. The upshot of all this is that in historical terms Birmingham sits at the periphery of some jurisdictions used by family historians and is very much at the heart of others.

So, for the family historian the question 'Where is Birmingham?' is best answered 'It depends'. Historically, Birmingham stood at the western-most edge

Birmingham used to sit at the boundary of Warwickshire, Staffordshire and Worcestershire. (Public domain)

of north-west Warwickshire. Maps show it to be effectively on a peninsular, bordered to the south-east and south by Worcestershire and to the west and north-west by Staffordshire. In medieval times, the ancient parish of Birmingham (St Martin) was contiguous with the Staffordshire parishes of Handsworth and Harborne, and was surrounded to the north and east by the much larger (and wealthier) parish of Aston. In the centuries that followed the growing town pushed against and then overflowed all these borders, so that by the mid-nineteenth century 'Greater Birmingham' was much larger than what was, by then, the Borough of Birmingham itself. Aided in particular by the railways, the urban area extended well into neighbouring districts, such as Aston, Bordesley, Edgbaston, Moseley, Kings Norton, Northfield, Harborne and Handsworth. At its closest point, Kings Norton in Worcestershire was less than two miles from St Martin's church, Birmingham's historic centrepiece. Handsworth, in Staffordshire, was a similar distance in the other direction.

In 1851 the various districts and parishes now covered by the City of Birmingham fell under several, and varying, jurisdictions. Birmingham districts were split between two Church of England dioceses (responsible for probate of wills prior to 1858); five civil registration districts (with frequent changes at sub-district level); and five poor law unions. The Archdeaconry of Coventry, the ecclesiastical area containing Birmingham, was moved between Anglican dioceses in 1836, meaning that diocesan courts in both Lichfield and Worcester have, at various times, had jurisdiction over Birmingham wills. Harborne, in Staffordshire, was in Kings Norton Poor Law Union, while Handsworth was in West Bromwich Poor Law Union. The courts of Quarter Sessions, a key source not just for criminal records but also for many civil and administrative records, were organized at county level: courts in Warwick, Worcester and Stafford all had jurisdiction over affairs within the Birmingham area. Until 1838, that is, when Birmingham acquired its own Quarter Sessions. Since it was granted city status in 1889, Birmingham's boundaries have been extended on several occasions, bringing areas and parishes from the surrounding counties into the Birmingham Corporation.

You get the picture: research in Birmingham can be complicated. You need to be constantly aware of where you are researching and which jurisdictions apply, and at which period.

For the purposes of this book, 'Birmingham' is defined as being **all of the area now covered by the City of Birmingham within its post-1974 boundaries**. This includes Sutton Coldfield, which historically was part of Warwickshire and only joined (some would say was 'annexed by') Birmingham in 1974. It has traditionally had, and continues to maintain, a distinct identity. Solihull, the metropolitan borough to the south-east of Birmingham, is also included within the scope of the book. Although still a separate administrative unit, it is a highly urbanized area contiguous with the City of Birmingham and researching there involves many of the same issues and sources. Together Birmingham and Solihull provide a natural focus for the family historian. Although all part of that man-made construct known as the West Midlands, their roots, traditions and linkages are distinct from both Coventry and rural Warwickshire to the east, and the Black Country to the west.

Principal Archives and Sources

The Birmingham area is served by a diverse range of archives, several of national and international significance. In common with public archives elsewhere, these face two major, and in some senses inter-related, challenges. On the one hand, there is the shift towards digital access and delivery, whilst at the same time an increasing strain on archive services in the wake of public sector cutbacks. Several archives are reviewing their service provision, amending opening hours and/or closing certain facilities in order to stay within their shrinking budgets. For these reasons, no information is given here on aspects such as opening hours or cost of services; you should check each organization's website for details before visiting. While information on online resources and collections is as up-to-date as possible, this too may change.

The main archives referred to in the text are listed below. The entries here merely summarize the services available and the relevant web addresses. Further details, including full postal addresses, are provided in the Annex and specific references are made throughout the text.

Birmingham & Midland Society for Genealogy and Heraldry (BMSGH)
www.bmsgh.org.uk and **www.bmsgh-shop.org.uk**
The main family history society (FHS) for researchers with interests in Birmingham and the surrounding counties: Staffordshire, Warwickshire, and Worcestershire. Through the indexing and transcription work undertaken by its volunteers, the BMSGH is now a major data provider in its own right. It operates a series of indexes, several of which contain data not available elsewhere. Many datasets are available as downloads or on CD-ROM. There is also a specialist BMSGH Reference Library in central Birmingham and a series of online directories covering Birmingham, Warwickshire and Worcestershire.

Library of Birmingham: Archives, Heritage & Photography (LoB)
www.libraryofbirmingham.com/archives
Unless otherwise stated, references in this book to 'Library of Birmingham' refer to the Archives, Heritage & Photography (AHP) department, located on Level 4 of the new Library. In its role as the main record office for the City of Birmingham, the AHP service holds an extensive range of material for tracing families in the Birmingham area, including in districts outside the city's historic boundaries. Original documents may be consulted in the Wolfson Centre for Archival Research, for which an appointment is required. Important sets of the Library's original records are available online at Ancestry, as the 'Library of Birmingham Collection' (**http://collections.ancestry.co.uk/search/UK/LibraryofBirmingham**).

Lichfield Record Office (LRO)
www.staffordshire.gov.uk/archives
Formerly the diocesan record office for Lichfield and now part of the Staffordshire & Stoke-on-Trent Archives (see below). Holds important collections of wills for the Birmingham area and other records relating to south Staffordshire.

Staffordshire & Stoke-on-Trent Archives (SSA)
www.staffordshire.gov.uk/archives
The records and archive service covering the historic county of Staffordshire. Many records relating to Staffordshire parishes now incorporated into Birmingham have been transferred to the Library of Birmingham, but the service still holds important collections originating from other (i.e. non-parish) sources. These include the records of Staffordshire Quarter Sessions, Staffordshire Police Force, and apprenticeships. The service currently operates across a number of sites and is planning to centralize many of its collections under one roof at an extended Staffordshire Record Office (SRO) site.

University of Birmingham, Cadbury Research Library (UoB)
www.birmingham.ac.uk/facilities/cadbury
Holds records from a wide range of organizations. These include missionary societies, Christian and other youth organizations, local authority associations, political organizations and trade associations. Other organizational archives include a number relating to Christian education and training, special education,

and British athletics. Business records, mostly relating to the West Midlands, and records of publishers and records of publishing presses are also represented.

University of Warwick, Modern Records Centre (WMRC)
www.warwick.ac.uk/services/library/mrc
WMRC has a focus on modern British social, political and economic history, in particular industrial relations and labour history. While many of its collections have a national remit, there is also a strong regional focus within Birmingham and the West Midlands. Holdings include the records of: trade unions and related organizations; trade associations, employers' organizations and related bodies; motor industry records; radical British political groups; and pressure groups and other organizations.

Warwickshire County Record Office (WCRO)
http://heritage.warwickshire.gov.uk/warwickshire-county-record-office
The records and archive service covering the historic county of Warwickshire. Many records relating to rural Warwickshire parishes now incorporated into Birmingham have been transferred to the Library of Birmingham. Collections remaining at the WCRO include the records of the Warwickshire Quarter Sessions, for many years the main legal and administrative jurisdiction for Birmingham. Other important sources include asylum and prison records.

Worcestershire Archives and Archaeology Service (WAAS)
www.worcestershire.gov.uk/info/20019/archives_and_research
The records and archive service covering the historic county of Worcestershire. Many records relating to Worcestershire parishes now incorporated into Birmingham have been transferred to the Library of Birmingham, but the service still holds important collections originating from other (i.e. non-parish) sources. These include the records of Worcestershire Quarter Sessions, wills proved in the diocese of Worcester, and electoral registers and bishops' transcripts for Birmingham parishes prior to their incorporation into the city.

Key online resources containing collections from these and other archives are listed in the Annex.

Local History

As well as providing a guide to genealogical records, this book discusses the history of Birmingham and the surrounding area. It is only possible to sketch the city's rich history in a volume such as this. Thus, the presentations provide snapshots around particular themes rather than exhaustive accounts. The subjects have been chosen in order to better understand how our Birmingham ancestors lived and to enable us to interpret the records they left behind.

If you wish to delve further into Birmingham's fascinating past, a whole variety of sources are available. Four texts by early historians represent the first

Corporation Street, around 1900. (Public domain)

attempts to capture the city's history and make interesting studies in their own right. These are:

- *An History of Birmingham*, William Hutton (1783)
- *Memorials of Old Birmingham*, Joshua Toulmin Smith (1863)
- *Old and New Birmingham*, Robert K. Dent (1880)
- *Showell's Dictionary of Birmingham: A History and Guide Arranged Alphabetically*, Thomas T. Harman and Walter Showell (1888)

Digitized versions of these are available online, for example through the Internet Archive (**www.archive.org**) and Project Gutenberg (**www.gutenberg.org**).

In the modern era, Chris Upton's *A History of Birmingham* (The History Press, 2011), Carl Chinn's *Birmingham: The Great Working City* (Birmingham City Council, 1994), and Victor Skipp's two titles, *The Making of Victorian Birmingham* (Brewin Books, 1996) and *A History of Greater Birmingham Down to 1830* (Brewin Books, 1997) are key reading. Gateway sources for the specific themes covered are indicated in each chapter.

Among periodicals, *History West Midlands* is a popular history magazine containing articles by the region's leading historians (**www.historywm.com**). *Brummagem* magazine, edited by academic and broadcaster Carl Chinn, is also a good read (**www.carlchinnsbrum.com**). *Midland History* is an academic journal, available on subscription, with certain articles free to download (search at **www.maneyonline.com**). The biographies of men and women who have shaped the city are profiled in a special project undertaken by the *Oxford Dictionary of National Biography* (ODNB) (**www.libraryofbirmingham.com/blog/News/odnb**).

Genhound has a set of brief obituaries of Birmingham people of note extracted from Showell's *Dictionary of Birmingham* (**www.genhound.co.uk**).

Connecting Histories was a project to document the stories of diverse communities and groups that make up modern Birmingham, concentrating on the history of the twentieth century. Although the project ended in 2007, the portal website remains active. It contains a wealth of material, including a series of research guides around specific themes created in conjunction with local people and communities (**www.connectinghistories.org.uk**).

Most districts and suburbs have their own local history society (sometimes more than one); website addresses are given in the Annex or contact the nearest Birmingham community library. William Dargue's *History of Birmingham Places & Placenames* also has much interesting material (**http://billdargue.jimdo.com**).

The Birmingham Collection, the local studies collection at the Library of Birmingham, is one of the largest and most comprehensive collections of its type in the country. Dating from the opening of the Birmingham Public Reference Library in 1866, it comprises a wide variety of materials from standard history books to theatre programmes, exhibition catalogues to DVDs. Certain items are located on open shelves within the Archive, Heritage & Photography search room on Floor 4 but much more is held in storage. The catalogue is in three parts: bound volumes pre-1941; card index for 1941–74; and the computerized LoB book catalogue (OPAC) post-1974.

How to Use This Book

This book aims to provide a comprehensive guide to genealogy resources for tracing your family history within Birmingham and the surrounding area. It also presents an introduction to different facets of the city's history.

Many general sources, such as censuses, parish registers, and civil registration indexes are now readily available online. Whilst these are addressed, the book also encourages you to go further and deeper, seeking out sources that you may not have considered previously. Only by digging down into the lives of our ancestors will we be able to understand how they lived and worked within the extraordinary place that is Birmingham. Hence, there is, hopefully, something for the beginner and the experienced researcher alike.

Where relevant, references are given to original sources within the catalogues of the archives concerned. As each archive operates its own unique cataloguing system, it is necessary to identify exactly which reference field is being used within each catalogue. The catalogue fields for the four main archives are shown in the table below, together with the URL (web address) for that service's search engine. Many archives use a commercial cataloguing system called Calmview, hence the use of this term within several of the URLs and the similar appearance of some systems. **Not all of the individual catalogues are online**, so if you are unable to locate a reference given in the text it may be necessary to check with the repository concerned.

Main Archive Catalogues and Search Engines

Archive	Catalogue Reference Used	Catalogue Search Address
Library of Birmingham, AHP	Ref No (Reference number)	http://calmview.birmingham.gov.uk (Archives only; see main LoB website for library book catalogue)
Staffordshire & Stoke-on-Trent Archives	DocRefNo (Document reference number)	www.archives.staffordshire.gov.uk
Warwickshire CRO	AccNo (Accession number) or DocRefNo (Document reference number)	http://archivesunlocked.warwickshire.gov.uk/Calmview/
Worcestershire Archives	ComputerRef No (Computer reference number)	http://e-services.worcestershire.gov.uk/CalmView/

Notes: 1. For Warwickshire CRO: AccNo generally begins 'CR' and is four-figure with no spaces; DocRefNo has other designations, such as 'QS' for Quarter Sessions, and is four figure with no spaces.

Within the text, original archive references according to the above system are given in square brackets [ ]. Thus, in relation to Warwickshire CRO for example, the reference [CR0677] means the document with accession number (AccNo) CR0677 within the Warwickshire CRO catalogue. The document, in this case the Solihull Window Tax, may be located by entering this reference in the search engine at the 'archivesunlocked' URL shown. Similarly, document series Q/RLv at Staffordshire & Stoke-on-Trent Archives is 'Victuallers and Alehousekeepers Recognizances'. In cases where the repository is not mentioned explicitly, the reference will include the archive's abbreviation. Thus, the above example may also appear as [WCRO: CR0677].

Website addresses generally appear in the text in conventional brackets ( ) and in bold, e.g. (**www.birmingham.gov.uk/register-office**). For the sake of brevity, only addresses that are referenced once (or on very few occasions) are written in full. General sources, such as main repositories and commercial websites, are given in the Directory.

Chapter 1

THE CITY AND ITS PEOPLE

Birmingham and Environs

The area we now know as Birmingham lies at the centre of the Birmingham Plateau, an upland area bounded by the rivers Avon, Severn and Trent. Its average height is around 125 metres (410 feet) above sea level. The upland is divided into higher plateaus and punctuated by a series of ridges and river valleys. From west to east the plateau is traversed by the River Tame, which runs south-east from Wolverhampton. The River Blythe runs northwards from Shirley to flow into the Tame near Shustoke, by which time it has been joined by the River Cole, another minor tributary. The River Rea rises in the Waseley Hills, south-west of the city, flowing through the historic centre of Birmingham to join the Tame at Gravelly Hill.

Exactly when and why people decided to settle on the Birmingham Plateau is unclear. Archaeological investigations have found evidence of Roman

St Martin's church in the Bull Ring, around 1900. (Public domain)

occupation: a Roman military fort at Metchley (Edgbaston); the Roman road in Sutton Park; farming at Kings Norton; and commercial-scale pottery manufacture near Holford. The discovery of the Staffordshire Hoard in a field near Lichfield is a reminder that the Kingdom of Mercia was home to a vibrant culture during the period known as the Dark Ages.

From a poor manor in Anglo-Saxon times situated at a crossing of the River Rea, Birmingham grew into a town of national industrial significance from the eighteenth century and by the nineteenth century was Britain's second city after London. The ancient manors that make up the modern city were previously part of the counties of Warwickshire, Worcestershire and Staffordshire.

For genealogical purposes, we can think of the Birmingham conurbation in terms of four distinct areas: the historic centre; the neighbouring but separate parish of Aston; the outlying villages that became the suburbs; and the medieval towns of Solihull and Sutton Coldfield, both of which retain distinctive identities.

The Historic Centre

Until the early 1700s Birmingham comprised only one parish, St Martin, which had more or less the same boundaries as the ancient manor of Birmingham. The parish consisted of the town, roughly what is now the city centre, and 'the foreign', an expanse of flat wasteland to the west known as Birmingham Heath, in today's Winson Green.

The area around the Bull Ring has been at the centre of Birmingham life for centuries. A market has been held here since at least the twelfth century and as early as 1403 there is evidence not just of agricultural produce and livestock being sold, but also linen, wool, brass and metal goods. By 1500, the town had a population of around 1000. Visitors described it as comprising around 200 houses, squeezed into a small area around Digbeth, Deritend and High Street. New Street was also beginning to take shape during this period – showing that it is not so new – and in the two centuries that followed provided the focus for much of the town's development.

As the economy prospered, by the early eighteenth century the town was outgrowing its medieval street pattern. A period of more planned development began, starting on land to the north of New Street donated by John Pemberton, a wealthy ironmonger. The centrepiece of the new Priory Estate was Old Square, for many years Birmingham's most prestigious address. Other lands nearby became the site of the town's second church, St Philip, consecrated in 1715. Throughout the Georgian period, the town marched steadily northwards as landowners took the opportunity to develop their estates. A number of distinctive 'quarters' grew up as artisans and craftsmen from particular trades clustered together in order to take advantage of each others' skills. The Gun Quarter and the Jewellery Quarter both emanate from this period, although only the latter is in evidence today.

By the late 1700s Birmingham was spilling out into its neighbour, Aston, as well as across the Birmingham Heath. Winson Green became the site of three major Victorian era institutions: the Borough Prison, the Borough Asylum, and

The Jewellery Quarter
The area known as the Jewellery Quarter developed from the New Hall Estate. In 1746, the Colmore family obtained an act of Parliament allowing them to rearrange the New Hall Estate, which they had owned since Tudor times, and grant leases. The new housing developed in the area started to attract artisan workers within the jewellery trade.

Jewellery-making is a complex activity, requiring many different skills and outworkers. Workers tended to specialize – as diamond cutters, stone setters, engravers, polishers, etc. – and an individual craftsman seldom worked on a piece from start to completion. For practical reasons these workers needed to be grouped together. Artisans purchased or rented houses which they lived in and used for their workshops. The quarter became established from the late eighteenth century, spurred in particular by the establishment of the Birmingham Assay Office in 1773.

After a period of recession, a resurgence in the jewellery trade during the 1830s and 1840s led to the quarter shifting to an area of Hockley bounded by St Paul's Square, Vyse Street and Warstone Lane. Eventually, virtually every house within the Jewellery Quarter was a workshop; often additional workshops were constructed in gardens. Meanwhile, the fronts of the premises were opened up as retail shops selling the finished artefacts. Other industries with similar needs, such as pen-making and button manufacture, became established in the same area.

The Quarter continued to expand throughout the nineteenth century, reaching its largest extent before the First World War when over 50,000 people were employed across all trades. Today, the Jewellery Quarter remains a major centre, accounting for around forty percent of the UK's jewellery production.

the Borough Workhouse. Lands to the south of the town were also developed, although not as intensively as in the north and east, which were the main routes for the railways and canals.

By the time Birmingham became a city in 1889 it was pushing against its boundaries in all directions and the adjacent areas had begun to take on its urban character. Less than two years after receiving city status, the first expansion occurred, with Harborne, Balsall Heath, Saltley and Little Bromwich being brought into the corporation in 1891. Over the next forty years, the city's boundaries were expanded on four separate occasions. The most significant of these was under the Greater Birmingham Act of 1911 which brought Aston, Erdington, Handsworth, Kings Norton, Northfield and Yardley into the city, effectively doubling the corporation area.

Table 1.1: Population of Birmingham

Year	Population
1538	c.1,300
1650	5,472
1700	15,032
1731	23,286
1778	42,250
1785	52,250
1801	73,670
1811	85,755
1821	106,722
1831	146,986
1841	182,922
1851	232,841
1861	296,706
1871	343,787
1881	400,774
1891	478,113
1901	522,204
1911	840,202
1921	919,444
1931	1,002,603
2011	1,074,000

Source: Wikipedia and Birmingham City Council

Aston

The district of Aston warrants special mention here as its development is intimately bound up with, but at the same time distinct from, its Birmingham neighbour. Many of the records of value to genealogists are split between Birmingham and Aston jurisdictions, especially during the rapid expansion of the nineteenth century. Aston had its own programme of church building, its own poor law union, and its own civil registration district.

The suburb of Aston was once part of a large parish in Warwickshire. It comprised a number of townships and stretched as far eastwards as Castle Bromwich. The parish church of St Peter & St Paul dates from the thirteenth century but was extensively rebuilt in the Victorian era. Aston Hall was built by Sir Thomas Holte in 1618 and is now owned by Birmingham City Council.

The townships of Duddeston & Nechells and Deritend & Bordesley were included in the borough of Birmingham in 1838. Aston Manor stayed outside Birmingham, along with other manors such as Erdington, Witton and Little Bromwich, but was often referred to as 'Aston-juxta-Birmingham'. From 1869, Aston Manor was governed by Aston Manor Local Board. It became an Urban District in 1903 and was finally absorbed into Birmingham in 1911.

Parish church of St Peter & St Paul, Aston. (Wikimedia, Creative Commons)

Aston was the first area to feel the encroachment of Birmingham's urbanization. From the early nineteenth century, Lozells and the area between Aston and Birmingham developed into a mix of workers' housing, small factories and workshops, and small shopping centres such as High St., Newtown, Six Ways, Aston and Lozells Road. Larger factories such as Aston Manor Brewery, Hercules Cycles, Hudson & Co. Whistles, Norton Motorcycle Works, Martindale's Crocodile Works, and HP Sauce helped to give the area its industrial character.

The Suburbs

The districts now forming the suburbs have their origins in a series of ancient parishes and manors that surrounded the small, and at that time very poor, parish of Birmingham. Like Birmingham, they were rural in character, typically comprising a manor house, a church, a mill and simple cottages for the workers. For centuries their village folk worked the land, in some cases supplemented by cottage industries such as nail-making. There is evidence of mills on the River Rea and the River Tame. Kings Norton, which appears to have been the wealthiest manor in the area, also had its own market.

All of this began to change as transport links improved. The turnpiking of major roads brought benefit to some localities, through the large inns needed to serve the stagecoaches. The arrival of canals led to the construction of wharfs and

774 Bristol Road South, 1964. (Geoff Thompson Archive, courtesy of Mark Norton)

lock-keepers' houses and immediately ended the isolation of rural communities. Kings Norton was one of the first areas to benefit, with factories being established at Lifford around the junction of the Worcester & Birmingham and Stratford canals. Routes into the Black Country also became built up.

However, the real change for the suburbs came with the railways. From the 1840s onwards, ribbon development began along all the main railway routes into Birmingham. To the east and south, areas such as Stechford and Acocks Green grew up around new railway stations. A similar pattern was seen around the Birmingham to Gloucester railway to the south-west, which spurred the growth of Selly Oak, Northfield and Kings Norton. Suburban development brought housing, but also industry. The ultimate example was Bournville where a whole community – established according to the Cadbury brothers' Quaker values – grew up around a model factory built in a rural setting.

From the late nineteenth century, the introduction of trams and omnibuses, and eventually of course the motor car, allowed the suburbs to spread away from rail lines and arterial roads. The house building boom of the 1920s and 30s led to many new housing estates, both municipal and private, a trend that continued in the post-war period. Having now filled virtually every conceivable space, Birmingham forms a seamless conurbation running from the urban areas of Solihull in the south-east, through the city centre and suburbs, to merge with the Black Country authorities – Dudley, Sandwell and Walsall – in the west.

Pockets of Birmingham's suburban villages still remain and are being preserved through conservation areas in districts such as Hall Green, Harborne, Kings Norton, Moseley, and Yardley (see **www.birmingham.gov.uk/conservationareas**). Several city-centre districts are also protected.

A research project, *Suburban Birmingham: Spaces and Places, 1880–1960*, led by the University of Birmingham, has generated a wealth of material on the development of the south-western suburbs (**www.suburbanbirmingham.org.uk**).

Sutton Coldfield

Although now part of Birmingham, the Royal Town of Sutton Coldfield differs from the other suburbs in terms of its history and character. Mentioned in the Domesday Survey, Sutton Coldfield became a royal manor in 1489 and remained in the hands of the crown until 1528. Bishop Vesey succeeded in getting Henry VIII to grant the town a charter of incorporation. This bestowed the title of Royal Town and established a Corporation of twenty-five men, known as the Arden, who held all the manorial rights, powers and liberties. Sutton retained its rural character until the nineteenth century, when it became a popular residential area for people from Birmingham and Walsall.

The gem of the district is Sutton Park, a remnant of an extensive forest that once covered much of the Midlands. The survival of the Park was enshrined in the Charter of 1528 and, despite minor encroachment, it has remained

Boating Lake, Sutton Park, around 1955. (Public domain)

remarkably untouched ever since. It gained national and international attention in 1957 when the Scout movement held its World Jubilee Jamboree there, attended by many dignitaries and thousands of scouts from around the globe.

Although incorporated into Birmingham in 1974, Sutton retains a strong sense of individuality and, in spite of being a residential suburb, still has significant areas of open countryside.

Solihull

Solihull is not mentioned by name in the Domesday Survey. It began to take shape around 1220 with the founding of St Alphege's church and by 1242 it was large enough to be granted a weekly market. Knowle became an ecclesiastical centre for the area, so the district grew around these two distinct centres with settlements and woodland in between. The town was known for its blacksmiths, a trade that led to the clearing of the woodlands to provide fuel for their fires. A visitor in 1840 found Solihull to be 'remarkably neat and rural in appearance'.

The late nineteenth century saw the transition to a dormitory town for Birmingham industrialists and artisans. Small villas were built in and around the old villages and larger houses along the main roads. The availability of land, particularly in the Shirley area, attracted some small firms and, at the beginning of the Second World War, the Rover Company occupied a factory in Lode Lane. From 1920, the infilling of the areas between the Coventry, Warwick and Stratford Roads began, with the construction of housing estates, schools, factories and playing fields.

In 1974 the Metropolitan Borough of Solihull was created by the merger of the Solihull County Borough and most of the Meriden Rural District. Areas on the Borough's western edge – Castle Bromwich, Chelmsley Wood, Elmdon, Olton and Shirley – have strong historical links with Birmingham (**www.solihull.gov.uk/localhistory**).

Finding People: Key Sources

Censuses

All of the publicly available censuses, 1841–1911, are available online through commercial sites and increasingly, also, through FamilySearch. The FreeCEN website has complete transcriptions of the 1841 and 1891 censuses for the whole of Warwickshire, including Birmingham, which are free to view; there is also partial coverage for 1861 (**www.freecen.org.uk**).

The four censuses taken prior to 1841 (i.e. 1801–1831) generally listed only the head of the household rather than the entire population. Coverage for these pre-1841 listings is extremely patchy and none are known to survive for any parishes within the Greater Birmingham area. Major localities within the three counties where some lists do survive, and which may be relevant in terms of migration, include Bromsgrove, Lichfield, Walsall, and Wednesbury. Gibson and Medlycott (1999) has details for these and similar (pre-1800) lists.

BMSGH's Warwickshire Pre-1841 Census Index has entries from around seventy pre-1841 indexes relating to forty parishes, some only surname lists with size of household; others give ages and occupations (see Annex).

Civil Registration

At the introduction of civil registration on 1 July 1837, England and Wales were divided into a series of registration districts based on the poor law unions introduced a few years before. The Birmingham area comprised five main registration districts, each with several sub-districts:

1. Birmingham: All Saints, Ladywood, St George, St Martin, St Mary, St Paul, St Peter, St Philip, St Thomas.
2. Aston: Bordeseley, Deritend, Duddeston, Erdington, Sutton Coldfield.
3. Kings Norton: Balsall Heath, Edgbaston, Harborne, Kings Norton, Moseley, Selly Oak.
4. Solihull: Acocks Green, Elmdon, Hall Green, Hay Mills, Shirley, Solihull, Sparkhill, Yardley.
5. West Bromwich: Birchfield, Handsworth, Perry Barr.

In addition, Sheldon fell within the Meriden registration district and Quinton fell within the Stourbridge registration district.

These divisions remained in place until 1924, although in the case of Birmingham with frequent changes at sub-district level. In 1889 Aston Manor became a sub-district within Aston registration district, and in 1912 Sutton Coldfield was taken out of Aston and became part of Tamworth registration district. In September 1924 the whole system was revised, introducing two new districts: Birmingham North (All Saints, Aston, Duddeston, Erdington, Ladywood, St Mary) and Birmingham South (Acocks Green, Balsall Heath, Edgbaston, Kings Norton, St Bartholomew, St Martin, Smethwick, Sparkbrook). Handsworth sub-district remained within West Bromwich and Sutton Coldfield remained within Tamworth. In October 1932 boundaries were changed again, creating a single Birmingham registration district (covering all of Birmingham North, Birmingham South and Handsworth) and a separate registration district for Sutton Coldfield. In 1962 sub-districts were abolished and following the local government reorganization of 1974 the Birmingham and Sutton Coldfield registration districts amalgamated to form a single administrative unit. GENUKI (**www.genuki.org.uk/big/eng/WAR/Birmingham**) and UKBMD (**www.ukbmd. org.uk/genuki/reg**) have further details of the evolution of registration districts within Birmingham and surrounding areas. GENUKI also has listings that cross-reference Birmingham locations (sub-districts) to churches and *vice versa*.

The Library of Birmingham has the complete GRO indexes of births, marriages and deaths on microfiche and is one of the major centres designated to receive the contemporary annual updates. The Library also holds the Adopted Children's Index (from 1927), Civil Partnerships Index (from 2005), and the Overseas/Miscellaneous Indexes (various dates). Copies and transcriptions of the GRO indexes are widely available online, including on non-commercial sites such as FamilySearch and FreeBMD.

Birmingham Register Office holds civil birth, marriage and death registers for historical registration districts in the Birmingham area (**www.birmingham. gov.uk/registeroffice**). Certificates may be ordered online and are usually delivered very promptly. In view of the frequent changes detailed above, the website has a useful list identifying registers held at Birmingham and other register offices. Staff will undertake searches in the indexes or you may search the indexes in person at their offices in Holliday Street; see website for opening hours and fees.

Family history societies in the Midlands are collaborating with the local registration services to transcribe their indexes and make them freely available online. Projects are underway, with varying degrees of success, in Shropshire (**www.shropshirebmd.info**), Staffordshire (**www.staffordshirebmd.org.uk**), and the Black Country (**www.westmidlandsbmd.org.uk**).

Wills

Since 1858, probate records for England and Wales have been administered centrally through the Principal Registry of the Family Division. Library of Birmingham has the National Probate Calendar available either via Ancestry (1858–1966), in book form (1942–1972), or on microfiche (1973–1998).

Registered copy wills proved at Birmingham between 1858 and 1941 may be viewed in the Wolfson Centre, Library of Birmingham. Registered copy wills proved at Lichfield 1858–1928 are deposited at Lichfield Record Office, and those proved at Worcester are deposited at Worcestershire Archives. Birmingham District Probate Registry has all original wills proved at Birmingham, as well as those proved at Lichfield and Worcester between 1858 and 1928 (see address in Annex). It also has a searchable database covering 1921 to the present. Searches for the will or probate of any person in the UK who died after 1858 can be made at **http://probatesearch.service.gov.uk**.

Before 1858 probate was proved in ecclesiastical courts. Warwickshire was in the Province of Canterbury and was split between the dioceses of Lichfield and Worcester. As a result, the main collections of probate records are outside of the historic county.

The ecclesiastical jurisdictions for Warwickshire parishes, including Birmingham, have changed on a number of occasions. The key dates are:

• From 1541 to 1836, north, east and north-western Warwickshire parishes came under the authority and jurisdiction of the Diocese of Lichfield & Coventry. The remainder of Warwickshire (south-west portion) came under the Diocese of Worcester (see list at **http://familysearch.org/learn/wiki/en/List_of_ Warwickshire_Parishes**). The Diocese of Lichfield & Coventry was extensive, covering, in addition to northern Warwickshire, the entire counties of Staffordshire and Derbyshire, as well as north Shropshire.

- In 1837, north Warwickshire (Archdeaconry of Coventry, which included all parishes within Birmingham and Aston) was transferred to the Diocese of Worcester. The name of the remaining diocese was changed to Diocese of Lichfield.
- Prior to 1858, certain areas were covered by smaller courts, known as peculiar jurisdictions or peculiars, and were exempt from the bishop's jurisdiction. These were usually in the hands of other church officials or, in a handful of cases, lords of manors. See lists at FamilySearch Wiki (Diocese of Worcester) and Staffordshire Name Indexes (Diocese of Lichfield).

Thus, the probate records for Birmingham and north Warwickshire are divided, at different times and for various places, between the Consistory Court of Lichfield and the Consistory Court of Worcester. It may be necessary to search in the records of both these courts and/or the superior court, the Prerogative Court of Canterbury (PCC), to locate a will. In general, probate jurisdictions within Staffordshire and Worcestershire have been more stable (dioceses of Lichfield and of Worcester, respectively), although peculiar courts still applied. Raymond & Churchill (2002) lists the location of probate records.

Most records for the Consistory Court of Lichfield are held at Lichfield Record Office; holdings are summarised in the *Handlist to the Diocesan Probate and Church Commissioners' Records* (2nd edn, 1978). There is a good nineteenth-century calendar to wills and administrations, 1516–1857, and a separate index to records of peculiars. Printed versions of these indexes to 1652 (published by the British Record Society) are less accurate. Most of the indexes are now available online through various providers (see Table 1.2). Once located, a copy of an original will or administration may be ordered from the LRO by post.

BMSGH has compiled an index to Birmingham Probates at Lichfield Record Office (including Aston, Handsworth, Edgbaston, etc.) 1500s to 1857. This index also covers Staffordshire; access via correspondence only (see BMSGH indexes in Annex). See also *Birmingham Wills and Inventories, 1551–1600*, abstracts compiled by Richard Holt.

Records for the Consistory Court of Worcester are held at Worcestershire Archives. There are printed indexes covering most periods 1451–1857, and original wills are on microfilm. The WAAS has a downloadable index of wills proved in Worcestershire peculiars.

In general, where someone held property or goods within one diocese only, the will was proved, or administration granted, in that court. If held in two dioceses, then the grant was made in the archbishop's prerogative court. Indexes to PCC wills are readily available online through The National Archives and commercial providers.

Many original wills for both Lichfield and Worcester are available on microfilm via LDS Family History Centres; details on FamilySearch.

Table 1.2: Online Sources for Birmingham and West Midlands Wills

Jurisdiction	Coverage	Website	Comments
Consistory Court of Lichfield	Calendar of wills & administrations, 1516–1652	Ancestry	Transcript by W.P.W. Phillimore, 1892. Also available at http://wishful-thinking.org.uk/lichdb/
Consistory Court of Lichfield	Calendar of wills & administrations, 1640–1760	Staffordshire Name Indexes	A modern index, more accurate than the 1892 version above.
Consistory Court of Lichfield	Calendar of wills & administrations, 1650–1700	Origins.net and Findmypast	Digitized version of British Record Society Volume 125 (2010). Also in BMSGH Library.
Worcester Probate Registry	Worcestershire Wills Index, 1858–1928	BMSGH	An index to Wills at Worcestershire Archives. Available as a download from the BMSGH Shop.

Local Photographs

The breadth and quality of the Library of Birmingham's Photographic Collection has received national and international recognition. The collection comprises around three million items: negatives, prints, lantern slides, photographic albums,

City in transition: John Bright Street, early 1960s, showing the redevelopment of the city centre. (Geoff Thompson Archive, courtesy of Mark Norton)

books and albums illustrated with original photographic prints, and a considerable collection of literature associated with photography. Subjects such as the history of Birmingham, the contribution of Birmingham and the Midlands to photographic history, portraiture, and theatre photography are all well represented.

Foremost among the collections is the Warwickshire Photographic Survey, a project founded in the 1890s to document the county's architectural and historical heritage. The collection runs to thousands of images and is housed in the Wolfson Centre [MS 2724]. It includes street scenes, architectural studies, and topographical views of Birmingham and Warwickshire. Original prints are not normally accessible, for conservation purposes. Extracts from the collection are being digitized and made available online (**www.libraryofbirmingham.com/ warwickshirephotographicsurvey**). The Digital Handsworth Project has digitized all of the images relating to Handsworth, Perry Barr, Kingstanding and Oscott (**www.digitalhandsworth.org.uk**).

The Photographic Album Collection, another collection of note, comprises around fifty albums, ranging from Victorian *cartes de visite* to Kodak Autographic and snapshot albums from the 1920s. There is also a collection of around 60,000 lantern slides, dating from around 1890 to 1940 by both commercial and amateur photographers, many with Birmingham subjects. In addition, there are extensive collections of photographs relating to both World Wars.

Other aspects of the LoB's collections of interest for family and local historians are listed in Table 1.3. Further information is available at the Archives, Heritage & Photography department's website and the Connecting Histories portal has a guide, *Visualising Birmingham: Reframing the Photographic Collections*.

The county record offices all have photographic collections for their areas. Staffordshire Views is a unique series of images of churches, public buildings, country houses and landscapes from all over Staffordshire, dating mainly from the 1830s and 1840s (**www.views.staffspasttrack.org.uk**). SSA's full photographic collection can be searched using the Gateway to the Past search engine (**www.archives.staffordshire.gov.uk**). Windows on Warwickshire is a searchable database of historic photographs and other items held at Warwickshire archives, museums and libraries (**www.windowsonwarwickshire.org.uk**). WCRO's full collection of photographs, prints and drawings can be searched via the online catalogue (**http://archivesunlocked.warwickshire.gov.uk**). WAAS has the Worcestershire Photographic Survey, with a downloadable index, as well as a separate online index to the entire county photographic collection (**http://tinyurl.com/q32pnkn**).

Pastscape is a portal to information on archaeological and architectural heritage across England, run by English Heritage (**www.pastscape.org.uk**). It has descriptions, and in some cases pictures, of sites and buildings referenced within historical sources, including around 2000 within the Birmingham area. A related service, ViewFinder, has historic photographs from the English Heritage Archive (**http://viewfinder.english-heritage.org.uk**). Information on all buildings that have received listed status is available at **www.britishlistedbuildings.co.uk**.

The work of amateur photographers of the late twentieth century is celebrated at two sites: **www.photobydjnorton.com**, dedicated to the work of Dennis John

Table 1.3: Library of Birmingham Photographic Collections for Family and Local History

Birmingham City Council Planning and Architecture [BCC: Acc:1999/077]	Street scenes and architectural views of Birmingham, 1940s-1970s.
Bill Brandt Collection [MS 1536]	Social photography from the mid-twentieth century, including back-to-back slums and municipal housing.
Birmingham Corporation and City Council Collection	Predominately twentieth-century gelatin silver prints and negatives from the Council's various departments. Card indexes for some collections available.
Birmingham Improvement Scheme Collection	Over 100 large albumen prints by Birmingham photographer James Burgoyne documenting the slums and streets cleared in the Birmingham Improvement Scheme c.1875.
Birmingham Industrial Exhibition (1886) Collection	Over 70 large albumen prints recording the exhibition stands, judges and events of the 1886 Birmingham Industrial Exhibition at Bingley Hall.
Dyche Studio Collection [MS 2912]	Wide range of portraits, 1910–1980, from early twentieth century music and variety hall artists, to the Asian and African-Caribbean communities.
Francis Bedford Collection [MS 4010]	Topographical and architectural views of Great Britain, 1860s-1870s.
Francis Frith & Co. Collection [MS 2911]	Topographical views of selected counties and areas of England, Scotland and Wales, 1870s-1970.
Harold Baker Collection	Over 200 albumen prints, largely architectural and archaeological studies of buildings and sites in and around Birmingham, c.1870–1880.
Metro-Cammell Collection [MS 99]	Includes over 100 photographic albums, rolling stock specifications, catalogues and pamphlets, c.1850 to c.1950.
Vanley Burke Collection [MS 2192]	Documentary photography, community photography and ephemera with an emphasis on African-Caribbean communities, 1960s-2010s.
Whitlock Studio Collection [MS 4151]	Portraits of local and national dignataries, local private commissions and group portraits, c.1879–1930.

Norton, and the Old Birmingham photo gallery set up by the late Keith Berry (**www.pbase.com/beppuu/old_bham**). The University of Birmingham has a large series of images taken by Phyllis Nicklin, former tutor in geography, documenting buildings and street scenes around the city during the 1950s and 1960s (**http://epapers.bham.ac.uk/chrysalis.html**). For other amateur and community sites see **http://birmingham.blogspot.co.uk** and **http://oldbirminghampictures. lefora.com**.

The photo-sharing site Flickr has many members and groups devoted to photography around and relating to Birmingham, both contemporary and historic. The gateway URL at **www.flickr.com/groups/birmingham** has a directory of Birmingham-related pages. Bill Dargue's History of Birmingham Places site has links to Flickr groups with an historical emphasis, some of which are not listed in the other directory (**http://billdargue.jimdo.com**). Of particular note is the Flickr page of Birmingham Museum and Art Gallery (BMAG), which has a selection of images from the city's collections (**www.flickr.com/ people/birminghammag**). Selected prints and images are available to purchase through **www.bmagprints.org.uk** and **www.bmagimages.org.uk.** Facebook and Twitter also have photo-sharing communities.

There are many Birmingham galleries within the Geograph database, which aims to collect geographically representative photographs and information for every square kilometre of Great Britain and Ireland (**www.geograph.org.uk**).

There are many books and websites presenting Birmingham and the surrounding counties through old postcards (see Publishers section in the Annex).

Maps, Gazetteers and Plans

The Library of Birmingham's Map Collection covers all types and periods. There are four editions of Ordnance Survey maps of Birmingham at the 1:2500 scale between 1884 and 1939: 1st edition 1884–1890, 2nd edition 1903–1905, 3rd edition 1915–1919, and 4th edition 1936–1939. Archives, Heritage & Photography holds copies of most of these editions for most parts of Birmingham. Another key part of the collection is the Pigott Smith map of 1855, a ten-feet to the mile survey of the centre of the town undertaken during improvements to the water supply and sewerage system.

The Tithe Commutation Act of 1836 abolished the in-kind payment of tithes and substituted rent charges (see Chapter 9). This required new maps of the whole country, measuring acreage and recording the state of cultivation. For some places the tithe maps were the first detailed maps, although the results were of variable quality. Together with the accompanying apportionment schedule, the tithe maps show who owned and who rented land. Most maps of the area covered by modern Birmingham were produced between 1839 and 1851.

In addition to the series listed above, there are many individual maps, estate plans and enclosure maps. Older maps of central Birmingham include the Pigott Smith map of 1825, and the Westley map of 1731, made by William Westley, a Birmingham surveyor. *The Village Atlas* (Village Press, 1989) is a collection of maps showing the development of Birmingham and the West Midlands from 1831–1907. A selection of high resolution maps from the LoB's collection is available to purchase at Mapseeker (**www.mapseeker.co.uk**).

In the county record offices: WCRO has an extensive series of printed maps, tithe apportionment maps for most parishes, and a large number of estates and farms dating from around 1600. SSA has similar coverage. WAAS has an online database of maps and plans, as well as downloadable guides to its maps on microfilm, and tithe apportionments and plans. Online catalogues are as listed for photographs above. FamilySearch has a facility to compile maps made up of various layers, such as parishes and poor law unions, to see how they relate to each other; very useful in a border area such as Birmingham (**http://maps. familysearch.org**).

Jenni Coles-Harris's Georgian Streets blog has commentaries on several eighteenth-century maps of the town (**http://mappingbirmingham.blogspot. co.uk**). Revolutionary Players has an article on maps and map-making in the West Midlands with links to many early maps, including James Sherriff's 1798 map of twenty-five miles around Birmingham (**www.search.revolutionary players.org.uk**). This flickr site has a set of 1933 maps of Birmingham and suburbs (**http://tinyurl.com/pabl4c7**).

Bill Dargue's website presents a history of the city's places and place-names, as well as a postcode gazetteer (**http://billdargue.jimdo.com**).

Newspapers

Newspapers are a valuable, but often underused resource for the family historian. They can be a gateway to a wealth of information, some of which is not available elsewhere; or they may lead on to other sources. The types of information to be found include: obituaries, birth, marriage and death announcements, business contracts, bankruptcies and dissolution of partnerships, name changes, court cases, school and university examination results, military appointments and promotions, and gallantry citations and awards.

Court cases and inquests are a staple of all local papers. Usually a reporter would be sent along and took down, verbatim, what was said. Witnesses, such as family members, would be questioned, perhaps revealing key information, such as marital infidelity or a separation. Obituaries also give a lot of information: as well as a summary of the deceased's life, they may mention family relationships and provide a list of people who attended the funeral. As the areas covered by newspapers often overlapped, and some of the content was

Banner of the *Birmingham Gazette*, 1937. The title was absorbed by the *Birmingham Post* in 1956. (Public domain)

Birmingham Gazette

Proprietors: The Birmingham Gazette Ltd.

LARGEST SALE—WITH ONE EXCEPTION—OF ANY PROVINCIAL MORNING NEWSPAPER

BIRMINGHAM, THE LARGEST PROVINCIAL CITY
Over a million people and over a thousand trades in the City

syndicated between titles, an event may not necessarily be reported (or have survived) in the nearest local newspaper.

The LoB has a substantial collection of newspapers from Birmingham and the surrounding areas available on microfilm (Table 1.4). As well as near complete runs of the *Birmingham Gazette*, *Birmingham (Daily) Post* and *Birmingham Mail*, there are many other titles, some of which only lasted a few years. On open shelves are an *Index to Obituaries in Aris's Gazette, 1741–1866* and *Birmingham Biography, 1872–1975* [BCol 78], a collection of newspaper cuttings compiled by library staff. A wide range of local and suburban titles are also held. Sports news is catered for by the *Sports Argus* and *Sporting Mail*.

Table 1.4: Main Newspaper Series at Library of Birmingham

(Aris's) Birmingham Gazette	1741–1956
Birmingham & Aston Chronicle	1882–1895
Birmingham Advertiser	1842–1844
Birmingham Argus	1828–1844
Birmingham Daily Globe	1879–1880
Birmingham Daily Mercury	1855–1857
Birmingham Daily Post & Birmingham Post	1857–2001
Birmingham Daily Press	1855–1858
Birmingham Daily Times	1886–1890
Birmingham Despatch	1983–1989
Birmingham Mail	from 1870
Birmingham Mercury	1850–1858
Birmingham Morning News (including the	
Birmingham Evening News and Birmingham Weekly News)	1871–1875
Birmingham News	1899–1959
Birmingham Planet	1964–1967
Birmingham Sunday Echo	1898–1906
Birmingham Weekly Mercury	1884–1918
Birmingham Weekly Post	1869–1960
Daily Argus	1895–1905
Evening Dispatch	1909–1955
Sporting Buff	1956–1960
Sporting Mail	1905–1953
Sports Argus	1897–2003
Sunday Mercury	1920–2000
Swinney's Birmingham & Stafford Chronicle	1775–1819

Key titles are accessible and searchable online through the British Newspaper Archive (BNA), a joint venture between the British Library and DC Thomson Family History (**www.britishnewspaperarchive.co.uk**). Coverage includes: *Birmingham Daily Mail* 1914–1918, *Birmingham Daily Post* 1857–1918, *Birmingham Gazette* 1741–1918, and the *Birmingham Journal* 1832–1869. There is also some coverage for other Midlands towns, such as *Berrow's Worcester Journal* 1800–1900

Spreading the News: The Growth of Newspapers

Provincial newspapers began to become established in England in the early eighteenth century. Before this news reached the English countryside through manuscript newsletters, printed newsbooks and newspapers produced in London. Politicians saw the growth of cheap newspapers as dangerous, fearing they would radicalise the lower classes, leading to social unrest and even revolution. Taxes were levied on paper and advertisements as well as a stamp duty on newspapers in an effort to restrict their growth. As the tax was per sheet of paper, the pages grew larger and larger and the print became smaller and smaller to accommodate more news. Most newspapers continued as so-called 'broadsheets' until recent times.

Birmingham's first regular newspaper was *Aris's Gazette*, launched on 16 November 1741. Thomas Aris had moved to Birmingham from London to set up business as a printer and publisher. *Aris's Gazette*, later called the *Birmingham Gazette*, was initially a four-page weekly paper (another means of avoiding stamp duty). Aris soon saw off imitators and rivals, enabling him to raise the price to two-pence. Advertising dominated in a bid to maximise revenue: foreign news was obtained from the London papers and local news was squeezed into a column on the third page. The rest of the paper was devoted to adverts for local events, property sales, and notices for patent medicines and other new inventions. This formula proved successful and the *Gazette* served as the town's main newspaper for more than one hundred years. *Swinney's Birmingham & Stafford Chronicle and Coventry Gazette* was another early paper, published (under varying titles) between 1773 and 1827.

Recognition of the importance of a free press and the relaxation of associated taxes led to a blossoming of provincial newspapers during the second half of the nineteenth century. By 1871, Birmingham was served by seven different titles, with many others in the surrounding counties and towns. There were over a hundred newspapers across the West Midlands as a whole. Prices decreased – the *Birmingham Daily Post*, launched in 1857, cost a penny – while readership increased. By the 1870s it had a daily circulation of 30,000.

and the *Staffordshire Sentinel* 1850–1949. Print, microfilm and digitized newspapers can be viewed at the Newsroom, the British Library's specialized reading room at St Pancras, London (**www.bl.uk/subjects/news-media**).

National newspapers can be an important source for legal and family announcements (especially for the upper classes). The *London Gazette*, published since the mid-1600s, is freely available online (**www.thegazette.co.uk**). National and some local titles are accessible through subscription services, such as the Gale Newspaper Database and The Times Digital Archive (1785–1985); many libraries offer free access either within library buildings or from home for library members.

Further Information

Susan Bates, *Solihull Past* (The History Press, 2001).

Jeremy Gibson & Else Churchill, *Probate Jurisdictions: Where to Look for Wills*, Fifth Edition (Federation of Family History Societies, 2002).

Jeremy Gibson & Meryn Medlycott, *Local Census Listings, 1522–1930: Holdings in the British Isles* (Federation of Family History Societies, 1999).

Roger Lea, *The Story of Sutton Coldfield* (History Press, 2003).

Paul Line, *Birmingham: A History in Maps* (History Press, 2009).

Chapter 2

CHURCH AND POLITICS

The Established Church

Principal Churches

The origins of St Martin-in-the-Bull Ring, Birmingham's original parish church, are unclear, but there is evidence of a church on the site since at least the twelfth century. The fabric of the building has been altered substantially over the years. In 1692 it was given a new red sandstone exterior (except the spire), keeping the interior mainly in tact. Further alterations were made in the 1780s and in 1873 the church was completely rebuilt by J.A. Chatwin, replacing everything except the spire and tower.

During the Middle Ages chapels-of-ease were licensed to enable parishioners to attend the Sunday service without going to their own parish church. This was especially convenient in large rural parishes, such as Aston which was ten miles across and had dangerous river crossings. By 1700, chapels-of-ease dependent on

The north prospect of St Philip's church, from the print by William Westley, 1732. (Public domain)

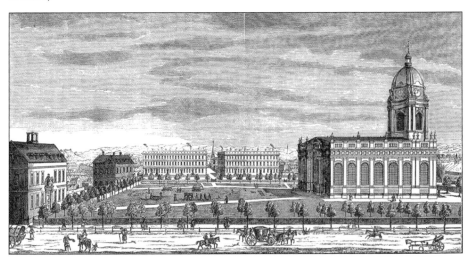

the Aston parish of St Peter & St Paul had been established at Deritend (St John the Baptist, founded in 1380), Ward End (St Margaret), and Ashted (St James the Less), all adjoining Birmingham. There were also chapels at Castle Bromwich, Water Orton, and Yardley. Although within Aston parish, Deritend, lying east of the river Rea, was part of the manor of Birmingham and for centuries St John the Baptist was effectively a Birmingham church.

By the early eighteenth century it was clear that a new church was needed to accommodate the town's growing population. A Commission of wealthy local landowners decided to build a church on the northern edge of the town, on land donated by the Inge and Phillips families. Designed by Thomas Archer, St Philip's church was consecrated but not completed in 1715. Built of brick and faced in stone, it was the first Birmingham building of Italianate design and one of only a few churches in the English baroque style.

The building made an immediate impression on the booming Georgian town and all those who visited. Recalling his first approach in 1741, William Hutton wrote:

> 'Upon Handsworth Heath, I had a view of Birmingham. St. Philip's Church appeared first, uncrowded with houses (for there were none to the north, New Hall excepted) untarnished with smoke, and illuminated by a Western sun. It appeared in all the pride of modern architecture. I was charmed with its beauty, and thought it then, as I do now, the credit of the place.

St Philip was made the cathedral church of the newly-formed Diocese of Birmingham in 1905 and is one of the smallest cathedrals in England.

During the mid eighteenth century three further churches were built to meet the needs of the town's growing population: St Bartholomew (consecrated in 1749), St Mary, Whittall Street (1774), and St Paul (1779). All were initially chapels-of-ease associated with St Martin before being assigned as separate parishes. Now standing in the city's only Georgian Square, St Paul is the sole survivor of these three churches.

Even with this additional capacity, there was concern that large numbers of the urban poor and working class were not catered for by the Established Church. At a Birmingham parish meeting in 1818 it was calculated that St Martin's and associated chapels offered only 7,360 seats for a population of over 60,000. Adding in St Philip, together with Deritend and Ashted (both in Aston, but physically part of the town), some 11,000 seats catered for over 80,000 people. Even not counting appropriated sittings of which there were very many, this amounted to eight people per seat.

In the 1820s two further districts were formed into the parishes of St George (consecrated in 1822) and St Thomas, Bath Row (1829); their construction was aided by Parliamentary grant. In 1836 the Birmingham Church Building Society was founded with the aim of erecting ten new churches in the poorer areas, though due to lack of funds only five were actually built. By 1865 another ten Anglican churches had been built, and the following four years saw the erection of a further ten churches, due to the financial aid of the Birmingham Church Extension Society.

Christ Church is one of Birmingham's least known central churches. It opened in 1805 at the corner of New Street and Waterloo Street, in what is now Victoria Square, and was the first Free Church in Birmingham, offering free seats to the poor. Towards the last quarter of the nineteenth century, however, congregations decreased as people moved out to the suburbs. The church closed in 1897 and was demolished two years later. Other churches were destroyed by German bombs during the Second World War, or were closed as part of the post-war slum clearance and redevelopment.

William Dargue's A History of Birmingham Churches website documents the history of all Anglican churches now within the City of Birmingham, including maps, illustrations and photographs (**http://ahistoryofbirminghamchurches. jimdo.com**). A similar list, with dates only, is available at the FamilySearch Wiki.

Church Plans Online, run by the Historic Churches Preservation Trust, has details of the architectural history of Anglican churches (**www.churchplans online.org**), while the Churches of Britain and Ireland site has photographs and old postcards from all denominations (**www.churches-uk-ireland.org**).

Anglican Records

The Library of Birmingham is the main repository for registers from Birmingham's Church of England parishes. Registers and other parish documents are listed in the Archives catalogue (Calmview) under series 'EP'; many parish entries have handlists of holdings to download. Certain registers (covering around eighty parishes in total) are now available on Ancestry; there is a list on the LoB site (**http://tinyurl.com/qa5ylk7**) and in the Archives Search Room. Ancestry also has a small collection of confirmations for Harborne, 1915–1931.

In addition to the LoB collection, many other registers for Midlands parishes are available online. Table 2.1 summarizes collections released through systematic efforts (official and unofficial); some sites also have miscellaneous records acquired through other means.

BMSGH maintains a series of marriage and burial indexes for Greater Birmingham and the adjoining counties which are open to postal and/or email enquiries; details are in the Annex. A separate index covers all of the St Martin registers, for which original images are available as downloads through the BMSGH Shop. The BMSGH also has three very useful online directories describing the coverage and locations of parish registers, bishops' transcripts, censuses and other records on a parish by parish basis. These are at the Tracing Your Ancestors in Birmingham, Tracing Your Ancestors in Warwickshire, and Worcestershire Parish Guide websites (see addresses in Annex).

Parish entries on the FamilySearch Wiki give summary information on the locations of parish registers, transcripts and other records for each parish. Steve Archer's site describes how the International Genealogical Index has been integrated into FamilySearch, and lists coverage of parish registers (all denominations) by batch number (**www.archersoftware.co.uk/igi/**).

Table 2.1: Online Collections of Birmingham and West Midlands Parish Records

Locality	Coverage	Website (and Holding Authority)	Comments
Birmingham	Composite registers (baptisms, marriages, burials), 1538–1812 Baptisms, 1813–1912 Marriages and banns, 1754–1937 Burials, 1813–1964	Ancestry (for Library of Birmingham)	Most Anglican parishes within the city's pre-1974 boundaries. Includes digitized images.
Staffordshire	Baptisms, 1538–1900 Marriages, 1538–1900 Banns, 1653–1900 Burials, 1538–1900	Findmypast (for Staffordshire & Stoke-on-Trent Archive Service)	Approximately 200 parishes. Excludes all Staffordshire parishes now within Birmingham, but includes Walsall, West Bromwich & Wolverhampton. Includes digitized images.
Shropshire	Baptisms, 1538–1900 Marriages, 1538–1900 Banns, 1760–1900 Burials, 1538–1900	Findmypast (for Shropshire Archives)	Anglican and non-conformist registers. Includes digitized images.
Warwickshire	Baptisms and burials, 1813–1910 Marriages and banns 1754–1910	Ancestry (for Warwickshire County Record Office)	Searchable by parish. Includes digitized images.
Warwickshire	Marriages, 1813–1837	Joiner Marriage Index	Covers rural parishes surrounding Birmingham and Aston: Curdworth, Edgbaston, Elmdon, Sheldon, Solihull, Sutton Coldfield. Some Staffordshire and many Shropshire parishes also included. http://joinermarriageindex.co.uk
Worcestershire	Baptisms, c.1540–1839 Marriages, c.1754–1812 Burials, various	The Genealogist	Unofficial but large-scale transcription effort by the Malvern FHS for registers held by the WAAS. Also available at www.fhs-online.co.uk
Worcestershire	Marriages, 1538–1836	Ancestry	Selected parishes, extracted or transcribed from original registers.
All	Burials, 1500s–1900s	Findmypast (National Burial Index)	See text

In its role as the Birmingham Diocesan Record Office, the LoB holds the official records of the Bishop and See, including some 'modern' (i.e. post-1837) bishops' transcripts [BDR/B/5]. Historic (i.e. mainly pre-1837) bishops' transcripts for Birmingham, Aston, Handsworth and associated parishes are at Lichfield Record Office.

When looking for vital events, do not be put off by the fact that St Philip's Church in central Birmingham is now Birmingham Cathedral. It only received this designation in 1905 and for the previous two hundred years had simply been a local parish church.

Clergy Ancestors

Crockford's Clerical Directory, first published in 1858, contains biographies of Anglican clergy in the UK. Selected directories from 1868 to 1932 are available on Ancestry. A typical biographical entry may include where the clergyman studied, when he obtained a degree and a work history of where and when he performed his clerical duties.

The Clergy of the Church of England Database (CCEd) has details of the clerical and educational careers of Church of England clergymen (**http://theclergy database.org.uk**). Staffordshire Name Indexes has indexes to the nomination papers of parish clerks for licences for the Diocese of Lichfield & Coventry, 1691–1836, and Diocese of Lichfield, 1836–1916 (**www.staffsnameindexes.org.uk**).

Roman Catholicism

The Heartland of English Catholicism

The Reformation of the sixteenth century caused a schism in English society. While some accepted the new Protestantism and its tenets – such as the Book of Common Prayer and the abolition of the Mass – others refused to comply. The West Midlands was one area where the Old Faith was kept alive. Oxford, south and west Warwickshire, neighbouring Worcestershire and parts of Staffordshire were all Catholic strongholds. The Gunpowder Plotters of 1605 were famously led not by Guy Fawkes, as many presume, but by Robert Catesby, who is thought to have been born in Warwickshire. When the plot was discovered, Catesby and his co-conspirators (many of whom were from the Midlands) fled London and made a stand at Holbeche House in Staffordshire.

The reign of James II, a Catholic, brought a brief resurgence and enabled a few new chapels to be built. In Birmingham, the Francisans built the Mass House in 1687 with a dedication to St Mary Magdalen and St Francis. The King himself gave the proceeds of 125 tons of timber towards the construction but it was destroyed after James's flight the following year; its memory survives in the street name Masshouse Lane.

The eighteenth century marked the lowest point for Catholicism in England. Although the Toleration Act of 1689 guaranteed freedom of worship for dissenting groups, Roman Catholics were expressly excluded and Catholic repression continued. Some ceremonies were held in secret during this period but most Catholics were baptized and married in Anglican churches and buried in Anglican churchyards. It was not uncommon for the Anglican minister to mark an entry in the register with 'papist' or 'recusant'. In the event of a Catholic marrying outside the Church of England, the authorities could prosecute the offending parties through the ecclesiastical courts.

Roman Catholic Cathedral Church of St Chad, built between 1839 and 1841. Designed by Augustus Pugin. (Tony Hisgett, Creative Commons)

The Catholic Relief Acts of 1778 and 1791 allowed new churches to be built. In Birmingham these included St Peter's in Broad Street, opened in 1786. Old Oscott College, in Sutton Coldfield, opened in 1794 for the training of priests and the education of boys. The Catholic Emancipation Act of 1829 and the appointment of Thomas Walsh as Bishop for the Midland District brought a change of fortunes. Churches were built to serve the growing population, which included many Irish immigrants who were moving into Birmingham and other Midlands cities.

Under the guidance of a series of outstanding characters, the Midlands became the focus for a Catholic renaissance, with Birmingham at its heart. Key figures included the architect Augustus Pugin, the theologian and writer Cardinal John Henry Newman, the missionary Dominic Barberi, and John Talbot, 16th Earl of Shrewsbury, a devout Catholic and generous benefactor.

In 1850, Pope Pius IX established the Diocese of Birmingham as part of the reorganization of the church in England and Wales. St Chad's Cathedral, the seat of the new bishopric, was the first Catholic cathedral to be built in England since the Reformation. Designed by Pugin, its soaring spires and impressive ironwork symbolized the revival of the Catholic community. Cardinal Newman, a convert to Catholicism, founded the Oratorian Congregation of Birmingham in 1848. The Oratory, an equally impressive building, stands in Hagley Road (**www.birminghamoratory.org.uk**).

Covering a huge swathe of central England, the new diocese had seventy-three missions (parishes), and a Catholic population of around 35,000. By 1900, the Catholic community in the Midlands had more than doubled, largely as a result of successive waves of immigration from Catholic countries; not only Irish, but also Italians, Poles and Ukrainians. In 1911 the diocese was elevated to the status of an archdiocese with five suffragan sees covering much of Wales and southern England.

Catholic Records

Following the introduction of civil registration in 1837, most Catholic congregations in England and Wales refused to hand over their parish registers to the Registrar General, as they were meant to do. Registers for Birmingham's Catholic churches are now held mostly by the Birmingham Archdiocesan Archives (BAA) based at Cathedral House, next to St Chad's Cathedral.

The BAA holds the episcopal and administrative records of the Midland District (1688–1840), the Central District (1840–1850), the Diocese of Birmingham (1850–1911), and the Archdiocese of Birmingham (1911–present). It is also the repository for all parishes in the Archdiocese, which comprises the ancient counties of Oxfordshire, Staffordshire, Warwickshire, and Worcestershire. Other collections include the archives of St Mary's College, Oscott; Sedgley Park School and Cotton College; Besford Court School and a wide range of Catholic charities, societies and organizations. Of particular note are the records of the Catholic Family History Society (Midlands Branch), which was disbanded in 2007. There is an online catalogue (**www.birminghamarchdiocesanarchives.org.uk**) but as yet none of the documents are available to view online. The registers of certain parishes remain with their incumbents (details on the website).

The persecution of Catholics (and non-conformists) from the sixteenth to eighteenth centuries generated various genealogical records. Recusant Rolls list dissenters or non-conformists and show the fines and property or land

Table 2.2: Catholic Sources in the Quarter Sessions Records

Category	Staffordshire	Warwickshire	Worcestershire
Oaths and Affirmations	Q/RRo	QS0018	1/6/1
Papists Estates, Registers of	Q/RRp	QS0062, QS0009	1/6/2, 8001/3/9
Popish Recusants	Q/RRr	QS0061	
Protestant Dissenters' Meeting Houses and Roman Catholic Places of Worship		QS0010	
Roman Catholics, Act for relief		QS0060	

Notes: 1. The references shown are for the catalogue of the relevant county archive: SSA for Staffordshire; WCRO for Warwickshire; WAAS for Worcestershire. For web addresses of online catalogues and other details see 'How To Use This Book' in the Introduction.

surrendered by the accused. Returns of Papists are records from audits of Roman Catholics taken nationwide at various times, arranged in dioceses by town or village. Some returns simply record the numbers of Catholics and not their names. Returns of Papists' Estates are registers of Roman Catholics who refused to take oaths of loyalty after the Jacobite Rebellion of 1715. All of these sources occur in the Quarter Sessions records (Table 2.2).

The Midland Catholic History Society promotes the study of post-Reformation Catholic History and recusants in the Midland counties and issues a regular journal (**http://midlandcatholichistory.org.uk**). Tracing Your Ancestors in Birmingham has a listing of Catholic religious houses (**www.bmsgh.org/TYAIB/religioushouses.html**).

Non-conformists

Birmingham has a long history of being home to, and tolerant of, many creeds and religions. Being exempt from the 'Five Mile Act' of 1665, which sought by law to enforce conformity to the established Church of England, Birmingham was seen as a safe haven for those who had undergone religious persecution. Over the next two hundred years the town saw the proliferation of a bewildering array of non-conformist denominations: Quakers, Baptists, Presbyterians, Congregationalists, Unitarians, Wesleyan Methodists, Calvinistic Methodists – to name just a few – all brought their dissenting voices to the ears of Birmingham's populace.

Interior of the Old Meeting House. (Public domain)

Between 1689 and 1829 the numbers of dissenting meeting houses in Birmingham and elsewhere were recorded at the Warwick Quarter Sessions [QS/10/4]. By 1830 there were at least twenty non-conformist chapels and meeting houses in the town, compared with twelve churches, two Roman Catholic chapels and one synagogue. Such was the strength of dissenting opinion that two of the meeting houses – one being the Wesleyan Chapel in Moor Street – were installed in theatres that had been shutdown due to religious opposition. Not everyone welcomed this firebrand radicalism and animosity against dissenters flared throughout the eighteenth century. In 1709 a mob sacked the Digbeth Meeting House and violence was sparked again in 1714 and 1715, at the time of the Jacobite rising. Sporadic riots against Wesleyans and Quakers continued through to the 1750s.

Being as concerned for the fate of the soul in this world as in the next, non-conformists promoted business and commerce and were at the forefront of campaigns for political and social reforms. Samuel Pearce, for example, minister at the Cannon Street Baptist church in the 1790s, was one of many who campaigned for abolition of the slave trade. In 1792, he founded the Baptist Missionary Society, which sent missionaries abroad. Others, such as the Birmingham Town Mission, aimed to spread the Gospel amongst the local populace.

Foremost among the town's non-conformist preachers during this period was Joseph Priestley. Minister of the Unitarian New Meeting House from 1780–91, and generally regarded as the discoverer of oxygen and father of modern chemistry, Priestley was the archetypal Enlightenment man. Within a few years of his arrival in Birmingham he had offended almost all of the Established Church and attracted a reputation as an anarchic and seditious figure. The situation came to a head in 1791 when, in loyalist reaction to the French Revolution, his house was destroyed during fierce anti-radical riots. As a result of these so-called Priestley Riots, Joseph Priestley fled Birmingham, never to return; he subsequently settled in the United States.

During the nineteenth century the 'Civic Gospel' inspired by non-conformist teachings played a major role in shaping politics in Birmingham and beyond (see below).

Non-conformist Records

The first systematic records are those of the Quakers, from 1656. Some books have a pre-printed style, e.g. Wesleyan, which predetermined the information given. Often the registers had been purchased by an individual within the chapel who considered it to be their property. In some cases the minister even took the register with him when he moved to a new chapel.

Prior to 1754, non-conformists could marry in their own chapels. Under Hardwicke's Act of 1753 marriages had to take place in a licensed Anglican parish church before an Anglican minister. Quakers (as well as Jews) were exempt from the new law. After the introduction of civil registration in 1837, all religious denominations were free to hold legal marriage ceremonies and were to keep their own registers. As very few chapels had their own burial grounds, individuals were either buried in the local Anglican churchyard or cemetery (some had areas set aside for non-conformists) or were sent further afield to an independent chapel which did have a burial ground.

The Library of Birmingham holds the registers for many, though by no means all, non-conformist places of worship. The Archives and Heritage Catalogue indicates which registers are held and the covering dates; lists are available in the search room and available to download under each place's catalogue entry. These use the catalogue designations: BC (Baptist), CC (Congregationalist), MC (Methodist), PC (Presbyterian), UC (Unitarian), and XC (for others). At present, these registers are not in the Library of Birmingham Collection on Ancestry.

Other notable collections at the LoB include a list of members of the Birmingham Meeting of the Society of Friends, 1789–1807 [MS 1071]; papers relating to Cannon Street Baptist church and the Baptist movement in Birmingham [MS 2646]; and various records relating to abolitionist organizations [MS 3173; IIR 62].

As with Catholic chapels, not all registers were surrendered to the Registrar General under the Non-Parochial Registers Commissions of 1837 and 1857. In Warwickshire, fifty-five chapels were deposited, together with forty for Worcestershire and seventy-seven in Staffordshire. These are now available at The National Archives [in Classes RG4 and RG8] and through the BMD Registers (**www.bmdregisters.org.uk**), Ancestry and The Genealogist websites. There are around twenty Birmingham chapels and meeting houses within this collection; a list is available (**http://tinyurl.com/qa5ylk7**). BMSGH has transcribed these registers, which are available as a download [B302D].

Other non-conformist records which may be of value include minute books (some denominations had to apply to leave and re-join the church when they moved area), account books (records of payment for burial), lists of members, Sunday school admissions, monumental inscriptions, magazines and year books (which may include obituaries).

Members of the Wesleyan Church who subscribed to a major fundraising effort launched in 1899 are listed in the *Wesleyan Methodist Historic Roll*. The names of most donors in Staffordshire, Warwickshire and Worcestershire can be found in *Volumes 21 and 22 – The Birmingham and Shrewsbury District*, available at the BMSGH Reference Library and the Archives of Westminster Methodist Central Hall (**www.methodist-central-hall.org.uk**). The Surman Index lists biographical information on Congregational and some other non-conformist ministers (**http://surman.english.qmul.ac.uk**), while the Unitarian Historical Society has an index to obituaries in Unitarian periodicals (**www.unitarianhistory.org.uk**). A major academic project is underway to document the dissenting academies in the British Isles from 1660 to 1860, including biographical data on tutors and students (**http://dissacad.english.qmul.ac.uk**).

The Library of the Religious Society of Friends, at Friends House, Euston Road, London, is the main repository for researching Quaker ancestors and publishes several research guides (**www.quaker.org.uk**). Some copies are held locally at the Library of Birmingham, the Friends Meeting House (Bull Street) and

Woodbrooke Quaker Study Centre (Selly Oak); details at the Quaker Family History Society (**www.qfhs.co.uk**). The LoB holds and is cataloguing the archives of the Society's Central England Area Meeting, 1662–c.2000.

For other non-conformist sources see specialist guides such as Ratcliffe (2014) and Milligan & Thomas (1999).

Cemeteries and Burial Grounds

Principal Cemeteries

During the population explosion of the eighteenth and nineteenth centuries Birmingham's churchyards quickly became full to bursting. In his 1781 *History of Birmingham*, William Hutton wrote of St Martin's Church that: 'the growth of the soil causes a low appearance to the building, so that instead of the church burying the dead, the dead would have, in time, buried the church'. Despite the opening of new churches with burial grounds, there was a desperate shortage of space. The last churchyard closed to new burials by 1873.

In order to address the issue, the General Cemetery at Key Hill was built, on what now covers twelve acres, in 1836 by private shareholders and designed by Charles Edge. Twelve years later the eleven-acre cemetery at Warstone Lane, adjacent to Key Hill in the Jewellery Quarter, was established in a park-like setting, designed by J.R. Hamilton. Both cemeteries were laid out on gently sloping ground on the outskirts of the town, on sites that had been worked as sand quarries. Each had a mortuary chapel and catacombs, which in the case of Warstone Lane were connected to the chapel by means of a hydraulic lift. J.A. Langford described Key Hill as being '...the most picturesque of our cemeteries, the grounds being tastefully and admirably laid out in walks, with ornamental lawns and shrubberies'. Notable people interred there include Joseph Chamberlain and his two wives, Harriet and Florence; John Henry Chamberlain, the architect; and three innovators involved with the Crystal Palace – Robert Chance, who supplied the glass, John Henderson, who erected the ironwork, and Thomas Osler, who made the fountain.

As commercial development encroached and public cemeteries were opened elsewhere, Key Hill and Warstone Lane were no longer as attractive as they once were. After being effectively abandoned by their owners, both sites were eventually taken over by Birmingham City Council. In recent years substantial restoration efforts have taken place at these cemeteries, alongside efforts by volunteers to index and transcribe their records (see below).

As a result of the Burials Act of the 1850s, which permitted local authorities to establish their own independent burial sites, the huge 102-acre municipal cemetery at Witton was opened in 1863. Until 1911, it was the only Corporation cemetery. Some of the authorities which were later incorporated into Birmingham also opened their own facilities. Sutton Coldfield (1880) and Yardley (1883) are Church of England; Lodge Hill Selly Oak, opened in 1895, has sections also for Catholics and Quakers; Brandwood End Kings Heath, opened in 1899 has sections for non-conformists and a Jewish section was added in 1919.

Handsworth Cemetery was opened in 1909 and Quinton in 1923. Also, most workhouses had their own burial grounds for the poor.

At certain times burial grounds and churchyards have been closed and the graves relocated in order to make way for new developments, especially the railway. In 1851 graves from the Quakers burial ground had to be re-interred to accommodate the new Great Western Railway; and in 1882 the burial ground of the Old Meeting House was destroyed for the enlargement of New Street Station. The Improvement Scheme of 1875 necessitated the closure and removal of a number of burial grounds in central Birmingham. In most cases the remains were re-interred at Witton Cemetery.

Scott's Burial Ground was established in 1779 for dissenters by Joseph Scott. It closed in 1878 and the bodies were re-interred at Witton and Key Hill. Catholic dead were buried from 1786 onwards at St Peter's in Broad Street and later re-interred, most likely at Witton, as was also the fate of Baptists originally buried at The Friends' and New Baptist Meeting Houses. Jewish cemeteries were situated at Granville Street (The Froggary) from 1783 and later in a passage named Betholom Row between Bath Row and Islington Row, consecrated in 1823. The original Jews' Burial Ground disappeared in 1845 with the building of the railway and New Street Station. The bodies from Betholom Row were later re-interred in the Jewish section of Witton Cemetery, which was added in 1869.

As well as a history of the city's burial grounds, McKenna (1992) has a gazetteer listing all cemeteries, churchyards and unorthodox burial places within the city's present boundaries. The latter is based on the work of Dr Richard Hetherington, a summary of which is available at the BMSGH website (**www.bmsgh.org/TYAIB/BurialGrounds.pdf**). GENUKI has a list of cemeteries and crematoria in the wider West Midlands area (**www.genuki.org.uk/big/eng/WAR/warcem.html**). Many cemeteries have 'friends' groups who can provide details of the history and layout of each site.

Insights into the Victorian way of death are on display at the Coffin Works, a museum in the Jewellery Quarter in the restored premises of Newman Brothers, coffin manufacturers (**www.coffinworks.org**).

Cemetery and Burial Records

The Library of Birmingham holds the burial registers of most Anglican and some non-conformist churches. The Archives and Heritage Catalogue indicates which churches had burials and the covering dates for the registers held; lists are available in the search room and available to download under each church's catalogue entry. Most burial registers for the period 1538–1964 are now available within the Library of Birmingham Collection on Ancestry. Catholic burial registers may be consulted at the Birmingham Archdiocesan Archives (see above).

The National Burial Index, available via Findmypast and to purchase on DVD, has good coverage for Birmingham churches and includes some non-conformist burial grounds (see **www.ffhs.org.uk/burials/war3.php**). Many rural parishes in Staffordshire, Warwickshire and Worcestershire are also covered. A separate

1865 Date of Burial	Running No.	No. of Grave	Depth Feet	Name of Deceased	Parents' Name, Relative, or principal connection	Last Residence	Age	Cause of Death	Officiating Minister
March 13	1899?	127 N Reopened		Mary Collins	Thomas Upton	114 Moland Street	56	Debility	John Brame
14	1899?	12 Catacomb? reopened		Robert Lucas Chance	Louisa Chance	Northfleet near Gravesend	82	Natural Decay	No service required
	1899?	16 Vault 2		Emma Whitehouse	Henry Whitehouse	Lower Camden Street	27	Phthisis	John Brame
	1899?	291 N Reopened		Ellen Isabella Gooch	Ephraim Gooch	Soho Hill	12 years	Typhoid Fever	John Brame
18	1899?	99 O	12	Joseph Hingley	Samuel Hingley	2 Court 13 house Ward Street	81	Natural Decay	Sampson Cocks
17	1899?	5 Vault Corridor		John Garlick	John Garlick	Bridge Street	53	Paralysis	John Brame

Burial register for General Cemetery, Key Hill, March 1865 showing the entry for Robert Lucas Chance of Chance Brothers, glassmakers. (Courtesy of BMSGH)

online index is available for Staffordshire parishes outside of Birmingham (**www.bmsgh.org/burialsearch**).

BMSGH volunteers have indexed and transcribed the registers for the four main central Birmingham cemeteries – Key Hill, Warstone Lane, Witton and Handsworth. These indexes are available to purchase either as a download or on CD-ROM, and are also on Findmypast (under 'Warwickshire Burials'). Following a major project to digitize the registers from all four cemeteries, BMSGH now offers a service whereby it is possible to search the indexes online and then purchase a high-resolution image of the original burial register entry.

The LoB has indexes for all local authority cemeteries in Birmingham from the dates of opening up to the mid-1980s (1973 for Brandwood End). For cemeteries not covered by the BMSGH indexes, you may be able to obtain additional information by contacting the cemetery or crematorium concerned (**www.birmingham.gov.uk/cemeteries**).

Although it has yet to include the main Birmingham cemeteries in its database, Deceased Online has records of disused and closed burial grounds and cemeteries held at The National Archives [class RG37] (**www.deceased online.com**). These include closed churchyards, such as St Mary and St Thomas, and burials re-interred in the main municipal cemeteries from various locations. Care should be taken, however, as the main referencing is by date of re-interment rather than date of death.

Monumental Inscriptions

Over the last forty years BMSGH volunteers have transcribed the monumental inscriptions ('MIs') from graves, tombstones and memorials across Staffordshire, Warwickshire and Worcestershire. Transcriptions for around 650 locations have been published; many of these are now available either on CD or as downloads. Indexes are also open to postal and/or email enquiries; details are in the Annex. In addition, copies of the MIs may be consulted at the BMSGH Reference Library, the Library of Birmingham, the Society of Genealogists in London, and relevant county record offices.

Other sources for information on deaths include newspaper announcements and obituaries, and wills (see Chapter 1).

Civic Gospels: Dissenters and Political Reform

Birmingham's reputation as a hotbed for dissenters was not confined to the religious sphere. The concerns of those, predominantly non-conformists, who aimed to improve the conditions of the rapidly growing urban population inevitably overlapped into the political arena. During the 1820s and 30s, Thomas Attwood of the Birmingham Political Union led campaigns to promote free trade and extend the voting franchise. Following the Reform Bill of 1832, Attwood and his associate Joshua Scholefield were elected as the town's first Members of Parliament.

In 1838, Birmingham was granted a Municipal Charter and became a Borough with its own Corporation, covering also Edgbaston, Bordesley, Duddeston and Nechells. However, responsibility for many aspects of urban administration, such as maintenance of the roads, still rested on the old parochial system – the Street Commissioners – which remained in place. By the 1860s the town council was still in the hands of a 'shopocracy': unprogressive tradesmen who lacked ideas and loathed spending money. Between 1853 and 1858 council expenditure actually decreased by one third.

Against this background of sterile local administration, a new civic philosophy began to take root. Known as the 'civic gospel', in Birmingham it was inspired by non-conformist preachers, implemented by a new generation of local politicians, and given expression in the work of artists and architects. Preachers such as George Dawson, Dr H.W. Crosskey and Robert Dale asserted in their teachings the importance of culture and civic pride alongside spiritual growth. A town council, they argued, should be responsible for the welfare of all within and subject to its authority, just as Parliament was for the well-being of the nation as a whole. Whilst they disagreed on elements of religious doctrine (they were each from different denominations), they were united in their belief that the municipal authority had a responsibility to work for and effect change.

In essence, the Birmingham civic gospel was an entrepreneurial gospel – one that proclaimed change, initiative and boldness. This dynamic outlook was a vital influence in shaping local politicians and business leaders, many of whom were regular attendees at non-conformist congregations. They included the young Joseph Chamberlain (who worked in the family screw manufacturing

Borough of Birmingham, 1839. (Public domain)

business), his brother Arthur (brass), his brother-in-law William Kenrick (hollow-ware), and R.F. Martineau.

In 1873 a reform-minded council selected Chamberlain as mayor; it marked the beginning of substantial efforts to put the principles of the civic gospel into practice. Within a few months Chamberlain was involved in negotiating the takeover by the council of the town's gas supply; municipalization of Birmingham's water supply soon followed. His crowning achievement as mayor was the Birmingham Improvement Scheme, launched in 1875 (see Chapter 7). Although Chamberlain left local politics in 1876, on being elected MP for Birmingham, he maintained a very close interest in the city's affairs. Most significantly, he helped to found the University of Birmingham in 1900 and became its first Chancellor.

By this time the civic gospel was being given physical expression through the work of a Birmingham-based school of architects and artists. Foremost amongst these was John Henry Chamberlain (no relation to Joseph), who saw each new building as 'the projection of values into space and stone'. His contributions included: Shenstone House, Edgbaston (1855, the first High Victorian building within the town); Birmingham Central Library (1882, demolished 1974); Oozells Street Board School, Brindleyplace (now the Ikon Gallery); Highbury Hall, Moseley (commissioned by Joseph Chamberlain); and the School of Art, Margaret Street (1881, generally considered his finest building).

Through a combination of moral philosophy, politics and architectural design, the civic gospel had, by 1890, led to Birmingham being called 'the best governed city in the world'. Whilst not without its critics – some said the Improvement Scheme was motivated by commercial interest rather than social ideals – it set a model for much of the city's later development.

Electoral and Voting Records

The Library of Birmingham holds electoral registers for the Borough and City of Birmingham from 1832. There are some gaps in the series, including 1914–17 and 1940–44 as registers were not compiled nationally during the world wars. Holdings start from the date at which an area became part of Birmingham (i.e. Handsworth and Kings Norton from 1911 and Sutton Coldfield from 1974). The Library has a small collection of poll books for Birmingham and some neighbouring counties and towns (e.g. Lichfield), and some early voters lists are in the Quarter Sessions records (Table 2.3). Voters lists for the period 1832–1955 – including electoral registers, burgess rolls, poll books, and absent voters lists – are available on Ancestry (for Birmingham and some of north Warwickshire). The Absent Voters List 1918 records those entitled to vote but who were not at home during the General Election of 1918. Similar lists were kept through to 1939, although the numbers covered reduced significantly.

Midlands Historical Data has a searchable index of Birmingham electoral rolls for 1920–1965, including absent voters lists (**www.midlandshistoricaldata.org**). For a map and details of current wards see the Birmingham City Council website

Table 2.3: Electoral Sources in Quarter Sessions Records

	Staffordshire	Warwickshire	Worcestershire
Electors – Parliamentary	Q/RPr	QS0113	1/7/3
Electors – County		QS0114	
Electors – Parochial	Catalogued by parish	QS0115	
Freeholders' and Jury Lists	Q/RJ	QS0076	1/11, 8001/3/2/5/12
Overseers' Voters Lists	Catalogued by parish	QS0112	

Notes: The references shown are for the catalogue of the relevant county archive: SSA for Staffordshire; WCRO for Warwickshire; WAAS for Worcestershire. For web addresses of online catalogues and other details see 'How To Use This Book' in the Introduction.

(**www.birmingham.gov.uk/wards**), while Wikipedia has information on current and former Parliamentary constituencies.

Political Records

The records of political parties may contain membership lists and, if an ancestor was particularly active, details of their involvement and contributions.

The University of Birmingham has the archives of the Midland Union of Conservative Associations, 1888–1944 [MUCA]; a file on the West Midlands Liberal Federation, 1894 [WMLF]; and papers relating to the British Union of Fascists and its successor organization, the Union Movement. Warwick MRC has the records of the West Midlands Regional Labour Party [MSS. 6], as well as some individual labour constituencies. The Library of Birmingham has minute books for the Birmingham Liberal Association, 1878–1888 [MS 440]; and a members' book for the Birmingham Liberal Club [MS 810].

Chartism and Trade Unions

Birmingham's association with the labour movement goes back to the very beginnings of organized labour and the political reform movement known as Chartism. The Reform Act of 1832 went only part of the way to meeting the demands of political reformers such as Thomas Attwood and his ilk in the Birmingham Political Union. During the 1830s a grassroots movement evolved around a wider campaign for political and social reforms. They unveiled their demands in a 'People's Charter', launched in London in 1838, and hence became known as the Chartists. The People's Charter had six main demands: the vote for all men aged over twenty-one, the abolition of a property qualification, secret ballots, fixed elections, equal-sized constituencies, and salaried members of Parliament.

Attwood – by then one of Birmingham's MPs – launched a national petition in support of the Charter, which attracted over one million signatures. By this time Birmingham was recognized as a town sympathetic to the Chartists' cause and becoming the focus for a national movement. Mass rallies were held regularly and in 1839 the first Chartist Convention moved to Birmingham from London, as it was felt to be a less threatening location. Throughout the summer of 1839 unease simmered between the Chartist supporters and the more conservative element on the new Borough Council. When the council sought police assistance from London, using the newly-opened railway line, violence erupted in the Bull Ring. Although no one was killed, the Bull Ring Riots led to many being arrested, including the Chartist leader William Lovett, and a tense standoff with police. The campaigners could now add violence by the state to their long list of political grievances.

Over the following two decades Birmingham's role in Chartism diminished as campaigners in other centres, notably London and Manchester, took up the cause. Its importance in providing the movement's early foundations can not be underestimated, however. The fruits of that campaign, in the form of cooperatives, trade unions and the organized labour movement, would eventually be taken up in Birmingham's factories and workshops. These made major contributions to improving the working and living conditions of the urban working class.

WMRC has substantial collections of trade union and labour movement archives. These files may include details such as membership lists, contributions books, minutes of branch meetings, wage rates, company files, and accident and mortality reports. The holdings range from long-defunct local organizations, such as the Birmingham and District Gun Workers' Union, formed in 1896 [MSS.21/3691], and the Pen Workers' Federation [MSS.42]; to Midlands branches of early national unions, such as the Birmingham district of the Amalgamated Engineering Union [MS 202 & 309]; to the national archives of current-day trade unions. Much of this collection, including digitized images of original record books, is now available on Findmypast (as 'Trade Union Membership Registers').

The Birmingham Trades Council was formed in 1866 as a coordinating committee for local unions; both WMRC and the LoB hold material. Other union-related archives include those of the Birmingham Trade Union Resource Centre [LoB: MS 2009] and the Indian Workers' Association [LoB: MS 2141].

For further details see Crail (2009) and that author's specialist websites: **www.chartism.net** and **www.unionancestors.co.uk**.

Further Information

Alan Betteridge, *Deep Roots: A History of Baptists in the English Western Midlands* (Matador, 2010).

Mark Crail, *Tracing Your Labour Movement Ancestors* (Pen & Sword, 2009).

Peter T. Marsh, *Joseph Chamberlain: Entrepreneur in Politics* (Yale University Press, 1994).

Joseph McKenna, *In the Midst of Life: A History of the Burial Grounds of Birmingham* (Birmingham Library Services, 1992).

E.H. Milligan and M.J. Thomas, *My Ancestors Were Quakers* (Society of Genealogists, 1999).

Richard Ratcliffe, *Methodist Records for Family Historians* (Family History Partnership, 2014).

J.J. Scarisbrick, *History of the Diocese of Birmingham 1850–2000* (Éditions du Signe, 2008). Available at www.birminghamarchdiocesanarchives.org.uk/book_history/index.html.

Roger Ward, *City-State and Nation. Birmingham's Political History 1830–1940* (Phillimore, 2005).

Christine Ward-Penny, *Catholics in Birmingham* (The History Press, 2004).

Chapter 3

CITY OF A THOUSAND TRADES: INDUSTRY

The Midlands Enlightenment

Something incredible happened in the West Midlands in the early years of the eighteenth century: people began to apply the growing body of scientific discoveries to the way things were made. The area was already well known for its metal-based industries. There had been smiths and forges in Birmingham since the Middle Ages and in the fifteenth and sixteenth centuries the town achieved a reputation for weaponry – first swords and later guns and munitions. In the Black Country, industries such as nail-making and chain-making were

Matthew Boulton's Soho Manufactory, Handsworth. (Public domain)

prevalent. These were all craft industries, where the skills were passed down from father to son, and from master to apprentice in a time-honoured way.

The key change brought by the eighteenth century was the notion of progress. Intellectuals and thinkers no longer saw mankind's place in the world as fixed, as the church taught, but as one that could be reasoned and improved. In this period, which we call the Industrial Revolution, the scientific knowledge built up over the previous 200 years began to be converted into useable technologies and manufacturing processes. This, in turn, brought the advent of mechanization and factory-scale industrialization.

Nowhere was this spirit of inventiveness and innovation as evident as in the English Midlands. In the early 1700s, Abraham Darby pioneered the use of blast furnaces at Ironbridge and the region was one of the most enthusiastic adopters of the Newcomen engine, used to pump out water in mines. During the 1760s a small circle of natural philosophers, physicians and manufacturers began to meet regularly to exchange knowledge and ideas both on practical matters and on the general social situation. As they met each month on or around the full moon, they became known as the Lunar Society. Over the next four decades the society's members, who never numbered more than fourteen, were responsible for pioneering work in chemistry, physics, engineering and medicine; for the application of these advances in manufacturing and commerce; and for campaigning for social reforms, notably abolition of the slave trade. They included the manufacturer Matthew Boulton (1728–1809), the Scottish engineers James Watt (1736–1819) and William Murdoch (1754–1839), the master potter Josiah Wedgwood (1730–1795), and Erasmus Darwin (1731–1802).

Matthew Boulton was undoubtedly one of the leading figures in what historians now refer to as 'The Midlands Enlightenment'. Born in Birmingham in 1728, he joined his father's button-making business and by his early twenties had taken over its management. In 1761 he leased thirteen acres at Soho in Handsworth. The site had a watermill to power machinery for grinding and polishing the metal components of the buttons, buckles and other trinkets he manufactured. He introduced many improvements in the manufacturing process, including installing one of Watt's new steam engines. Recognizing the potential of this new technology, Boulton then went into business with Watt and others to bring it to fruition. He also established a mint at Soho for making coins.

The achievements of Boulton, Watt and their contemporaries put Birmingham on a course to become the world's first town with an economy dominated by manufacturing. Over the next 150 years the foundations they established enabled Birmingham to be at the forefront of a whole variety of manufactured goods, from guns and jewellery, to bedsteads and pen-nibs, railway locomotives and bicycles, and eventually, of course, the motor car. They also left a commitment to philanthropy: the notion that entrepreneurs have a responsibility to use their wealth for the social good.

Although the Soho Manufactory has not survived, Boulton's former home, Soho House, has been restored as a museum (**www.bmag.org.uk/soho-house**). The papers of Boulton and his circle are in the Archives of Soho, a Library of Birmingham collection of international importance; highlights are presented in the Library's online collections. The achievements of the Lunar Society are described in Jenny Uglow's award-winning book *The Lunar Men* (2002) and at two websites: Revolutionary Players (**www.revolutionaryplayers.org.uk**) and Soho Mint (**http://sohomint.info**).

The Brass Industry

Brass was one of the first industries to become established in Birmingham and underpinned many others with which the city subsequently became associated. Originally, brass – an alloy of copper and zinc – was imported from Bristol and Cheadle and goods were finished in Birmingham. This started to change in 1740 when Turner's brass works was established in Coleshill Street.

Most goods were made in a foundry by casting, which involved pouring the molten alloy into sand moulds. Braziers, a separate trade, wrought goods by hand from sheet brass. Later, demand was for more specialized products, like fittings for carriages, cabinets, furniture, keys and bolts. In the nineteenth century, huge new markets opened up in supplying brass fittings for steam engines, railway carriages and gas lamps. Birmingham was also Europe's largest exporter of brass, mostly to France.

Both brass founders and braziers had their own guilds or companies established in London in the fourteenth century. As it was not a guild town, Birmingham attracted workers and entrepreneurs from far and wide, many of whom brought certain skills with them; for instance, from the chain and nailmaking trades of the Black Country. In 1770 there were thirty-eight brass founders in Birmingham; by 1788 this figure had risen to fifty-six, reaching seventy-one in 1797.

When the price of copper rose dramatically in 1780, the Birmingham industrialists decided to produce their own. This resulted in the founding of the Birmingham Metal Company off Broad Street (now Brasshouse Passage) and in 1790 the establishment of the Birmingham Mining and Copper Company (BMCC), which ran mines in Redruth (Cornwall) and Swansea (Wales). In 1781 it was estimated that more than 1000 tons of brass were used in the Birmingham manufactories. Prices dropped after the establishment of the BMCC, from around £84 to £56 per ton.

Following the appearance of brass manufacture in the town, Birmingham's inventors and entrepreneurs quickly developed their own innovations. In 1767, William Chapman was granted a patent for '*Refining copper and manufacturing brass and brass wire*'. In 1769 the production of brass articles by means of stamp and die was introduced by Richard Ford, who adopted a process patented by John Pickering, a London gilt toymaker, in his Birmingham factory. David Harcourt took out the patent for the first automatic press in 1835 and the same machine was still in use in the family's manufactory almost a hundred years later. Further technological advances took place in the 1830s. Firstly, a new technique of mixing copper and zinc directly in the crucible meant quicker and more efficient production. Secondly, new iron moulds began to replace the old sand ones, enabling far more precision in the making of brass goods.

The brass trade was highly skilled, requiring both manual dexterity and scientific knowledge. The production of an eagle for a church lectern, for example, required a mould made up of twenty-five separate pieces. Braziers wrought intricate patterns on many of the goods they produced, but by the nineteenth century their work had largely been taken over by machine stamping. Writing in 1865, W.C. Aitken noted that Birmingham workers had 'a special qualification for the manipulation of metals' which was '… hereditary, transmissible and transmitted from sire to son'.

By 1831, 1,800 workers were involved in the brass trade, ten years later this number had almost doubled. The larger brass companies were Messenger (employing 250 in the early 1800s), Ryland (150 in 1812, though essentially an iron and steel company), Jenkins (250 in 1833), and Wingfields (100 in 1835, rising to over 700 in 1860). However, the majority of the companies were smaller factories employing 20–30 workers. By 1870 the brass trade was providing 10,000 jobs.

The Avery Historical Museum is a private museum devoted to W.T. Avery Ltd, a leading manufacturer of weighing equipment (**www.averyberkel.com/ museum**); it stands on the site of Matthew Boulton's Soho Foundry.

The Gun Trade

The gun trade is one of Birmingham's oldest industries. The making of flint-lock guns and pistols was firmly established by the early 1690s, when Birmingham gunsmiths contracted to supply the government with 200 muskets per month. Subsequent wars, demand at home and a growing colonial trade – especially with the west coast of Africa – all helped to consolidate military small arms as a staple manufacture. During the Napoleonic wars, 1803–1815, Birmingham gunmakers accounted for two-thirds of the firearms used by the British army, with around 1.7 million guns being delivered to the Board of Ordnance. Large numbers of swords and cutlasses were also supplied for the army and navy. By the end of the eighteenth century, Birmingham was the foremost arms producer in the world, manufacturing a million items more than London, its nearest rival.

Firearms was a specialized trade: the production of a gun involved many stages, from the forging and manufacture of component parts to the assembly, finishing and decorating of completed weapons. Initially, all the operations were carried out by individual gunsmiths, but as production methods changed and different styles of weapons were introduced, people began to specialize in the manufacture of the various component parts. Component manufacturers included breechers, borers, stock makers, barrel welders, bayonet forgers, socket and ring stampers. These parts were then assembled by the 'setters up' who assembled the finished article, such as polishers, engravers, browners, and sighters. Each finished gun would have gone through about fifty different hands.

The need for so many different processes and skills led workers to cluster within the same area. By the 1820s there were several thousand people employed in the gun trade, most working in an area around St Mary's church, which became known as the Gun Quarter. Centred on Weaman Street, Whittall Street and Loveday Street, the Quarter was a mixture of factories of moderate size, small factories and 'shoppings' – workshops let out to individual outworkers. A gunsmith who wished to set up his own business would rent a space from either the parish or another gunmaker. It was close, cramped and higgledy-piggledy, with early Victorian tenement buildings pushing in between buildings of an earlier time and function.

Sketchley's Directory of Birmingham for 1767 lists a total of sixty-two workshops involved in gunmaking. There were thirty-five gun and pistol makers, eight gun barrel makers and filers, five gun barrel polishers and finishers, eleven gun lock makers, forgers and finishers, and three gun swivel and stock makers. An 1860 trades directory lists forty-eight different gun-related trades. In 1851 there were around 2,900 workers in the Birmingham gun trade. This had grown to nearly ten thousand workers by 1865. *Kelly's* directory for 1874 lists 329 names connected with the gun trade in Birmingham, 210 of which had premises in the Gun Quarter.

The trade was given a further boost in 1813 with the establishment of the Birmingham Gun Barrel Proof House. Private proof houses run by individual gunmakers had existed before this and were available for use by others, but were not used by the less reputable gunmakers. Many saw the need for compulsory independent proof as was available in London. As a result a local facility was established by Act of Parliament, at the request and expense of the Birmingham trade. Still situated in its original premises in Banbury Street, the Birmingham Proof House is the only official proof house outside of London. It now houses a museum dedicated to the gun and ammunition trades of the Birmingham area (**www.gunproof.com**).

One of the sector's biggest success stories was the Birmingham Small Arms Company (BSA), which opened a factory in Small Heath in 1860. When demand for guns fell following the Crimean War, BSA turned its attention to making the new Otto bicycle. The company subsequently diversified into bicycles and later motorcycles and cars, only increasing gun production again during the Boer War and the Great War.

The Birmingham Gun Museum website (**www.birminghamgunmuseum.com**) is dedicated to the city's gun trade heritage and efforts to establish a specialist museum. It lists information on the Gun Quarter, a list of gun trades, profiles of leading companies, and a detailed history of two of the major manufacturers, BSA and Webley & Scott. Records of the Birmingham Gun Trade Association 1856–1989, including a register of members, are held privately; application via Library of Birmingham [NRA: 33255 Birmingham Proof].

The Jewellery Trade

Precious metals have been worked within Birmingham since at least the fourteenth century. The industry started to flourish around 1660, when Charles II brought back fancy buttons and shoe buckles on his return from exile in France. These items soon became very fashionable and created a large demand for the

The Cartwheel twopenny piece minted at Matthew Boulton's Soho Mint. (Wikimedia, Creative Commons)

work of Birmingham craftsmen who specialized in the manufacture of small metal goods.

The establishment of the Birmingham Assay Office in 1773 was a defining moment. With their own assay facility, the Birmingham jewellers no longer had to suffer the impracticalities and expense of sending their wares to London or Chester for assaying. This, together with Matthew Boulton's dedication to quality in his own manufactory at Soho, completely changed the perception of the Birmingham industry which had previously acquired a reputation for shoddy workmanship.

The depression that followed the Napoleonic Wars caused a major slump in the industry and by 1825 it was close to extinction. However, Queen Victoria's accession in 1837 made wearing jewellery fashionable again. Many poorly paid industrial workers in Birmingham set up their own 'peg' (workshop), often from home, allowing them to improve their standard of living considerably.

The Birmingham assay mark. (Public domain)

Then, as now, the trade was divided into manufacturing and non-manufacturing jewellers. The former provided raw rings, brooches, chains, etc. for the non-manufacturing jewellers to turn into finished items. As with gun makers, jewellery production required many different trades and skills. One craftsman would seldom work on a piece from start to completion; workers would specialize, for example as diamond cutters, stone setters, engravers, or polishers. Craftsmen began to group together in order to collaborate effectively, eventually congregating in the Hockley area which became known as the Jewellery Quarter (see Chapter 1).

A technological milestone in the trade came in 1840, when George Richards Elkington and his partner John Wright developed a new method of electroplating silver. Their patented process, applied at Elkington's Works in Newhall Street, was so revolutionary that it rendered the old method, which was very unreliable, obsolete. Elkington subsequently dominated the jewellery market, creating demand among the new Victorian middle class for affordable gold- and silver-plated jewellery. The development gave rise to the expression 'Brummagem ware' for mock or imitation goods.

The period from 1866 to 1886 is known as the Silver Jewellery Period, when silver was actually more popular as a raw material than gold. During this period much civic regalia were produced in Birmingham and diamonds were being increasingly used. Decorative boxes and household items such as brush backs were also being manufactured in silver. Employment in the jewellery trade increased from 7,500 to 16,000 by 1890, when a further slump set in.

In 1887, the Birmingham Jewellers and Silversmiths Association was set up, partly through the efforts of Joseph Chamberlain, followed a year later by the Jewellers' School in an attempt to raise standards and thereby protect the industry from decline. This, coupled with the cheap gold prices around 1900, led to another boom in trade. By 1913 the jewellery trade reached its zenith, providing at its peak employment for 22,000 Birmingham workers. The sharp fall in demand for jewellery during the First World War and the ensuing depression in the 1920s caused many firms to close. Today, the trade in jewellery is again a key feature of Birmingham's economy.

The story of the Jewellery Quarter and Birmingham's renowned jewellery and metalworking heritage is told at the Museum of the Jewellery Quarter (**www.bmag.org.uk/museum-of-the-jewellery-quarter**). This award-winning museum is housed in the artisan jewellery factory of Smith & Pepper, a manufacturing firm that closed in the early 1980s. Working life is also on display at the Evans Silver Factory, a workshop maintained by English Heritage. The Jewellery Quarter Research Trust researches the history and heritage of the area and has its own archive (**www.jqrt.org**).

If your ancestors sold jewellery to the public they may have had their own hallmark. The Birmingham Assay Office maintains the register of all hallmarks issued in Birmingham, only part of which has been published (**www.theassayoffice.co.uk**). Register entries record the date of registration, the location of the shop or workshop, and a description of the mark, sometimes with an illustration. The register may be consulted at the Assay Office's library, or the library staff will conduct research on your behalf; charges apply in both cases. A new project starting in 2015 aims to digitize the catalogue and make it available online.

Further information on Birmingham's jewellers and their work is given in Mason (1998) and the Birmingham Jewellers & Silversmiths Association's fiftieth anniversary publication (1937). The Clocks and Watches Research site has a table of hallmarks for the Birmingham Assay Office as well as a list of local clock and watch makers (**www.clockswatches.co.uk**).

The Toyshop of Europe

Alongside high-value items, such as guns and jewellery, Birmingham became a centre for the manufacture of all manner of metal articles, collectively referred to as 'toys'. These were not playthings but utility items such as tinder boxes, steelyards, pokers, fire-shovels and tongs, metal tools, domestic utensils, and household fittings of all kinds. In a debate in Parliament in 1777 Edmund Burke famously referred to Birmingham as 'the great toyshop of Europe', a moniker that stuck for many years after.

One characteristic of these new 'toy' industries was that they employed metals other than iron. Copper and brass were in demand, both for decorative work and for the manufacture of domestic utensils. Steel, a much harder metal than brass and therefore less easy to work, became popular for ornamental objects; it did not rust and could be polished to a sparkle. In the late seventeenth century small quantities of the metal were emanating from south Staffordshire. A few years later at least two furnaces for converting iron into steel were established in Birmingham itself.

Many of these items were subject to the vagaries of fashion, so the industry had to be continually alert to new opportunities. The declining popularity of buckles at the end of the eighteenth century led many buckle fabricators to apply their skills to the production of buttons. By the 1780s the fashion was for large

A Royal visit to Gillott's pen manufactory, watching the women workers during the slitting process. (Wellcome Images, Creative Commons)

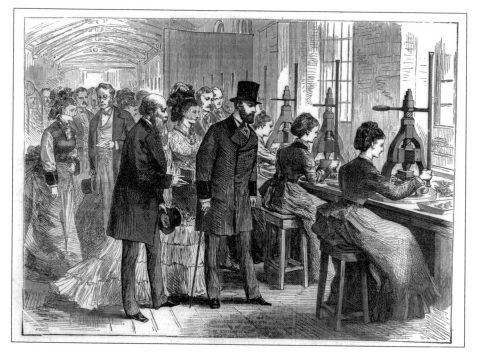

plated buttons, worn on all possible garments. Some of the leading industrialists were involved, such as the partnership of Matthew Boulton and John Fothergill. Indeed, of twenty-one button patents applied for between 1770 and 1800, nineteen were from Birmingham. Traditional buttons were supplemented by cloth-covered buttons (patented 1825), silk buttons (1837) and linen buttons (1841). *Slater's Directory 1852* lists twenty major button manufacturers in the town.

This period marked the high point of the button industry. The abolition of import duty in the 1840s brought a flood of cheap imports, while mechanization led to a streamlining of the workforce. By the 1860s there was considerable over-production of buttons and the industry was in decline. The exception was the pearl button trade: due to the delicate nature of the materials, these had to be turned on hand or foot lathes. They were therefore mostly produced in smaller home-based shops, which were less vulnerable to fluctuations in wages and prices. The hand production of pearl buttons and pearl-based jewellery continued in Birmingham until the late twentieth century.

The manufacture of steel pen nibs was another of what might be called Birmingham's 'signature' trades. The growth of literacy, as well as commercial writing and bookkeeping, led to a search for more durable alternatives to quill pens. The quest attracted the attention of Birmingham's entrepreneurial and inventive minds. Renowned for their skill with metal, they began experimenting with the use of steel as a writing implement. John Mitchell was the first to mass produce steel pens, in 1822, having observed the handpress production of small metalware items such as buckles and buttons. Others added improvements, notably Joseph Gillott and Josiah Mason, both of whom were incomers to Birmingham. As with other industries, the pen trade benefited from the ready availability of raw materials (coal, iron and steel from the Black Country) and good transport links (canals and later railways) for transporting materials and distributing the finished goods. Later, Sheffield took over as the sole source of steel.

Early pens were so simple that even small manufacturers produced their own models and introduced improvements. At the height of the trade, around 1870, there were over 130 steel pen manufacturers in the town, and it was estimated that around two-thirds of everything that was written down around the world was written with a Birmingham pen. Visiting Gillott's factory, the Victoria Works in Graham Street in 1868, the American Consul in Birmingham, Elihu Burritt was awestruck by the activity, energy and ingenuity. Birmingham pens were, he noted, used 'in ten thousand school houses scattered over the American continent between the two oceans'. Amalgamations and bankruptcy reduced the number of independent suppliers until, by the end of the nineteenth century, only twelve large manufacturers remained.

The talents of the pen makers of Birmingham, both the employers and the workers, are celebrated in the Pen Museum operated by the Birmingham Pen Trade Heritage Association (**www.penroom.co.uk**). The museum is situated in the Argent Centre in the Jewellery Quarter, in a building that was once the factory of pen maker, W.E. Wiley. The Library of Birmingham has the records of the Association of British Steel Pen Makers and various pen manufacturing companies covering the period 1834–1970, including trade catalogues [MS 2718].

Food and Drink Industry

As elsewhere in the country, tea drinking became popular in Birmingham in the eighteenth century. Advertisements in Aris's *Birmingham Gazette* in 1742, for instance, show Benjamin Mansell had a tea warehouse just below the Bull Ring in Edgbaston Street, and was offering fine teas on wholesale terms. As no canal or rail transport was available then, the supplies obtained from London warehouses would have been conveyed to Birmingham by road, a slow and hazardous journey. By 1812, there were over twenty-five tea dealers in the town, both retail and wholesale. The increasing popularity of tea spurred demand for associated metal articles, such as Britannia tea bells, teaspoons, teapots and tea kettles, all made by Birmingham's skilled workers. Later, the success of Elkington's new electroplating process brought attractive silver-plated utensils within the reach of many more tea-drinking households.

In 1903 a Birmingham grocer and wine merchant called John Sumner decided to introduce a new blend of fine-leaf tea which he thought better suited to the modern palette. He invested £200 – a fortune for the time – on packaging and advertising, adopting the name 'Typhoo' Tipps; thus one of the great tea brands was born. Ty-Phoo Tea remained in Birmingham for many years and is now under Indian ownership.

Alfred Bird invented his egg-free instant custard in Birmingham in 1837. By 1843, Alfred Bird & Sons Ltd was promoting its custard powder nationally and also making the newly-invented baking powder. By 1895, the company was producing blancmange powder, jelly powder, and egg substitute. In the First World War, Bird's Custard was supplied to the British armed forces. Production was relocated to Banbury in 1964 (along with the factory gates, featuring the company logo), and Bird's factory in Gibb Street has since been adapted as the Custard Factory business centre.

Originally invented and developed in Nottingham, HP Sauce became associated with Birmingham after the recipe and brand were acquired by Edwin Samson Moore, the founder of the Midlands Vinegar Company, in 1903. The site in Aston was once bisected by the A38(M) and had a pipeline carrying vinegar over the motorway, from one side of the factory to the other.

Probably the most iconic Birmingham food business is the chocolate maker, Cadbury. John Cadbury started his one-man grocery business in Bull Street in the 1820s, selling tea and branching out into the luxury market of preparing drinking chocolate and cocoas. His business flourished, there was endorsement from royalty and the chocolate became refined and eatable. With his health failing, in 1860 John passed the business on to his two sons, Richard and George. The artistically inclined Richard concentrated on sales while the more methodical George concentrated on the manufacturing side. It was a precarious business but motivated by the Victorian work ethic and their Quaker beliefs the two young men drove the business forward.

With the business flourishing, in 1879 the Cadbury brothers moved their factory to a rural location four miles south of the centre. As well as a modern factory, their new village – which they named 'Bournville' – had well-built cottages with large gardens for the workers, together with open spaces for recreation and leisure. The story of the Cadbury family, their business and philanthropy is told at Cadbury World, a heritage centre-cum-factory tour at the Bournville site (**www.cadburyworld.co.uk**). The University of Birmingham Special Collections holds an extensive archive relating to Cadbury Brothers Ltd and the Cadbury family, housed appropriately within its Cadbury Research Library.

Brummies have always liked a pint, so it is hardly surprising that the area was the home to several successful breweries. Ansells Brewery was founded by Joseph Ansell, a hop merchant and maltster, at Aston Cross in 1858. By 1901 it had 388 licensed houses and in the decades that followed acquired several smaller local brewers. Mitchells & Butlers Brewery (M&B) – another Midlands icon – was formed in 1898 through the merger of Henry Mitchell's old Crown Brewery and William Butler's Brewery (both of which originated in Smethwick). Henry Mitchell's site in Cape Hill became the company's main brewing location and had its own rail link to the national railway network via the Harborne line. Both Ansells and M&B (or their successors) have now relocated to Burton-upon-Trent and their premises demolished, although the war memorial from the Cape Hill site has been retained and restored. SSA has the archives of the Birmingham and Midlands Counties Wholesale Brewers Association, 1895–1940 [D3163].

Other Industries

Its dominant position in metalworking of all kinds put Birmingham in the ideal position to develop more technologically-based engineering industries. The mid to late nineteenth century saw the emergence of businesses making increasingly sophisticated engineering-based products. Initially these were agricultural machinery, bicycles, and railway locomotives and rolling stock. There was then a natural progression into areas such as motor cycles, and eventually motor cars, trucks and commercial vehicles. Birmingham's involvement in these transport-related industries is described in more detail in the next chapter.

Manufacturing is a capital-intensive business, so it is hardly surprising that the town attracted bankers keen to finance the new factories. Sampson Lloyd III, a wealthy Quaker ironmonger, was one of the first to recognize the importance of a stable system of business loans in the development of industry in the town. In 1765 he formed a company with the button manufacturer, John Taylor, to set up the town's first bank. Taylor and Lloyd's Bank on Dale End was a forerunner of the Lloyds banking group we have today. The other half of what became the Lloyds TSB Group also had its origins in Birmingham. The Birmingham Municipal Bank, which later became the Trustee Savings Bank, was set up in 1919 as part of efforts to encourage rebuilding after the First World War (see **www.bmbhistory.org.uk**).

Birmingham had no mining activity of its own, the nearest being the coal mines of the Black Country (which helped give the area its name). The South Staffordshire thick coal-seam (some thirty feet deep) was a unique feature in England, and was vital to the region's development before and during the

Industrial Revolution. In 1875, the Hamstead Colliery Company was formed to buy and develop land at Hamstead (near Handsworth) purchased from the Calthorpe family of Perry Hall. On 4 March 1908 disaster struck when a fire started near the bottom of the main shaft. Rescue efforts failed and a total of twenty-five men died. The colliery lost a total of 114 men between 1875 and 1965; the 1908 incident was the largest single loss of life (details at **www.cmhrc.co.uk**). The Hamstead Miners Memorial Trust documents the history of the mine and maintains a memorial to all those who died (**www.hamsteadminers.co.uk**).

Trade and Commercial Directories

As a centre dependent on the production and sale of manufactured goods, trade directories were an essential means for Birmingham firms to publicize their wares. In the early years Birmingham tended to be covered as part of county directories for Warwickshire (and sometimes neighbouring counties as well); later on, as the town's importance grew, dedicated directories were produced. Most directories provide a history of the locality and descriptions of amenities such as schools, workhouses and churches. As well as businesses, some directories list every resident or building and/or the members of local councils and other administrative bodies.

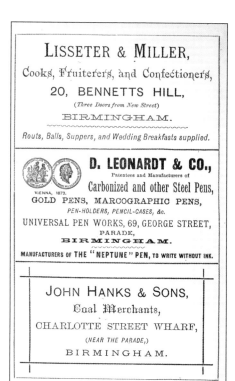

Trade advertisement from 1877: everything from fruit and pen nibs to coal was on sale in Birmingham. (Public domain)

The Library of Birmingham has a large collection of trade and commercial directories covering not just Birmingham and the Midlands but many parts of England and Wales. These are produced by well-known publishers such as Bartholomew, Holden, Hulley, Kelly, Pigot, the Post Office, Slater, and White. William Cornish, a Birmingham-based publisher and bookseller, started to produce his own directory around 1860; this later became *Cornish's Birmingham Year Book* and around 1940 the *Birmingham Post Year Book and Who's Who*. The earliest directory generally available is *Sketchley's Birmingham Directory 1767*. The Library also has a pseudo-directory of Birmingham for 1663 based on other sources, compiled by Joseph McKenna.

Historical Directories of England and Wales, part of the University of Leicester's Special Collections Online, has many digitized trade directories for Staffordshire, Warwickshire, Worcestershire and other Midlands counties from the 1760s to the

1910s, which are free to download (**http://specialcollections.le.ac.uk**). Midlands Historical Data offers digitized copies of trade and commercial directories to purchase on CD-ROM; subscription and pay-as-you-go options are also available (**www.midlandshistoricaldata.org**). The BMSGH Reference Library, the Society of Genealogists and The National Archives all have good runs of Midlands directories.

The introduction of the telephone brought the need for a new type of listing. The first telephone directory for Birmingham was published in 1906. The Library of Birmingham has a full set from this date through to the present day. For ancestors who worked in the Post Office, Ancestry has the British Postal Service Appointment Books, 1737–1969.

Apprenticeship Records

Apprenticeship was a feature of Birmingham's economy for many years. Essentially, it involved a contract – both legal and moral – whereby the young person learnt a trade that would equip them for gainful employment and the master undertook to pass on his knowledge to his young protégé as he assisted him in his work (apprentices were generally but not exclusively boys).

The legal contract, known as an apprenticeship indenture, was made between the master and the parent or other legal guardian of the young person. The master contracted to provide training, clothing, board and lodging, in exchange for a sum of money paid to him at the outset of the contract. The apprentice contracted to work for the master for a set period of time, to be of good behaviour – avoiding drinking and gambling for example, and (in the case of boys) not to get married during the period of the contract. The length of the apprenticeship might be a set number of years, often seven (reflecting a sixteenth-century regulation). In other cases the apprenticeship lasted until the apprentice reached a certain age, such as 18 or 21 years. Girls were usually apprenticed until 21 years of age or until their marriage.

So-called trade apprenticeships were arranged privately, where a young person's parents could afford the fees. Others, known as parish apprenticeships, were linked to the Poor Law administration: pauper children would be apprenticed either by the overseers of the poor or by the trustees of charities established for that purpose. The apprenticeship indenture named the apprentice, the master and his trade, and in some cases the parents and the fee paid.

For trade apprenticeships, the majority of surviving records are from registers kept by the Board of Stamps and Taxes (Inland Revenue). Stamp duty was imposed on premiums payable under apprenticeship indentures, from 1710 until 1815. This tax resulted in most indentures being registered centrally in London (irrespective of where the master lived), either in the city registers (when the tax was paid in London) or the country registers (when the tax was paid in the regions). The registers are held at The National Archives (in series IR 1) and both the registers and indexes can be consulted online (various offerings through Ancestry, Findmypast, Origins and the TNA websites). BMSGH has an index of seventeenth- and eighteenth-century London Guildhall apprentices from Staffordshire, Warwickshire and Worcestershire.

Staffordshire Name Indexes has around 12,500 entries for apprenticeships arranged within the county, mainly parish apprenticeships in the period prior to 1838. An index to Worcestershire apprenticeships is available to download at the WAAS website; follow the 'Online Indexes' link on the 'Search Our Records' page. As well as locating apprenticeships within Worcestershire parishes, this can be useful in identifying the many young people from the county who were apprenticed to Birmingham masters. Fines could be levied for practising a trade without having served an apprenticeship; cases appear in Quarter Sessions records.

The other main category of occupation-related records for the working class – trades union membership – is discussed in Chapter 2.

Other Business Records

Trade catalogues provide a detailed picture of a company's activities and products. The Library of Birmingham has a substantial collection of trade catalogues for Midlands businesses since the mid-nineteenth century [BCOL L62.65]. A card index, arranged by company name and product/service type, is available in the Archives Search Room. There is a separate index of sales catalogues of properties and businesses.

The Birmingham Collection at the LoB contains many published company histories; these include some self-published studies not available elsewhere. Grace's Guide is a database of historical information on industry and manufacturing with profiles of industries and firms, as well as obituaries of prominent engineers (**www.gracesguide.co.uk**).

Solicitors' records of their business clients may include information of interest to the family historian: business accounts and correspondence, partnership agreements, bankruptcy papers, patents, newspaper cuttings, land purchases and factory plans, sales particulars, leases and contracts, and apprenticeship indentures. These archives are generally deposited at county record offices but can be difficult to identify, as you need to know which firm of solicitors a business engaged and where they were located. As a regional centre, Birmingham solicitors may have worked for businesses across the Midlands. On the other hand, as many businesses were multi-site or acquired companies elsewhere, they may have used solicitors in other Midlands towns (or indeed anywhere in the country) and the relevant records may have been deposited at local repositories. Hence, if the relevant firm is known it is worth looking in neighbouring towns and cities. The National Archive's Discovery catalogue (formerly Access to Archives) is the best way in. Even then, the deposits may not be catalogued in sufficient detail to identify individual client companies. The LoB holds the archives of Wragge & Co. (1639–1929) and Pinsent & Co (1693–1902), both major firms of Birmingham solicitors, among others.

Like households, businesses paid rates and will be recorded in the rate books, many of which are now available online (see Chapter 7). Fire insurance registers include the name, status, address and occupation of the policy holder, who was often a homeworker or small business. The London Metropolitan Archives has

Patented Dec. 24, 1946   2,413,272

UNITED STATES PATENT OFFICE

2,413,272

TILTING CAMERA

Bernard Wheelwright, West Smethwick, England

Application June 19, 1944, Serial No. 541,055
In Great Britain September 22, 1943

11 Claims. (Cl. 95—50)

1

My invention relates to photographic apparatus and more particularly is concerned with apparatus designed for taking "oblique" photographs from aeroplanes, but which may also be used with advantage for taking photographs from fixed high altitudes, as for example church towers, and for taking photographs of high buildings from ground level.

As is well understood photographs taken from high altitudes and photographs from ground level of high buildings have certain defects or distortions technically termed "tilt" and "side rocking," these distortions being due to the fact that the camera is always more or less tilted from a level or horizontal plane at the moment of exposure.

My invention has for its object to provide photographic apparatus whereby oblique photographs can be taken which are practically free from the defects or distortions aforesaid.

Broadly my invention resides in photographic apparatus for the purpose specified characterised in that the camera embodies a focal plane or nega-

2

only of the stand being shown in the said figure and the parts being in the positions which they occupy when the camera base is horizontal and in which condition the optical axis of the lens, or lens system, is normal to the vertical plane occupied by the sensitive or other surface whereon the image is received.

Figure 2 is a similar view to Figure 1 showing the parts of the apparatus in positions which they may occupy or assume relative to each other when the optical axis of the lens, or lens system, is deflected downwardly for directing the same towards a target or landscape when taking photographs from high altitudes.

Figure 3 is a similar view to Figures 1 and 2 showing the parts in positions which they may occupy or assume when the optical axis of the lens, or lens system, is given such degree of elevation as may be requisite or desirable for photographing a high building from ground level or for focussing a target or object which is at a height above the camera level.

Figure 4 is a front elevation of the apparatus

US Patent on photographic equipment, granted to Bernard Wheelwright, a relative of the author, 1946. (Author's collection)

the records of the Sun and Phoenix insurance companies for towns across the country, including card indexes and insurance maps (**www.cityoflondon.gov.uk/lma**).

If your ancestor had an invention patented then their design will still be on record. The Library of Birmingham's Science Department holds historical patents dating back to the seventeenth century and has access to specialist databases of historical material. These can be difficult to use, however, for those not trained in the intricacies of intellectual property, so be prepared to ask the staff for help. Under an on-going project, patents of historic interest are being added to the esp@cenet database (**http://ep.espacenet.com**), managed by the European Patent Office.

Running a business could be a risky undertaking: unforeseen events, such as a customer defaulting on a debt, price rises as a result of war or bad weather, or simply changes in fashion, led many businesses to go to the wall with their owners declared bankrupt. Notices of bankruptcy were published regularly in the *London Gazette* and other newspapers, and original case files may survive in Quarter Sessions records at county record offices. The National Archives has an online guide to bankrupts and insolvent debtors, describing the holdings available for different periods including county court bankruptcies.

Virtually every industry or trade had an association, some of them highly specialized, and their records may list individual or company members, or provide insights into company history. LoB has the records of the Midland section of the Society of Chemical Industry 1905–1980 [MS 1227], as well as the Birmingham Steel Stamp and Letter Cutters' Association 1918–1940s, with volumes organized according to the name of the firm [MS 788]. WMRC holds the records of many UK trade associations, trade unions and employers; there is an online guide listing available sources by occupation.

J.G. Phelps' *Illustrated Midland Business Review* of 1897 gives a picture of business life in Birmingham and other Midlands towns, while 'notable professional and business men of the Midlands' are profiled in a supplement to *Notable Londoners: An Illustrated Who's Who of Professional & Business Men*, published in 1924.

Further Information

Carl Chinn, *The Cadbury Story: A Short History* (Brewin Books, 1998).

Carl Chinn, *Birmingham: The Great Working City* (Birmingham City Council, 1994).

Malcolm Dicks (ed.), *Matthew Boulton: A Revolutionary Player* (Brewin, 2009).

Eric Hopkins, *Birmingham: The First Manufacturing Town in the World 1760–1840* (Weidenfeld & Nicolson, 1989).

Brian Jones (ed.), *People, Pens and Production in the Birmingham Steel Pen Trade* (Brewin Books, 2013).

Shena Mason, *Jewellery Making in Birmingham 1750–1995* (Phillimore, 1998).

Shena Mason (ed.), *Matthew Boulton: Selling What All the World Desires* (Yale University Press, 2009).

Birmingham Jewellers & Silversmiths Association, *Record of the Work of the Birmingham Jewellers & Silversmiths Association from 1887–1937* (Birmingham Jewellers & Silversmiths Association, 1937).

Douglas Tate, *Birmingham Gunmakers* (Safari Press, 1997).

Jenny Uglow, *The Lunar Men: The Friends Who Made the Future* (Faber, 2002).

David Williams, *The Birmingham Gun Trade* (History Press, 2009).

Ken Williams, *The Story of Typhoo and the Birmingham Tea Industry* (Quiller, 1990).

Chapter 4

TRANSPORT

Highways and Turnpikes

Birmingham has always been a communications hub. Its early importance as a trading and manufacturing centre was due, at least in part, to the wheel-like pattern of roads, which had radiated out from the town since medieval times. The historian William Hutton described twelve roads going out from Birmingham 'which point to as many towns', and complained of them being 'worn by the long practice of ages into deep holloways'.

By the early 1700s the strain on these ancient roads and trackways was becoming intolerable. Many routes were impassable to carts, forcing goods to be brought in by pack-horses: eighty packhorses per day struggled into the town from Evesham and Droitwich, bringing commodities such as fruit, vegetables and salt. The roads to the Black Country used to carry iron, coal and other raw materials were equally overcrowded and dangerous, especially during wet weather. Responsibility for the roads fell upon local parishes, whose residents could afford little more than basic maintenance.

The advent of turnpikes, a form of privatized road network, brought relief to this situation. Key arterial roads, funded by tolls and administered by local trusts, opened up a new era in land transportation. Toll houses and barriers were erected between each section of road and a toll was charged for access: these barriers were known as turnpikes as they had spikes on them to stop horse riders jumping over to avoid the toll.

Announcement of Nicholas Rothwell's Birmingham to London stagecoach, May 1731. (Public domain)

Roads in the Birmingham area began to be turnpiked in 1726, the first being the all-important Stratford Road, which went on to London. The Warwick Road, another important route, was turnpiked in the same year; those to Bromsgrove, Wednesbury and Walsall soon followed. By 1767, when the road to Alcester was turnpiked, ten toll-managed roads converged on the town.

The improvement in journey times led to the rise of stage coaches as a popular form of travel for those who could afford them. Nicholas Rothwell initiated the first regular weekly stage coach between London and Birmingham in 1731. It made the journey in two and a half days; down from four days in 1659 and three days in 1702. The service operated from the *Swan Inn* in New Street, one of several inns and coaching houses established to cater for the new clientele. By the 1770s *Aris's Gazette* was full of advertisements for new coach routes and services, each claiming to be faster or more comfortable than their competitors. Fifty-two services were travelling to London and sixteen to Bristol, some run by inn keepers as well as independent companies.

The condition of the highway was not the only hazard on eighteenth-century roads: highway robbery was a frequent occurrence. In May 1742 an infamous highwayman called Mansell Sansbury, who worked the roads near Banbury, was finally arrested with an accomplice after stealing from a London to Birmingham stage coach. He was found in a nearby cornfield, sleeping off the effects of the alcohol he had found on board.

The records of turnpikes mainly relate to those involved in establishing and managing turnpike trusts, who were generally drawn from the upper classes. Each trust required its own Act of Parliament, which had to be renewed roughly every twenty years. The Act included a list of the trust's subscribers, who were effectively shareholders investing in the scheme for a commercial return. These ranged from the local aristocracy and gentry, to prominent landowners, farmers and merchants. Once established, each turnpike trust would have to issue regular reports on its activities, which were reported at the Quarter Sessions. Fines imposed on stage coach drivers for various infringements on turnpikes would also be levied there. Catalogue references for these categories are shown in Table 4.1.

Table 4.1: Highway Related Sources in Quarter Sessions Records

Category	Staffordshire	Warwickshire	Worcestershire
Highways and Bridges (Public Works)	Q/AH, Q/AB	QS0023, QS0024, QS0047	1/3/2
Stage Coach Drivers, Hawkers, etc (Penalties)	Q/RLb	QS0017	
Turnpike Trusts	Q/RUt	QS0084	1/9/2

Notes: The references shown are for the catalogue of the relevant county archive: SSA for Staffordshire; WCRO for Warwickshire; WAAS for Worcestershire. For web addresses of online catalogues and other details see 'How To Use This Book' in the Introduction.

Canals

The Golden Age

Turnpiking improved the speed and reliability of road transport but did little to reduce its cost, especially for heavy goods. Birmingham industrialists reliant on selling their wares into national and international markets looked for a new solution. In January 1767 'a meeting of Inhabitants' was called 'to consult about making a Navigable Cut ...to run as near as possible thro' the Center of the Colleries' (i.e. the Black Country) and 'it was unanimously agreed to have it Survey'd'.

For their survey the 'Inhabitants' turned to James Brindley, who had made his name building canals in Manchester and Staffordshire. At a meeting at the *Swan Inn* on 4 June 1767 (no doubt surrounded by stage coach passengers), Brindley outlined his plan for a canal between Birmingham and the Black Country coalfields. Such was the enthusiasm for the scheme that within two months £50,000 in shares had been raised. By February the following year the necessary Act of Parliament had been passed. A mere twenty-one months later, on 6 November 1769, the canal's first ten miles was opened, running from Wednesbury colleries to the wharf off Paradise Street.

Canals offered two benefits for Birmingham's cost-conscious businessmen. Firstly, they made it cheap and convenient to move basic supplies within the manufacturing district itself. Secondly, they made it relatively easy to transport heavy loads – raw materials coming in, finished goods going out – over long distances, firmly connecting this fledgling manufacturing town with both its customers and suppliers. Being without navigable rivers, it is unlikely that Birmingham would have progressed to the industrial superiority it later attained without its canals.

The Birmingham Canal ran from Birmingham through Smethwick, West Bromwich and Dudley to Wolverhampton. With its completion shipment times plummeted and the price of coal in Birmingham halved. An extension to Autherley in 1772 gave access to the Staffordshire & Worcestershire Canal, completed in the same year, and from there on to Bristol via the Severn. By 1793, one hundred boats a day were plying their trade on the Birmingham Canal.

A Golden Age of canal building followed. Completion of the Grand Trunk Canal in 1777 gave access to Liverpool via the Mersey, and Hull via the Trent and Humber. Within a few years Birmingham had direct connections to the northern ports via the Birmingham & Fazeley Canal (opened in 1789); to Bristol via the Worcester & Birmingham Canal (opened in 1815); and to London, via the Warwick & Birmingham Canal (opened in 1799). By the mid-nineteenth century the Birmingham Canal Navigations (BCN), which from 1848 incorporated all the Black Country canals, had become the hub of the national canal system.

The old adage that Birmingham has 'more miles of canal than Venice' is difficult to substantiate but the excellence of the systems setup by its canal entrepreneurs is beyond dispute. After being neglected for a long period, today canals have again come into Birmingham's consciousness and form the centrepiece of many of the regeneration efforts seen in the city in recent years.

Canal People

The people who lived on the canals were, in many senses, a breed apart. In the early days the boatmen were a new elite, skilled men who earned a good wage. They had to operate the boat, look after the horse, deal with toll tickets, and keep a record of expenses. Many were probably villagers who had become unemployed due to the enclosure of the land, rather than gypsies or ex-sailors as often assumed. The work on the canals was hard but the pay was better than in the factories or agriculture.

With the coming of the railways competition increased, eventually leaving the boats with only the low value trade. As conditions worsened, the boatmen were forced to cut costs and their families moved onto the boat. By the 1870s their pay had dropped to well below the factory wage. Large families were forced to live in very cramped conditions, with everyone expected to contribute: often the wife would steer the boat while the children walked along the towpath with the horse or mule.

George Smith's 1875 report *Our Canal Population* brought the problem of the living conditions on the boats to public attention. An Act of Parliament, passed in 1877, required the registration and regulation of canal boats used as dwellings, but did little to improve the situation of the boatmen and their families. In the early twentieth century Canal Boat Missions were set up to provide schooling opportunities for canal boat children; once educated many never went back to

Canal boat in Birmingham, early 1960s. (Keith Berry collection)

the boats. The hardships of the Second World War and the disastrous winter of 1962–63 effectively brought an end to this way of life.

The decline of canals and the canal way of life has proved an attractive topic for photographers. Sources include: British Waterways Archive's Photographic Collection [BW192] (see below); Jack Haddock Photographic Collection at Walsall Local History Centre [162]; and two publications: Rolt (1997) and WFHA (1998).

Canal Records

The canal age has left a huge legacy of records and archives. The National Archives holds the bulk of the surviving canal company records: minute books, wage books, correspondence, deeds of partnership, bankruptcy orders, canal share certificates and shareholders' registers, prospectuses, pamphlets, accounts, maps, deposited plans, photographs and surveys, etc. Canal records are archived with docks, road and railway records in addition to many other categories. Relevant authorities include the Board of Trade, Ministry of Transport, and the British Waterways Board and its predecessors. TNA Research Guide *Domestic Records Information 83 (Canals)* gives an overview of the many types of record available. See also Wilkes (2011) and a checklist compiled by the London Canal Museum (**www.canalmuseum.org.uk/collection/family-history.htm**).

Important collections relating to canals are held within Midlands repositories. These are of three main types:

1. *Records of the Canal Companies*
   These cover the initial planning and construction of the canals and their subsequent operation, including employee records. They include plans, maps, letter books, correspondence (for example, negotiations between canal and railway companies), and other records.

   Library of Birmingham holds the archives of the Birmingham Canal Navigations (BCN) from the early nineteenth century (mainly legal and financial papers and some boat registers) [MS 86 & MS 626]; and records of the Birmingham & Midland Canal Carrying Co., 1909–1982 [MS 856]. Walsall Local History Centre also has records relating to BCN [refs 33 & 365].

   WCRO houses the British Waterway series [CR1590], a major archive covering the Oxford, Grand Junction, Grand Union, Warwick & Birmingham and Warwick & Napton Canals from 1791–1962. As an example of the detail to be found here, the records from the Hatton and Hillmorton depots include: lists of canal employees exempted from military service 1916–1918 [CR1590/439]; lists of canal employees and their pay rates 1946–1948 [CR1590/479]; engineers' wage books [CR1590/488–9] and rent books [CR1590/492 and 1603]; accident reports for 1951–1959 [CR1590/1552–3]; local keepers' pay schedules and conditions for 1949–1955 [CR1590/1008], among others. Warwick Quarter Sessions records include many canal maps and plans [QS0111].

   Many of the canal companies' records have found their way into the British Waterways Archive at Gloucester Docks. Virtual Waterways (**www.virtual waterways.co.uk**) is an online resource for canal history. Its catalogue covers the British Waterways and other repositories with major canal archives, such as Gloucestershire Record Office and WCRO. A series of articles on using canal records and how to begin your research is also available.

2. *Canal Boat Registers and Inspection Reports*

An Act of 1795 required vessels using navigable rivers and canals to register with the local Clerk of the Peace; the legislation seems only to have lasted a few years. Where they survive, registers of vessels and applications to register vessels under the Act are found in the Quarter Sessions records. Registers are available at WCRO for the Oxford Canal [QS0095] (with an index published by Eureka Partnership, 2009); and SSA [Q/Rub/1] with an online index at **www.staffsnameindexes.org.uk**.

Later records relate to inspections of inhabited vessels under the Canal Boats Act, 1877. LoB has official registers of boats and inspections from 1879–1957 [MS 316], comprising boat registers 1879–1960, inspection records 1934–1957, and examining officers' reports 1912–1943.

Archive services within the Black Country, such as Dudley Archives, Walsall Local History Centre and Wolverhampton City Archives, hold similar registers (details in Wilkes, 2011).

3. *Miscellaneous Documents and Correspondence:*

Documents relating to the canal era may be found in non-official sources, such as letters, diaries, estate papers, railway company records, and newspaper cuttings.

Prosecutions under the Canal Acts will appear in the Quarter Sessions records. The Staffordshire Quarter Sessions, for example, has a number of convictions of boatmen for wasting water from locks, allowing a boat to hit lock gates and so on. Depositions (witness statements) may have names of canal workers or boatmen if they were accused of theft or other crimes.

Canal people lived an iterant life and therefore you may need to search for them across a wide area. The Virtual Waterways website above is a useful gateway into the catalogues of relevant CROs.

Railways

The Railway Era

In the summer of 1837 an army of navvies was closing in on Birmingham from all directions. Three companies – the London & Birmingham Railway (LBR), the Grand Junction Railway (GJR) and the Birmingham & Derby Junction Railway (BDJR) – were racing to connect the town to the country's rapidly expanding railway network. The GJR was the first to arrive. In fact its progress from Liverpool was so swift that the intended terminus in Curzon Street was not ready and a temporary alternative had to be constructed at Vauxhall (Duddeston).

Curzon Street, Birmingham's first central railway station, opened the following the year, serving both the Grand Junction and London & Birmingham railways. The station, designed by Philip Hardwick, celebrated the achievement.

Newspaper announcement for Curzon Street, Birmingham's first railway station. (Public domain)

Passengers were greeted by a grand building adorned with magnificent triumphal arches and ionic columns (**www.libraryofbirmingham.com/curzon streetgallery**). There was a 'refreshment saloon' and a ticket office, whilst the trains arrived and departed from a parade of iron sheds a little way off.

An *Obsourne's Guide* of 1838 describes the novelty of railway travel:

> Porters with ladders are mounting and placing luggage on the tops, passengers are taking their seats, and arranging themselves for the journey, [...] You look round, and see several engines with red-hot fires in their bodies, and volumes of steam issuing from their tall chimnies. One of them moves slowly towards you. The huge creature bellows, at first, like an elephant. Deep, slow, and terrific are the hoarse heavings that it makes, [...] spouting up steam like a whale. You feel a deep, strong, tremulous motion throughout the train, and a loud jingling rattle is heard, analogous to what is experienced in a cotton mill. The conductor has done his part and is seated; the guard is in his box at the back of the first carriage; a bell is rung as a signal for starting – and you are off.

The engineers of the period faced enormous technical and geological difficulties. Birmingham's geography made it more cost effective to approach the town along the valleys to the north-east, creating an extraordinary congestion of lines in the area now known as Heartlands. The London line, in particular, posed major difficulties for builders George and Robert Stephenson and their navvies. Its opening on 17 September 1838 connected the most important manufacturing districts in the country, Birmingham and Manchester, with both London, the nation's capital, and the great seaport of Liverpool.

A frenzy of railway building followed. The BDJR opened its station in Lawley Street in February 1842, close to the Curzon Street terminus, and a year later the Birmingham & Gloucester Railway also arrived there, abandoning its previous terminus in Camp Hill. Despite its early success, Curzon Street was hardly convenient for customers as it was a mile, or one shilling in cab fares, from the town centre. It was decided to build a more central station at New Street, on the site of a notorious slum. New Street station opened on 1 June 1854, serving the trains of the London & North Western Railway (LNWR, formed from the merger of GJR and the LBR) and Midland Counties Railway (MCR, a successor to the other Birmingham companies). In the meantime, the Great Western Railway (GWR) had established its own station at Snow Hill, opened in 1852 (see photo gallery at **www.libraryofbirmingham.com/localrailwaystations**).

Of course, the inter-city routes through Birmingham are only half the railway story. Commuter lines, such as those to Harborne and Kings Heath, were key elements in Birmingham's expansion. In places like Moseley, Balsall Heath, Northfield and Kings Norton ribbons of Victorian terraces followed the rail links, transforming rural villages into suburbs. Suburban lines had recreational value as well. Day-trippers from the city packed the trains to Sutton Park, with additional services being laid on at bank holidays. Meanwhile, the mainline termini were the starting point for workers' annual seaside holidays.

Although (with one exception) the original Victorian buildings have long gone, Birmingham's stations have seen a renaissance in recent years. New Street station has been completely overhauled, expunging the ghastly innards constructed in the 1960s. Snow Hill, together with Moor Street, has found new life catering for trains to and from London Marylebone as well as a host of regional services. Having been long abandoned, Curzon Street, including Philip Hardwick's magnificent facade, is being proposed as the site for the Birmingham terminus for HS2, the high speed link to London and other major cities.

Railway Industries

Birmingham did not just benefit from the railways as a form of transportation: it also provided locomotives and rolling stock for this new market. From supplying Brunel with screws for fastening rails to sleepers, the town's involvement expanded to take in the whole panoply of rolling stock and railway equipment. Much of this industry was concentrated in Saltley, alongside the lines that converged on that area.

A steam engine at New Street Station, early 1960s. The building in the background is the Queen's Hotel, Stephenson Street. (D J Norton, courtesy of Mark Norton)

Joseph Wright, a London coachbuilder, was one of the first to realize the opportunity. Recognizing that railways would soon replace his stage coach business, he set up a factory manufacturing passenger coaches for LBR and other railways. In 1845 he relocated the business from London to Saltley. By the 1880s the Metropolitan Carriage and Wagon Co., as it became (later Metro Cammell), employed around 1,200 people. Brown Marshall & Co., another carriage business nearby, employed a similar number. Across the city, on the boundary with Smethwick, was the Birmingham Railway Carriage & Wagon Company. These companies and others became major exporters, supplying rolling stock and equipment to railways around the world.

As well as being a museum, the Tyseley Locomotive Works (formerly the Birmingham Railway Museum) restores, maintains and services steam and other heritage locomotives and coaches (**www.tyseleylocoworks.co.uk**). The site is based at the former GWR locomotive works.

Railway Records

The National Archives holds the records of many of the railway companies that existed prior to nationalization in 1947; these are catalogued in the TNA Class RAIL. Many are employment related, including staff registers (the commonest type), station transfers, pension and accident records (which can include date of death), apprentice records (which can include father's name), caution books, and memos. The main series, more than two million records in total, is available on Ancestry [search for 'UK Railway Employment Records, 1833–1963']. For further information on railway staff records see specialist guides: Hawkings (2008), Hardy (2009) and Drummond (2010).

With the industry relying so heavily on safety, rail workers were actively rewarded for taking action that prevented possible accidents, the good deed being marked in red ink on their personal records and rewards of up to two weeks wages issued. BMSGH has a download of the *Register of Red Ink Staff for the Tyseley Goods Depot, 1899–1907* [M035D].

Inquisitions and assessments for compensation for land acquired by railway companies are in Quarter Sessions records. There may also be references in the personal or estate papers of the families concerned. For example, the files of the Anson family, Earls of Lichfield, at SSA, have correspondence with various railway companies about constructing lines over their lands during the 1830s and 40s [D615].

The Metro-Cammell collection at the Library of Birmingham comprises over 100,000 railway rolling stock drawings on microfilm as well as photographic albums, rolling stock specifications, catalogues and pamphlets [MS 99]. David Millin's site at **http://metcam.co.uk** is dedicated to the history of Metro-Cammell Ltd through to its closure in 2005; see also Beddoes, *et al.* (1999). The business records of the Birmingham Railway Carriage & Wagon Company are at SSA [D831 & D4663].

Library of Birmingham has a major collection of railway material, including over 5,000 books and periodicals, timetables (including *Bradshaw's*), maps, architectural drawings and plans, and over 20,000 photographs and postcards of locomotives. It also houses the Wingate Bett Transport Ticket Collection, comprising over one million tickets from all over the world. In addition, the Birmingham Railway Heritage Study Centre, based at Acocks Green library, has a large collection of railway books available for loan (**www.libraryof birmingham.com/acocksgreenlibrary**).

The Midland Railway Study Centre in Derby is a specialist archive relating to the former Midland Railway Company assembled from various collections. The website has a staff index and online catalogue (**www.midlandrailway studycentre.org.uk**).

Trams and Buses

Creeping urbanization during the nineteenth century brought the need for short-distance transport options. In 1828, John Doughty, a fishmonger, started a horse-drawn omnibus service between the *White Swan* in Snow Hill and the *Sun Inn* in Bristol Road. Another early arrival was the service from the *Beehive Inn* near Handsworth to the *White Horse* in Steelhouse Lane. These early horse-bus services operated between public houses as they were considered 'short stage carriages' and so not allowed to stand on the streets. A double-deck service was introduced on the Bristol Road by Joseph Brookes in 1846.

Taking their inspiration from the railways, omnibuses running on fixed rails were introduced. From the 1870s a spider's web of tramways spread across the suburbs, pulling them closer to the inner city. The Corporation built the

The last horse-drawn tram leaving Nechells, 30 September 1906. (Public domain)

tramways itself and leased them to private operators. The first horse-drawn tram service went into operation on 20 May 1872 between Colmore Row and Hockley, connecting to a route that already ran through to Dudley. A second route down the Bristol Road was opened four years later, and 1882 saw the introduction of steam trams. As the catchment area grew, the 1880s and 90s was a period of intense competition between omnibuses and tramways, with frequent name changes as companies came and went.

The situation eventually consolidated around two main operators: Birmingham Corporation Tramways, which from 1904 obtained powers to operate the tramways once existing leases expired; and the Birmingham & Midland Motor Omnibus Co Ltd (BMMO), the ultimate result of a long line of mergers and takeovers, and commonly known as 'the Midland Red'. The first Corporation tram ran from Steelhouse Lane on 4 January 1904, and by 1911 the Corporation had control of all the tramways in the city. Following an experimental period some years earlier, the Midland Red motor omnibuses started regular operations in May 1912, one of the initial routes being from New Street to the *Kings Head* in Bearwood.

During the twentieth century, Brummies grew to love their 'buzzes' and some routes have become iconic. The No. 8 'Inner Circle' and the No. 11 'Outer Circle' (both introduced in 1926) give panoramic tours of the city. A bus trip down the Bristol Road to the Lickey Hills was a popular outing on weekends and holidays.

The Aston Manor Road Transport Museum (**www.amrtm.org**) and the Wythall Transport Museum (**www.wythall.org.uk**) both have interesting collections covering the area's bus and tramway heritage. Several local history societies present details of the development of public transport services within their areas (see Annex for addresses). Old Birmingham Garages profiles petrol stations, transport companies and coach operators that once operated in the Birmingham area (**www.obgt.pwp.blueyonder.co.uk**). British Tramway Company Buttons and Badges is a reference site for collectors and historians (**www.tramway badgesandbuttons.com**).

The Midlands-based Kithead Transport Archive holds the records of bus and coach operators from across the country, including the Midland Red and the archives of the Birmingham Transport Historical Group covering five public authorities within the West Midlands (**www.kitheadtrust.org.uk**). It also has a location list for early private motor vehicle records, mostly those first registered before about 1948.

The Motor Industry

During the twentieth century, no industry came to epitomize Birmingham more than the motor car.

It all began in the 1890s when Frederick Lanchester, works manager at the Forward Gas Engine factory, started experimenting with car design. After a series of prototypes, one of which is in the Science Museum in Kensington, he settled on a twin-cylinder engine with a separate crankshaft – a highly innovative design for the time. The Lanchester Engine Company was formed in November 1899 and took over part of the National Arms and Ammunition Works in Montgomery Street, which became known as Armoury Mills.

The Lanchester Car Company's involvement in the early days of the motor car was prolific. Of thirty-six early design initiatives on cars, Lanchester contributed eighteen, including patenting the first disc brake. In 1931 the company was taken over by BSA after running into financial difficulty and production was moved to Coventry as part of the BSA/Daimler Group.

The first decade of the twentieth century was something of a gold rush for car production, with all sorts of companies and entrepreneurs keen to muscle in on this new technology. Other early arrivals included: Enfield Autocar Company, founded by Albert Eadie in 1904; Calthorpe, an early bicycle manufacturer based in Bordesley, which diversified into cars and motorcycles; and Alldays and Onions, which had been in business since 1650 and decided to try its hand in cars and motorcycles.

In Alma Street, Aston the Wolseley Sheep Shearing Company, a manufacturer of sheep shearing equipment, thought there might be a future in this new-fangled technology and asked their 27-year old manager, Herbert Austin, to investigate. Austin designed a three-wheel vehicle for Wolseley which was exhibited at Crystal Palace in 1896. Other vehicles were manufactured and production was successful enough for a separate business, the Wolseley Tool and Motor Company to be formed in 1901 with Austin as manager. Unlike some companies, who were merely assemblers, Wolseley made most of the parts itself.

After a disagreement with the company in 1905, Austin resigned and cycled around Birmingham looking for an appropriate place to start his own automotive business. On the outskirts of Northfield he came across a derelict tin printing works at Longbridge. After some haggling he bought the site and started to build what would become one of Britain's largest car plants. By the end of 1905 he had shown plans of his first car at the Olympia Motor Show; the 25hp Endcliffe Phaeton went into production the following year and cost £650.

From the 120 cars made in the first year, production increased rapidly reaching around 1000 per year by 1914 with 2000 employees. Over the next few years the factory exploded in size, mainly due to the war effort, so that by 1918 there were around 20,000 employees mostly women. During this period the factory supplied armoured cars, ambulances, generators, searchlights, 2000 trucks, 2000 fighter aircraft and 6.5 million shells. Herbert Austin was knighted for his services to the war effort and for a short time served as MP for Kings Norton. After struggles that brought it to the brink of collapse in the early 1920s, the company hit on the Austin Seven, a whole new class of small car that secured its future.

The later history of 'the Austin' is well known. After successes during the inter- and post-war period, by the 1970s and 80s Longbridge had come to symbolize all that was wrong with British industry, especially the motor industry: poor management practices, shoddy products, a lack of innovation, and trades union militancy all contributed. Amalgamations with other car companies into the unwieldy British Leyland group and a series of ill-judged takeovers and business deals sealed its fate. The site eventually closed in 2005.

In the early years of the twentieth century a separate tier of companies began to appear which specialized in supplying components and assemblies to the fledgling motor manufacturers. In Hockley, Joseph Lucas, a former paraffin oil salesman, started making lamps and other automotive electrical components. In 1901, the Dunlop Rubber Co Ltd was set up to manufacture tyres for bicycles, cars and lorries, eventually expanding to a 120-hectare site known as Fort Dunlop. Meanwhile, Guest, Keen and Nettlefolds (GKN) operated facilities across the Midlands supplying sheet metal pressings as well as forged products, such as crankshafts. These and a myriad of other businesses, large and small, prospered as Birmingham developed its reputation as 'Motor City'.

WMRC has a substantial archival collection relating to the British motor industry. This includes the records of: Austin Motor Company Ltd, 1919–1961; British Leyland Motor Corporation and its predecessors, 1952–1974; Jensen Motors Ltd., 1936–1994; MG Car Company Ltd, 1930–1958; Morris Motors Ltd and associated companies, 1926–1973; Riley Motors Ltd, 1938–1968; Rover Company Ltd, 1890–1996 (back to its origins as a cycle manufacturer); and Standard Motor Company Ltd., 1903–1973. These are mostly business records, such as annual reports, annual returns, minutes, etc., but some files include press-cuttings, wage books, patent applications and other records identifying individual employees. A trade unionist's view on life at the Longbridge plant is provided by the papers of Richard (Dick) Etheridge, who worked as a shop steward at the Austin Motor Co in the 1940s and 50s and later became a district official for the Amalgamated Engineering Union [MSS.202/S].

The archives of BSA across all of its businesses – guns, tools, cycles, motor cars – are also at WMRC, covering the period from 1877 through to the 1960s

[MSS.19A]. There is also a small archive relating to the Motor Cycle Association for 1921 [MSS.204].

A specialist archive on the British motor industry, including films, DVDs and a substantial picture library, is managed by the British Motor Industry Heritage Trust (**www.heritage-motor-centre.co.uk** and **www.bmiht.co.uk**). Access is by prior appointment only.

The history and memories of the Longbridge works are chronicled at John Baker's Austin Memories (**www.austinmemories.com**), whilst Lucas Memories (**www.lucasmemories.co.uk**) documents the history of the Lucas Company. Chris Myer's site has a history of Kynoch & Co, one of Birmingham's best-known engineering companies, now known as IMI plc (**http://tinyurl.com/mpjqxhd**).

Further Information

Eric Armstrong, *Birmingham's Horse Transport* (History Press, 2008).

Gillian Bardsley & Colin Corke, *Making Cars at Longbridge* (History Press, 2006).

K. Beddoes, C. Wheeler, S. Wheeler, *Metro-Cammell: 150 Years of Craftsmanship*, (Runfast Publishing, 1999).

Di Drummond, *Tracing Your Railway Ancestors* (Pen & Sword, 2010).

Frank Hardy, *My Ancestor was a Railway Worker* (Society of Genealogists, 2009).

David T. Hawkings, *Railway Ancestors: Guide to the Staff Records of the Railway Companies of England and Wales, 1822–1947* (History Press, 2008).

Terry Moors, *Lost Railways of Birmingham & the West Midlands* (Countryside Books, 2008).

Ray Shill, *Birmingham Canals* (History Press, 2013).

Sue Wilkes, *Tracing Your Canal Ancestors: A Guide for Family Historians* (Pen & Sword, 2011).

Sonia Rolt, *A Canal People: The Photographs of Robert Longden*, (Sutton Publishing, 1997).

WFHS, *Canal Miscellany: A Compilation of Records & Memories of Canal Family Life in & around Warwickshire & the Midlands* (Warwickshire Family History Society, 1998).

Chapter 5

EDUCATION, HEALTH AND INSTITUTIONS

Birmingham Corporation and City Council

When William Hutton wrote, in 1795, that Birmingham was 'a Town without shackle', he was referring to its lack of a municipal corporation. In the eighteenth century the powers of the Street Commissioners seemed adequate to supply the needs that were outside the scope of manorial or parochial government. A petition for a Charter in 1715 met with little support and it was not until after the passing of the Municipal Corporations Act of 1835 that there was any marked enthusiasm in Birmingham for the town to become incorporated.

The municipal borough was to have the same boundaries as the parliamentary borough, that is, it was to include Edgbaston, Deritend and Bordesley, and Duddeston and Nechells. Municipal elections were held in December, and before the end of the year the first Council had met and chosen a mayor, William Scholefield. Incorporation was followed by the establishment of a Coroner's Court, Quarter Sessions, and a Commission of the Peace.

By the Charter of Incorporation of 1838 the borough was divided into thirteen wards, governed by a Council comprising a mayor, sixteen aldermen, and forty-eight councillors. Over the next fifty years ward boundaries changed on a number of occasions as a result of changing population densities and the extension of municipal suffrage; however, the size of the Council remained the same.

Birmingham became a County Borough under the Act of 1888, and in the following year was granted a Royal Charter, conferring city status. The Mayor was raised to the dignity of Lord Mayor in 1896. Further rearrangements and additions of council wards were made following the successive enlargements of the City in 1891, 1909, 1911 and 1928.

The Corporation acquired control of the Police Force in 1842 and, under the Birmingham Improvement Act of 1851, took over the functions of the Birmingham Street Commissioners. In the 1870s the Council's activities extended more strikingly, and this period of municipal growth is particularly associated with the mayoralty of Joseph Chamberlain (1873–76). Under his leadership, Birmingham was transformed as the council introduced one of the most ambitious improvement schemes outside London. Between 1875 and 1900 the Corporation gained control of the water supply and initiated a major scheme to bring water from the Elan Valley in Wales; took over gas supply, replacing two private companies; and municipalized the electricity supply, albeit limited at the time. Other new powers included the Corporation taking over responsibility for Education from the Birmingham School Board in 1903, and in 1930 becoming directly responsible for the administration of the Poor Law.

In essence, the philosophy of Chamberlain and those who came after him was to apply the economics of the marketplace – massive borrowing, takeovers and shrewd long-term planning – to local government. Income from utilities provided a healthy income for the council, which was re-invested into the city to provide new amenities. It was a model that was adopted by cities across Britain and in the early twentieth century would be extended to housing as well (see Chapter 7).

The Library of Birmingham holds the records of Birmingham City Council and its committees, departments and affiliated bodies from the eighteenth century through to modern times [in class BCC]. The records of adjoining predecessor authorities are also held: Aston Borough Council [BCA]; Erdington District Council [BCE]; Handsworth Urban District Council [BCH]; Kings Norton and Northfield Urban District Council [BCK]; Perry Barr Urban District Council [BCP]; and Yardley Rural District Council [BCY].

Into the Workhouse

The Workhouse System

The use of workhouses to house the poor began with the introduction of the Poor Law Act of 1601 and witnessed a rapid growth during the eighteenth century. Birmingham's first workhouse was erected in the 1730s on Lichfield Street. The building cost £1,173 and was intended to accommodate 600 people. Two wings were later added to provide an infirmary and a workshop. Further efforts to make the system profitable were made in 1789 when Josiah Robins, a worsted maker in Digbeth, was given permission to set up a workshop in premises adjoining the workhouse and to employ the inmates.

A local Act of Parliament in 1783 gave Birmingham greater control over the management of poor relief, replacing the parish administration that existed previously. The new Incorporation was empowered to set up its own workhouse. Proposals were made to build a massive new workhouse on Birmingham Heath which, it was promised, would solve Birmingham's poor law problems 'at a stroke'. The scheme failed to materialize, however, and the existing parish workhouse remained in use for a further seventy years.

In 1797, an Asylum for the Infant Poor was opened on Asylum Road, at the east end of Summer Lane. William Hutton recorded that 'The manufacture of pins, straw-plait, lace, &c., is carried on for the purpose of employing the children, whose labour produces a profit to the parish. There is a bath, garden, playground, school, and chapel connected with this institution.' The Asylum closed around 1852.

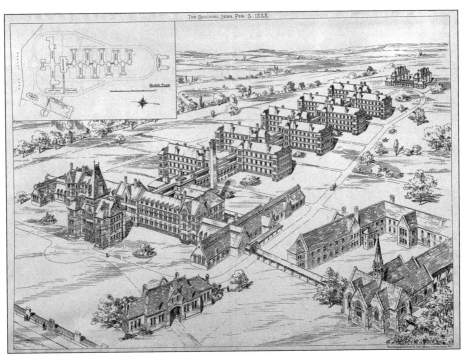

Plans for the Birmingham Workhouse Infirmary, Winson Green, 1888. A central corridor a quarter of a mile long linked the nine 'pavilions'. (Wellcome Images, Creative Commons)

Under the Poor Law Amendment Act of 1834 responsibility for administering poor relief passed to new poor law unions. The Act had been passed in response to the rising costs involved in providing poor relief, and allowed parishes to group together in order to tackle the problem jointly. Birmingham's status as an Incorporation made it exempt from most of the provisions of the 1834 Act, with the Lichfield Street workhouse remaining in use. Eventually, it was decided that a new workhouse was needed. A site at the junction of Dudley Road and Western Road in Winson Green was chosen. The building, designed by J.J. Bateman, opened on 9 March 1852. Accommodation was provided for 700 adults, 600 children, and an infirmary for 310. A separate workhouse infirmary was built in 1889.

Workhouses were run by a Board of Guardians elected by ratepayers and made up of respectable traders, businessmen and the local gentry. The Guardians employed a master and matron, as well as medical officers, nurses, teachers and other staff. They oversaw a regime that was grim and unforgiving. On admission, inmates were stripped of all their clothes and given a bath, for many the first of their lives. They would then be put into workhouse clothes (it was an offence to abscond while wearing them) and segregated by age and gender. The daily routine was hard work, with education or training for the children, interspersed by unnutritious, unappetizing meals.

Strict principles of segregation were enforced, in particular to differentiate between the 'deserving' and 'undeserving' poor. Not only was there separation between men and women, but also between the elderly/infirm and those who were deemed fit enough to work. A report on the Birmingham Union Workhouse in the 1850s records that:

> 'The principal features of the design are the isolation of each from the other of the workhouse, the infirmary, the tramp department, and the asylum for the children, and of the perfect separation of the classes in each department. The asylum for the children has every accommodation for their maintenance and education, with a view to promoting habits of industry and self-reliance in their future career.'

In 1911, Birmingham merged with the adjacent Aston and Kings Norton unions to form the enlarged Birmingham Poor Law Union. All three workhouses subsequently became incorporated into or replaced by hospitals. The Birmingham Union Workhouse stands next to Dudley Road Hospital and almost all of the original workhouse buildings have now been demolished; Kings Norton Union Workhouse became Selly Oak Hospital; and Aston Union Workhouse became part of Highcroft Hospital. Peter Higginbotham's **www.workhouses.org.uk** and the Rossbret website, **www.institutions.org.uk**, have lists of institutions, as well as some histories and photographs.

Workhouse Records

Workhouses were a feature of daily life before the welfare state and most people's ancestors would have come into contact with them at some point in their lives.

The Board of Guardians generated an enormous amount of records. Admission and discharge registers generally show full name, date of admission, date of birth, abode, occupation and marital status, and date of discharge. Creed registers were a way of ensuring inmates' religious needs were met. Apprenticeship records document those indentured to local tradesmen and Servants Registers show who was put as hired hands to factories or farms, or into domestic service. Punishment books include name, date, offence, punishment and often a comment on character. Other records cover the administration of the workhouse and those who worked there. Minutes of meetings were produced and often reported verbatim in the local newspaper. There are also reports from sub-committees formed to investigate and report back on various subjects, and details of tenders received from local traders and who was awarded the job.

The Library of Birmingham holds collections from all three Poor Law Unions within the Birmingham district:

- *Birmingham Poor Law Union [series GP B]*: The main surviving records are those of the Guardians and the administrative structure which was used to run the Union. No admission or discharge registers have survived and there are few other records relating to the inmates themselves. The best sources are: poor

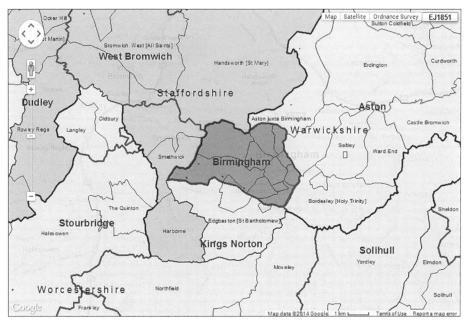

Poor law unions in the Birmingham area, circa 1850. (Courtesy of FamilySearch)

ledgers for non-resident and non-settled inmates, 1824–1861 [GP B/3/5–6]; papers relating to apprenticeship indentures, 1869–1889 [GP B/11/1]; emigration of pauper children, 1898–1911 [GP B/11/2]; settlement and removal orders [GP B/12]; Relieving Officers' records [GP B/25]; and vaccination registers (mainly post-1912) [GP B/29]. Whilst committee minutes contain occasional references to individual paupers, they are not a comprehensive source.

• *Aston Poor Law Union [series GP AS]*: Aston Union was made up of the ecclesiastical parishes of Aston, Sutton Coldfield, Curdworth, Minworth and Wishaw. The surviving records are sparse, comprising mainly inmates admitted for care in the asylum [GP AS/4/1], those receiving out-relief [GP AS/7/1], and vaccination registers [GP AS/29]. Series GP AS/11 contains some registers for adopted children, deserted children, and servants and apprentices (mainly early twentieth century). There are also some passing references contained within the committee minutes. Records relating to Aston Union post-1912 are to be found in the Birmingham Union collection [GP B].

• *Kings Norton Poor Law Union [GP K]*: Kings Norton Union covered the ecclesiastical parishes of Kings Norton, Edgbaston, Northfield, Harborne and Beoley. The main series comprises Relieving Officers' report books [GP KN/25] and vaccination registers (split across four different districts) [GP KN/29]. There is also a single admission and discharge register for 1901 [GP KN/22]. Records relating to Kings Norton Union post-1912 are to be found in the Birmingham Union collection [GP B].

Table 5.1: Poor Law and Asylum Sources in Quarter Sessions Records

Category	Staffordshire	Warwickshire	Worcestershire
Asylums (County and Private) – Public Works	Q/Al	QS0024	1/3/6
Lunatics (Criminal, Pauper)	Q/Rl	QS0019, QS0021	1/3/6/5, 7
Poor Relief	No single reference, see catalogue	QS0020	1/3/7
Settlement Certificates and Returns, Bastardy Orders		QS0050	1/3/7/5

Notes: The references shown are for the catalogue of the relevant county archive: SSA for Staffordshire; WCRO for Warwickshire; WAAS for Worcestershire. For web addresses of online catalogues and other details see 'How To Use This Book' in the Introduction.

Staffordshire Name Indexes has an online index of admissions and discharges for Staffordshire workhouses between 1836 and 1900 (**www.staffsnameindexes. org.uk**); this includes neighbouring Poor Law Unions such as Stourbridge and Tamworth where Birmingham paupers may have been returned. Note that Harborne and Smethwick – both in Staffordshire – were part of Kings Norton Poor Law Union. Handsworth was part of West Bromwich Poor Law Union; records are at Sandwell Archives.

The pre-1834 poorhouses were supervised by the overseer of the poor, but there was no legal requirement to keep records of those housed. References to inmates are most likely to be found amongst the papers of the parish overseer. A Warwickshire Poor Law Index, including Birmingham records prior to Incorporation, has been transcribed and published by Midlands Historical Data. The BMSGH has a similar index for Warwickshire, compiled separately, which is open to email enquiries (see Annex). Minute books and other early workhouse records are in LoB series MS 754–6. Settlement records related to the poor law are discussed in Chapter 7.

Children's Homes

By the late nineteenth century there was increasing recognition that the workhouse was not an appropriate environment for orphaned or destitute children. New institutions were set up away from the workhouse in airy rural locations, organized along the lines of a village community. These so-called 'cottage homes' provided accommodation for pauper children from aged three upwards. One of the first was erected by the Birmingham Board of Guardians at Marston Green, in the parish of Coleshill, and opened in January 1880.

The scheme included seven homes each for boys and girls, together with a probationary home, school infirmary, swimming baths, workshops, bakehouse, a superintendent's house and offices. Each cottage was under the care of foster parents and could house around thirty boys or girls, giving accommodation for a total of 420 children. The boys learnt various trades and the girls household work. A chaplain attended the homes regularly to give instruction and conduct religious services.

Similar cottage homes were built by the Aston Poor Law Union (at Fentham Road, Erdington) and by the Kings Norton Poor Law Union (at Shenley Fields, Northfield). In 1905, Birmingham established a children's Receiving Home, known as Summer Hill, at 19 Summer Hill Terrace, Ladywood. Children coming into the Union's care were sent here for assessment and medical examination before being transferred to Marston Green or homes elsewhere. Summer Hill also provided accommodation for children who were frequent short-term visitors, so-called 'ins-and-outs'.

During the twentieth century the nature of the homes changed, becoming less of a training facility for children who would otherwise have been taken to the workhouse, and much more of a care and education residential facility. No longer reserved for the destitute and orphaned, they also gave shelter to those whose family life was considered unsuitable: children who were abused, disabled, or not attending school.

The Marston Green Cottage Homes closed in the 1930s but those at Erdington and Shenley Fields lasted much longer. In the 1960s the institution of the cottage homes was broken up and each house became a children's home run independently of all the others. After the Second World War the facilities provided by the city for children in care expanded tremendously, so that by the 1960s and 70s there were almost a hundred other council-run homes.

In addition to homes run by the Boards of Guardians, other institutions aimed to provide care for orphaned or destitute children. Many orphanages were run by charities or philanthropic organizations, such as Josiah Mason's Orphanages in Erdington set up by the Birmingham pen entrepreneur; and the Handsworth Nursery opened by the Waifs and Strays Society in 1945 (on a site formerly occupied by the Calthorpe/Handsworth Home for Girls). Reformatories and industrial schools were another category, where juvenile offenders could be committed by the courts. The Middlemore Children's Homes specialized in emigration (see Chapter 7). Lists of homes, with some histories, are available at the Connecting Histories portal, as well as the Former Children's Homes (**www.childrenscottagehomes.org.uk**) and Peter Higginbotham's Children's Homes websites (**www.childrenshomes.org.uk**).

The Library of Birmingham has records for many of the city's children's homes [BCC 10/BCH]. In general these are much more complete and detailed than workhouse records. Those for the cottage homes are particularly comprehensive. For example, the Marston Green Cottage Homes records include: admission and discharge books 1887–1933; registers of children sent to service 1893–1914; registers of baptisms 1917–1931; and punishment books 1924–1930 [BCC 10/BCH/1]. However, due to confidentiality rules, many of these records remain closed for one hundred years.

The experiences of children in Birmingham's children's homes have been documented in a major project entitled *The Children of the Homes*. This focused primarily on the Erdington Cottage Homes but included information on council homes across the city [LoB: MS 2838]. The results are presented in a website –

containing a directory, essays and oral histories (**www.connectinghistories. org.uk/childrenshomes.asp**) – as well as in a book, *The Children of the Homes* (Limbrick, 2012). The project found mixed experiences among those who had been through the cottage homes. Some people felt that the homes rescued them from a bad situation and gave them shelter; others received poor treatment and felt their time there damaged them forever.

Hospitals

Birmingham's transformation into a manufacturing town during the eighteenth century brought a need for more organized medical provision. In general, Birmingham was perceived as a healthy town, and its labourers, kept in constant employment, purportedly enjoyed good health. Joseph Priestley, the chemist and discoverer of oxygen, pronounced that the air was 'equally pure as any he had analysed'. Hard work kept the workers' bodies fit and their minds employed.

The town's industrial wealth and thriving middle class attracted many medical practitioners. In 1767, at least twenty surgeons and three physicians were serving the local population. There was a gap in provision, however, in that the workhouse infirmary, in Lichfield Street, only catered for parishioners of Birmingham, whereas many of those working in the town lived in neighbouring parishes and so were not entitled to any relief. John Ash, a local physician, launched a campaign for a voluntary hospital to serve the entire local population. After prolonged delay due to shortages of money, the General Hospital finally

The first General Hospital, Summer Lane. (Wellcome Images, Creative Commons)

opened its doors in Summer Lane in September 1779, complete with forty beds, four nurses and physicians, and a barber.

Over the next century, many similar institutions were established: the Orthopaedic Hospital (1817), the Birmingham Eye Hospital (1823), the Queens Hospital (1841), the Ear and Throat Infirmary (1844), the Dental Hospital (1858, the first in the country), the Children's Hospital (1861), the Women's Hospital (1871), and the Skin Hospital (1881). The General Hospital expanded with two wings and additional beds until, in 1897, it transferred to a grand new terracotta building in Steelhouse Lane. The Workhouse Infirmary was the only one of the city's hospitals directly supported on the rates, the others being supported by charities or through subscriptions. Many workers were members of friendly societies, an early form of health insurance.

Birmingham's tradition in medical education started with William Sands Cox, who founded the Queen's College as a teaching establishment in 1828. He went on to set up the Queen's Hospital in Bath Row where his students could gain practical experience. Homeopathy was still in the mainstream of medical treatment in the Victorian period; the Birmingham & Midland Homeopathic Hospital (opened in 1875) received around five thousand patients a year [WCRO: CR1646].

In the 1930s, the Queen Elizabeth Hospital was built, along with the adjoining Medical School, next to the University of Birmingham at Edgbaston, for the first time linking clinical and academic medicine on a single site. In order to keep pace with modern developments, in 2010 the old QEH was, in turn, replaced by a new state-of-the-art facility at the same location.

Jonathan Reinarz's *Health Care in Birmingham: The Birmingham Teaching Hospitals 1779–1939* (Boydell Press, 2009) surveys the development of Birmingham's hospitals. Other publications, such as Waterhouse (1962) and Ayres *et. al* (1995), focus on the history of particular institutions. The Voluntary Hospitals Database has detailed time series and statistics on the growth of individual hospitals from the mid-nineteenth century, such as number of beds, number of nurses, and expenditure on in-patients and out-patients (**www.hospitalsdatabase.lshtm.ac.uk**).

Although Midlands repositories have substantial holdings relating to the region's hospitals, individual patient records seldom survive and those that do are subject to strict confidentiality conditions. Patient records are closed for up to 100 years but close relatives may be able to gain access by filing a Freedom of Information Act request to the relevant authority. The Wellcome/National Archives Hospital Records Database is the best finding aid: it documents the existence and location of the records of UK hospitals (more than thirty within Birmingham alone), based on information provided by the repositories concerned (**http://apps.nationalarchives.gov.uk/hospitalrecords**). Some establishments, such as the Children's Hospital, include staff records [HC/BCH/5].

For doctors, see the UK Medical Registers, 1859–1959 on Ancestry, covering all those who were licensed to practise in the UK. As well as housing many of the records catalogued in the Wellcome database [under series HC], the Library of Birmingham holds the archive of the Birmingham District Nursing Association,

1898–1950 [MS 934]. The University of Birmingham has the records of the British Medical Association, Birmingham & Midland Counties Branch, 1854–73 [MS129 & MS706]. BMSGH has transcribed the monumental inscriptions from the General Hospital, available as a download [I050D].

Asylums

Whilst the general populace were well catered for in terms of health care, the same could not be said for the mentally ill. A proposal for an asylum for 'lunatics' alongside the town's General Hospital was suggested in 1779 but was not acted upon. Special provision for these neglected individuals was eventually made in 1850 with the construction of the Birmingham Borough Lunatic Asylum in Lodge Road, Winson Green, near to the workhouse and prison.

By 1881 Winson Green Asylum (also known as All Saints' Hospital) was receiving around 3,000 admissions a year [LoB: HC/AS]. The pressure for accommodation led to the building of a second asylum at Rubery Hill, Rednal, which opened in 1882 [LoB: HC/RH]. A third asylum, Hollymoor Hospital, Northfield, opened in 1905 [LoB: HC/HO]. In 1908, Birmingham, Aston and Kings Norton set up a Joint Poor Law Colony at Monyhull, near Kings Norton, to accommodate up to 210 'sane epileptics and feebleminded persons'. The site later became Monyhull Hall Hospital and closed around 2000.

The Victorians had a rather sweeping definition of the term 'insanity': many of the inmates were suffering from post-natal depression, epilepsy, alcoholism or other minor afflictions. From 1871, the census returns made special provision for those with mental health problems, describing patients as either 'idiots', 'imbeciles' or 'lunatics'. The distinctions are somewhat vague and overlapping but those suffering from dementia were mostly described as 'imbeciles'.

Such was the demand for places, and the willingness by the authorities to commit, that patients would often to be sent to hospitals many miles from their homes. Aston Poor Law Union, for example, used a hospital near Northampton. Other asylums in the region which may have taken patients from Birmingham include: Barnsley Hall Hospital, Bromsgrove; Droitwich Lunatic Asylum; Highcroft Hospital, Erdington (formerly the Aston Union Workhouse and Infirmary) [LoB: HC/HI]; Midland Counties Asylum at Knowle (later Middlefield Hall Hospital); St Margaret's Hospital, Great Barr (a 'colony' set up jointly by Walsall and West Bromwich Unions); Staffordshire County Asylum at Burntwood; Warwickshire County Asylum at Hatton; and Worcestershire County Asylum at Powick.

The history of asylums and the treatment of mental illness are chronicled at Andrew Robert's website (**http://studymore.org.uk**), which includes a comprehensive list of such institutions across England and Wales. See also Peter Higginbotham's **www.workhouses.org.uk** and the Rossbret institutions website, **www.institutions.org.uk/asylums/index.htm**. Peter Allen's history of St Margaret's Hospital, Great Barr is at: **http://myweb.tiscali.co.uk/greatbarrhall/hospital_history.htm**.

Probably the most useful and widely available asylum records are the admission registers, which show that patients were often admitted and discharged within a short space of time. As with hospital records, these are closed to the public for 100 years but may be accessed by close family members. The authorities had little respect for patients' identities and it is not uncommon to find just initials or first names listed in institution registers and census returns. In addition to the references given above, the LoB has a general index to patients in Birmingham mental hospitals, 1894–1954 [MS 1602].

The George Marshall Medical Museum has a searchable database of records from the Powick Lunatic Asylum (**http://medicalmuseum.org.uk**). Charles Oram, for example, a currier from Birmingham was admitted on 8 March 1856 and diagnosed with 'Monomania of Suspicion'. He had been discharged from Birmingham Asylum previously and had been found to be living in 'an irregular and desultory manner'. He was admitted after threatening his wife and removed back to Birmingham Asylum on 20 May 1856. WAAS has a downloadable index of admission registers for Powick, 1954–1906.

Many asylums, or former asylums, are included in the Wellcome / National Archives Hospital Records Database (see above). WCRO has the records of the Warwickshire County Asylum, Hatton [CR1664], including admission papers for patients transferred between Birmingham and Warwick, 1873–1921. Public works aspects are in series CR3162 and in the Quarter Sessions records [QS0024]. Walsall Records Centre holds the records for St Margaret's Hospital, Great Barr [ref 178]. Some patient lists from county asylums can be found at The National Archives (series MH).

Schools

The Growth of Education

The increase in the population of Birmingham has logically been accompanied by a corresponding need for schooling. A survey carried out by the Statistical Society for the Improvement of Education in 1838 showed that twenty percent of the town's 45,000 children between five and fifteen years were attending day schools, and roughly a half were attending some kind of school, be it a private 'dame' (young ladies) school or Sunday school. However, the investigation noted that many of these children were simply learning by rote or practising writing and received little actual instruction.

The most prestigious school was what is known today as King Edward's School. Founded by Edward VI in 1552 as the Free Grammar School, it stood on the south side of New Street. Having been housed at that site in two splendid buildings (demolished in 1707 and 1830 respectively), it later moved south to Edgbaston, where it remains today. The Blue Coat School, the town's second oldest, was founded as a charity school in 1722 by the rector of St Philip's church and was located on St Philip's Square. Initially the school clothed, fed and educated around thirty boys and twenty girls aged 9–14 from poor families in the area. In 1930 it too relocated to Edgbaston and is now a preparatory school.

King Edward's School, New Street, shortly before its demolition in 1936. (Courtesy of Chris Myers)

During the early nineteenth century many different varieties of schools emerged, divided broadly between private and charity. The National Society for Promoting the Education of the Poor in the Principles of the Established Church aimed to provide a basic education whilst stemming the influence of non-conformists. Birmingham had three such schools, in Pinfold Street, Handsworth and Erdington, all founded around 1813. Dissenters had their own provision, such as the Protestant Dissenting Charity School in Graham Street and the Wesleyan School, Cherry Street. There were also many small private academies dotted around the town and surrounding areas where better-off girls were taught music, deportment and other necessary skills.

Joseph Lancaster devised a system of charitable provision based on 'a new, expeditious and cheap plan'. By using older children as monitors, one teacher was able to run a school of 400 or more children, accommodating a range of ages and literacy levels. The system was employed at his Lancastrian Free School that opened in Severn Street in 1809.

Ragged schools, such as those founded by William Chance in Windmill Street (1845) and Digby Street (1848), provided basic elementary schooling for around two hundred children. Most ragged schools were attached to and founded by local Anglican churches, though dissenters were not necessarily excluded. The intention was, through practical tasks such as making and mending clothes and shoes, to equip their young charges for a life of labour. A report on the St Philip's Ragged School in Lichfield Street noted that the children were 'watched over carefully; their faults patiently and kindly corrected, so as to win them by persuasion and gentleness from the idleness and errors into which they may have unfortunately fallen'. In 1849 this school moved to become the Gem Street Industrial School, the first of a new breed teaching trades and industrial occupations besides the '3Rs'.

To these can be added other religious schools, such as the Hebrew National School in Hurst Street (founded 1843), and St Peter's Roman Catholic School in Broad Street (1828). Specialist schools included the Royal School for the Deaf in Church Road, Edgbaston, founded in 1812.

In the era when tuberculosis and malnutrition were rife, the School Medical Service launched open-air schools as part of a national movement. As a result of the vision and patronage of Barrow and Geraldine Cadbury, Birmingham's first three open-air schools were founded at Uffculme, Cropwood and Hunters Hill around 1911, followed by Marsh Hill, Haseley Hall and Skilts. Children suffering from anaemia, debility, respiratory problems and many other ailments were admitted and restored to health and strength by a unique regime of medical treatment, fresh air, rest, showers, regular exercise and nourishing food (see Wilmot & Saul, 1998).

By 1868 around two-fifths of children aged five to fifteen were engaged in full-time education, double the figure of forty years earlier. Older children were less likely to remain in school, however, due to the pressures to get out and earn a living. Two Birmingham-based bodies, the Birmingham Education Society (founded by George Dixon) and the National Education League, started a campaign for free compulsory education. Their demands were partially met by the Education Act of 1870, but it was not until 1891 that the Birmingham School Board was able to abolish fees completely.

School Records

The Library of Birmingham has a large collection of school records, under catalogue class 'S', running to nearly three hundred separate files in total. Certain historic collections, such as the records of the Blue Coat Charity School, 1722–1989, are held separately [MS 1622]. Holdings vary and may include log books, admission registers, attendance registers, school magazines, minute books, and correspondence with parents. Staff records, for example completed applications for pupil teacher indentures, may also have been retained. In some cases there may be a history of the school, produced to celebrate a key anniversary. All registers, log books, health and punishment records are subject to a 100 year closure period; other material too may be subject to closure. See also records of the Birmingham Class Teachers Association, 1910–1945 [MS 872], and the Birmingham Head Teachers Association, 1920–1957 [MS 1102].

The records of King Edward's School have been published by the Dugdale Society in six volumes. Microfilms of the school's records are available through LDS Family History Centres. Genhound has a list of benefactors to the Blue Coat Charity School, 1722–1859, extracted from annual reports (**www.gen hound.co.uk**).

Elkington Street Junior School, around 1907. (Author's collection)

Lichfield Record Office has nomination papers for schoolmasters within the Lichfield Diocese, 1671–1866, covering Staffordshire and part of Warwickshire; the collection is incomplete but has been indexed [B/A/11/3].

The Archives and Records Association has launched a project with DC Thomson Family History, owners of Findmypast, to digitize pre-1914 registers from schools across England and Wales. It is not clear yet which Midlands schools will be included. Findmypast already has the records of the Teachers Registration Council, 1914–1948, while BMSGH has compiled the Birmingham Teachers Index, 1856–1899, available as a download [M007D].

Universities and Colleges

The University of Birmingham has its origins in Mason Science College, founded in 1880 through the philanthropy of pen magnate, Josiah Mason. Its first home was in the city centre, near to the Town Hall. It incorporated as University College in 1896, and was finally made a university in its own right in 1900. Joseph Chamberlain was the university's first chancellor and oversaw its early development, most notably the move to a new purpose-built campus at Edgbaston, south of the city centre.

Over the next hundred years or so, as demand for tertiary level education expanded, three other Birmingham institutions followed the same progression from college to university. In 1964 the College of Technology at Gosta Green became the University of Aston in Birmingham. Its origins were as the Birmingham Municipal Technical School, founded in the 1890s as an offshoot of the BMI. Now known simply as Aston University, it operates from a number of sites and has a strong focus on technological and management subjects. The other institutions are Birmingham City University, formerly Birmingham Polytechnic, and Newman University, named after Cardinal John Henry Newman.

All of the universities have alumni offices, which maintain registers of their graduates. In some cases they are willing to pass on enquiries and requests to former students, subject to data protection regulations. The University of Birmingham's registers have been published for the pre-computer era (roughly up to 1980). The Cadbury Research Library holds the official records of the University of Birmingham and its predecessor and associated organizations, as well as archives on the work of its staff and students.

Charities and Friendly Societies

The juxtaposition of avid social reformers alongside conditions of grinding poverty made Birmingham a natural breeding ground for charitable efforts. Outraged by the plight of the urban poor, persons of a charitable disposition – many though not exclusively non-conformists – banded together to perform social works. Their targets were numerous. Women and families were frequent recipients, in particular children and unmarried mothers; the elderly and infirm, prostitutes and drunkards were cared for too. Some operated their own homes,

Membership card for 'Band of Help', a children's charity, around 1910. (Wellcome Images, Creative Commons)

BAND OF HELP IN CONNECTION WITH
THE BIRMINGHAM & DISTRICT CRIPPLES UNION.

Having AGREED TO DO ALL HE CAN TO HELP THE CRIPPLED CHILD, IS NOW A MEMBER OF THE BAND OF HELP.

SECRETARY: MRS. ONGLEY, DAIMLER HOUSE, PARADISE ST., BIRMINGHAM, TO WHOM ALL LETTERS SHOULD BE SENT.

refuges and schools, whilst others sent volunteers out into the communities. Missions overseas were also supported, especially by church groups.

The Birmingham Medical Mission was one of the earliest organizations to cater for the spiritual and medical needs of the urban sick and poor. Created by an interdenominational committee of philanthropists, the Mission opened its first dispensary on Park Street in 1875. During its first ten months dispensary staff conducted over 3,400 consultations; by the next year this figure had risen to over 14,000. Funds were raised for the construction of a new purpose-built dispensary on Floodgate Street, opened in 1880. During the twentieth century the Mission continued to offer medical and spiritual aid, especially during the world wars, as well as distributing food to the poor.

Another influential charity is the Birmingham Settlement, founded in 1899. It concentrated originally on providing support to women and families in the deprived area of St Mary's, now known as Newtown. In 1907, it opened the first kindergarten in Birmingham, which was followed shortly after by an Out of School Club. It continues to offer support for all elements of the community.

The Library of Birmingham holds the records of many charitable organizations, including the Birmingham Medical Mission, 1899–1931 [MS 4038]; the Society for Administering Comfort to Poor Lying-in Women, 1813–1828 [MS 954]; the Society for the Relief of Infirm Aged Women, 1825–1948 [MS 886]; and the Birmingham Association for the Unmarried Mother and Her Child, early 1900s-1980 [MS 603]. The University of Birmingham has the records of local Christian charities and Sunday schools, such as the Birmingham Council of Christian Education, 1848–2001 [LCEC]. It also houses the national archives of several major charities: Church Missionary Society, 1799–1959 [CMS]; the Young Men's Christian Association, 1840–2008 [YMCA]; Save the Children, 1915–2006 [SCF]; and TocH, 1912–2012 [TocH].

Various non-political mutual societies were established to assist members financially in time of illness, old age and hardship. They were funded and governed by their members and included friendly societies, building societies, loan societies, trade unions and industrial and provident societies. By law, society rulebooks had to be submitted to the Quarter Sessions and sometimes these

Table 5.2: Charity and Society Sources in Quarter Sessions Records

Category	Staffordshire	Warwickshire	Worcestershire
Charities and Trusts	Q/RSb	QS0069–0071	1/10/3
Freemasons	Q/RSm	QS0087	1/10/6
Friendly Societies	Q/RSf	QS0083	1/10/4
Savings Banks, Building Societies, Loan Societies	Q/RSb, Q/RSl, Q/RSs	QS0088	1/10/5

Notes: The references shown are for the catalogue of the relevant county archive: SSA for Staffordshire; WCRO for Warwickshire; WAAS for Worcestershire. For web addresses of online catalogues and other details see 'How To Use This Book' in the Introduction.

include membership lists as well; later records are held by The National Archives. Under the Unlawful Societies Act of 1799 freemasons also had to register with the Clerk of the Peace of the local Quarter Sessions.

Further Information

J.G. Ayres, C.J. Ellis and O.H.D. Portsmouth, *East Birmingham's Hospitals 1895–1995* (Tector, 1995).

Robert Burlison, *Tracing Your Pauper Ancestors: A Guide for Family Historians* (Pen & Sword, 2009).

Simon Fowler, *Poor Law Records for Family Historians* (Family History Partnership, 2011).

Jon Glasby, *Poverty and Opportunity: 100 Years of the Birmingham Settlement* (Brewin Books, 1999).

David Hawkings, *Pauper Ancestors: A Guide to the Records Created by the Poor Laws in England & Wales* (History Press, 2011).

Peter Higginbotham, *The Workhouse Encyclopedia* (History Press, 2012).

Gudrun Jane Limbrick, *The Children of the Homes: A Century of the Erdington Cottage Homes* (WordWorks, 2012).

Jonathan Reinarz, *Health Care in Birmingham: The Birmingham Teaching Hospitals, 1779–1939* (Boydell Press, 2009).

Royal Orthopaedic Hospital League of Friends, *Years of Caring: The Royal Orthopaedic Hospital* (Brewin Books, 1997).

Rachel Waterhouse, *Children in Hospital: A Hundred Years of Child Care in Birmingham* (Hutchinson, 1962).

Frances Wilmot & Pauline Saul, *A Breath of Fresh Air: Birmingham's Open-Air Schools, 1911–1970* (Phillimore, 1998).

Chapter 6

LAW AND ORDER

The Judicial System

Historically, the judicial system in England and Wales relied on Assize courts and Quarter Sessions, a system that dated back to the twelfth century.

Assizes were the higher of the two courts. Judges rode on horseback from one county town to the next, trying all those charged with the most serious criminal offences. By the middle of the sixteenth century six assize circuits had developed, each under the control of a Clerk of the Assize. The Assizes were normally held twice a year in Lent and Summer. In some counties the Assize was an annual

Victoria Law Courts, Corporation Street. (Wikimedia, Creative Commons)

event and therefore people could spend many months in prison awaiting trial. Warwickshire, including Birmingham, was part of the Midland Circuit, with the assizes held initially at Warwick. Staffordshire and Worcestershire were part of the Oxford Circuit, with assizes held at Stafford and Worcester respectively. Birmingham gained its own Assizes in 1884, held at the newly-built Victoria Law Courts in Corporation Street.

Quarter Sessions dealt with the lesser, non-capital crimes. As well as dispensing justice, these courts collected taxes and other monies due to the monarch. The courts were presided over by knights, called Keepers of the Peace, latter known as Justices of the Peace (JPs). A statute of 1388 required that these sessions should be held in every quarter of the year – Easter, Trinity, Michaelmas and Epiphany – to be presided over by three JPs, and hence they became known as the Quarter Sessions. JPs were appointed at the start of each reign by the new monarch, and had to swear an oath of allegiance. They were required to possess 'justice, wisdom and fortitude' and latterly, to have a private income in excess of £100 a year.

Changes in Tudor times saw the Quarter Sessions administering the Poor Law and therefore replacing the Sheriff as county administrator. In the centuries that followed they acquired a whole range of other administrative responsibilities, from registering boats and barges, to licensing gamekeepers, printing presses and county militia. Thus, Quarter Sessions records cover much more than petty crime and are a key source for the family historian (see box). In 1846 County Courts, dealing with civil cases, were created. In 1894, many of the administrative functions of the Quarter Sessions, including the Poor Law, were transferred to the new County Councils, although they retained responsibility for licensing, betting and gambling.

Regular Petty Sessions courts began in the eighteenth century, due to the increase in workload for the justices of the Quarter Sessions. These met far more often – daily by the nineteenth century – and dealt with minor crimes, licensing, juvenile offences and civil offences such as bastardy and child maintenance.

Reform of the judicial system in 1971 led to the abolition of all three tiers, to be replaced by the present arrangement of High Courts, Crown Courts and Magistrates Courts.

Court Records

Assizes

The records of the Assize courts are held at The National Archives. For the Midlands Circuit these comprise Minute books, 1818–1893 [ASSI 11], Indictments, 1860–1957 [ASSI 12], Depositions, 1862–1945 [ASSI 13], and Miscellaneous, 1870–1890 [ASSI 15]. Equivalent records for the Oxford Circuit are under ASSI 2–6 (**www.nationalarchives.gov.uk**). LoB has a calendar of prisoners tried at Birmingham Assizes, 1884–1893 (see below).

Quarter Sessions

Following its incorporation as a borough, in 1839 Birmingham established its own Quarter Sessions and Petty Sessions courts. The Quarter Sessions records are more limited than those of the county courts for two reasons. Firstly, relatively few of the early judicial records have survived. Secondly, by the time the court came into operation many of the administrative functions associated with Quarter Sessions had been abolished or transferred to other authorities. As the

---

Quarter Sessions Records for Family Historians

The courts of Quarter Sessions acquired a wide range of responsibilities, from hearing criminal cases, to implementing various aspects of county administration, to the filing of certain statutory returns to Parliament. The Quarter Sessions records are therefore a key, though often underutilized, source for the family historian.

Being positioned at the boundary of three historic counties, the area covered by modern-day Birmingham was split between several court jurisdictions. Warwickshire Quarter Sessions, which covered Birmingham and Aston parishes, sat at Warwick (records are held at WCRO). Staffordshire Quarter Sessions, covering adjacent parishes in south Staffordshire, sat at Stafford (records at SSA), while Worcestershire Quarter Sessions, covering parishes within north Worcestershire, sat at Worcester (records at WAAS). Although the courts had similar responsibilities, there is no uniformity in the way their records are stored within modern-day archives. Each county record office has adopted its own cataloguing system, which sometimes makes it difficult to identify equivalent record sets across archives.

Throughout this book there are a series of tables that provides such a mapping for various categories of Quarter Sessions records. Each table lists, as far as possible, the catalogue references for specific Quarter Sessions sources for each of the three county record offices: SSA, WCRO and WAAS. Birmingham had its own Quarter Sessions court from 1839, although its records are more limited – see main text.

Within the wider West Midlands there were also: historic Quarter Sessions at Lichfield and Coventry (dealing mainly with local matters); and borough Quarter Sessions at Wolverhampton and West Bromwich (established late nineteenth or early twentieth century). Records are in the relevant local record offices.

Only the records related to the courts' overall running and judicial functions are listed within this chapter; others are under the relevant thematic headings. Further details about the catalogues (online and offline) of the relevant repositories and the reference fields used within these catalogues are given in the Introduction. In addition to the sources mentioned in the main text, records from all three courts are available on microfilm through LDS Family History Centres.

Table 6.1: Judicial Sources in Quarter Sessions Records

Category	Birmingham	Staffordshire	Warwickshire	Worcestershire
Courts of Quarter Sessions				
Order Books		Q/SO	QS/40	1/2/12, 8001/3/3/2
Minute Books	QS/B/1/1–5	Q/SM	QS/39, QS/41	1/2/8, 8001/3/3/3
Indictment and Presentment Books		Q/SPi	QS/33	1/2/2, 1/2/9
Recognizance Rolls & Registers		Q/SPr	QS/54–59	1/2/10, 8001/3/10/1, 8001/3/2/5/3
Depositions		Q/SBd	QS/30	1/2/3
Session Bundles, Rolls or Files		Q/SB, Q/SR	QS/32	1/1
Fines, Fees & Estreats	QS/B/19	Q/SPe	QS/31	1/2/5
Judgment Rolls and Books	QS/B/11 QS/B/1/6–29	Q/SPj,		
Calendars of Prisoners	QS/B/20	Q/SPc	QS/26	1/2/11, 8001/3/2/5/2/1, 8001/3/4/3
Printed Orders of Court		Q/SOp	QS/43	
Appeals and Traverses	QS/B/2	Q/SPa, Q/SPk, Q/SPt		QS/25, QS/49 1/2/4, 1/2/6
Other Courts				
Assize Court	At TNA	Q/CA (and at TNA)	QS/41b (and at TNA)	At TNA
Insolvent Debtors		Q/SB	QS/34	1/3/4/6, 8
Coroners Court	CO	No single reference, see catalogue	QS/8, QS93/f	1/3/4/9
Petty Sessions	PB	No single reference, see catalogue	QS/116	1/3/4/14, 15, 23–25, 30
Summary Convictions, Registers of Convictions and Juvenile Offenders	No single reference, see catalogue	Q/RC	QS/51	1/3/4/15, 8001/3/2/5/7

Notes:

1. The references shown are for the catalogue of the relevant archive: LoB for Birmingham; SSA for Staffordshire; WCRO for Warwickshire; WAAS for Worcestershire. For web addresses of online catalogues and other details see 'How to Use This Book' in the Introduction.
2. Library of Birmingham entries refer to the main nineteenth-century series only – see main text.
3. All judicial records are subject to 100 year closure.

judicial holdings are subject to the 100-year closure rule, this leaves a relatively small set of records open for inspection.

The Library of Birmingham holds the records for Birmingham Quarter Sessions 1839–1971, under series QS/B. The main collections that are at least partially open are: Registers of convictions, 1839–1857 [QS/B/11]; Court minutes, 1839–1971 [QS/B/1]; Appeals minutes, 1839–1971 [QS/B/2]; Calendars of prisoners, 1880–1971 [QS/B/20]; and Gaol Sessions minutes, 1849–1964 [QS/B/23–24].

These series and those of other Quarter Sessions courts are summarized in Table 6.1, with further explanation in the 'Quarter Sessions Records for Family Historians' box. The county courts will mainly be of relevance in the following instances: i) post-1839 cases outside the jurisdiction of the Birmingham Quarter Sessions; and ii) pre-1839 cases within Birmingham or surrounding areas.

Petty Sessions

The records of Birmingham Petty Sessions and Magistrate Court, 1839–1968 are in series PS/B. Although the Sessions started in 1839, no registers survive before 1899. The holdings are extensive and listed in the paper catalogue in the Wolfson Centre, including the records of the Juvenile Court [PS/B 1/1/8]. There is also a long series for Sutton Coldfield Petty Sessions, 1866–1966 [PS/SU], and more limited files for Handsworth [PS/ST], and Perry Barr [MS 277].

BMSGH has an index of petty fines in Birmingham courts, 1839–1852.

Crime: From Petty Theft to the Peaky Blinders

What would our ancestors' experiences of crime have been in the eighteenth or nineteenth centuries?

The judicial records in the Quarter Sessions, as well as newspaper accounts, show that the most common prosecutions were for offences against local licensing and byelaws, non-payment of tithes and taxes, and Poor Law offences, particularly vagrancy, settlement and removal and bastardy orders. Allegations relating to infringements against apprentices indentures and child maintenance were also a frequent occurrence.

The most common felonies dealt with were burglary; highway robbery (especially in the pre-railway era); stealing horses or livestock; breaking down fences, hedges or railings; trespass; theft of clothes or other personal possessions; and robbing from orchards and gardens. Even eavesdropping was considered a crime. More serious offences, such as murder, manslaughter, assault, rape, riot, or receiving stolen goods would be referred to the Assize, although certain towns could try such cases themselves, and even pass the death penalty.

Before regular police forces were introduced in the mid 1800s, the responsibility for reporting crime and identifying and catching the culprits usually fell on the victim. They would be aided by companions or a parish constable (lists in the Quarter Sessions). The accused would be held in the local 'lock-up' until they could be examined by a magistrate. Statements would be made and signed and then the magistrate had to decide how to proceed. As well

Birmingham City Police, criminal record card with drawing of tattoos, around 1916. (West Midlands Police Museum, Creative Commons)

as the Assize and the Quarter Sessions, there was the option to try minor offences 'summarily' before two magistrates at Petty Sessions.

Many records relating to all offences exist and are worth examining (see Table 6.1 above). Papers may include calendars of prisoners in the county gaol: gaolers were amongst a number of occupations that were paid on a per capita basis by the Quarter Sessions on receipt of detailed lists (see 'Prisons' section below). These can provide valuable leads to other sources of information regarding transportation, subsequent death of prisoners, etc. Start by checking the Index and/or Minute Books which give a summary of each case, then once the identity of an individual has been established, the full papers for the case in the Session bundles can be reviewed. Further detail on a case may survive in the Depositions and in solicitors' papers at county record offices.

Criminal ancestors may also be listed in the Criminal Registers compiled by the Home Office between 1805 and 1892. These are held at The National Archives (in series HO 27). They cover persons charged with indictable offences and are arranged by county. The registers are being transcribed and made available on CD-ROM by Family History Indexes (**www.fhindexes.co.uk**).

Other sources of note are:

• Order and Indictment Books for Warwickshire Quarter Sessions, 1625–1690: digitized versions available to purchase through the BMSGH Shop

- Index for Worcestershire Quarter Sessions, 1830 and 1850–1854: download available at WAAS site.
- Institutions set up to cater for juvenile offenders or potential offenders, such as Industrial Schools, Reformatory Schools, Approved Schools, Borstals and Remand Homes. LoB holds extensive records.
- Birmingham Pub Blacklist, 1903–1906: on Ancestry, a list of 'habitual drunkards' compiled by the City of Birmingham Watch Committee.

The Victorian Crime and Punishment website looks at the workings of nineteenth-century justice and has a small database of actual prisoner records (**http://vcp.e2bn.org**).

Towards the end of the Victorian era a new crime began to emerge: gang violence. Excluded from the economic benefits of the empire, industrialized cities such as Birmingham became breeding grounds for violent gangs of a kind not seen before. In the overcrowded slums and tenement blocks, life was cheap, many died in infancy and only the Poor Law provided a safety net against poverty and old age. Violence was part of day-to-day existence and came from all directions. Seeing safety in numbers, those youngsters who had survived childhood – a feat in itself – sought comradeship, protection and, above all, excitement in the few hours not taken up by earning a living. Whilst the middle and upper classes grappled with problems through political channels, the town's youth found their own expression through outbursts of raw and often violent exuberance.

Each city had its own breed of gang. In Birmingham they were called first Sloggers – a 'slog' was a fight – and later Peaky Blinders, after the fringe of hair or cap peak they typically wore over one eye. In recent years, the latter have achieved notoriety through the BBC drama series of the same name. Such gangs offered some protection against the police and the magistrate, as only the most foolhardy tended to get caught. Gooderson (2010) and Chinn (2014) tell the true story of the Peaky Blinders and other Birmingham gangs.

Policing the Town

During the early nineteenth century, policing in Birmingham was the responsibility of three main authorities. The Street Commissioners employed street keepers and nightwatchmen who were given uniforms and sworn in as constables to deal with the protection of the public and property, as well as traffic obstructions. Justices of the Peace, on behalf of the Quarter Sessions, were responsible for keeping the peace and enrolling special constables. Meanwhile, the Court Leet – an ancient parochial body – appointed two constables every year who were responsible for suppressing riots and public disorder; they also executed warrants issued by the courts.

In the absence of a regular police force, during the Chartist riots of 1839 local magistrates had to call for help from the Metropolitan Police. A contingent of 100 officers arrived and was sworn in as special constables to help quell the disturbances. As a result of the violent scenes, an Act of Parliament was passed to allow the borough to set up its own police force and appoint a chief

Badge of Birmingham City Police, 1839–1974. (West Midlands Police Museum, Creative Commons)

commissioner, empowered to recruit a sufficient number of 'fit and able men' as constables.

On 1 September 1839 local barrister Francis Burgess was appointed as the town's first Police Commissioner. Birmingham Police took charge of the streets on 20 November that year, with 260 men. They were paid 17 shillings a week and supplied with a uniform. After an administrative hiccup – the enabling Act expired and a replacement had to be passed hastily – the Birmingham Police was reconstituted in September 1842 and put on a permanent basis.

Over the next hundred years or so the strength of the force grew in relation to the city, expanding with each administrative change. In 1974, following the reorganization of the local authority boundaries, Birmingham City Police was incorporated into the newly-formed West Midlands Police. Reilly (1989) chronicles the history of policing in Birmingham.

Police records can reveal many aspects of an ancestor's service in the force as well as their family life. This may include postings, pay, disciplinary hearings, commendations or rewards, a physical description, and family details. The records of Birmingham City Police and its predecessors are held by the West Midlands Police Museum. These comprise staff records from 1839–1974 but are subject to closure for seventy-five years. Registers of Aliens compiled during the First World War are also held. The museum is open by appointment only: enquiries should be directed to Sparkhill Police Station via contactus@west-midlands.pnn.police.uk.

Records from Staffordshire Police have been indexed and made available online as: Staffordshire Police Force Registers, 1842–1920 and Disciplinary Index, 1857–1886 (**www.staffsnameindexes.org.uk**). The Staffordshire Police website has a short history of the force (**www.staffordshire.police.uk/about_us/history**). Bob Pooler's site has a database of officers who served in the Worcestershire Police Force, 1833–1967, as well as the author's book on the force (**www.worcestershirepolicehistory.co.uk**); original records are at WAAS. The Warwickshire Police website has a history produced to celebrate the force's 150th anniversary (**www.warwickshire.police.uk**).

It should be borne in mind that 'policeman' was a general term. Parish constables and railway policeman may also appear as policemen on census returns: their records will be found in the parish records and railway company archives respectively. See also specialist sources such as Wade (2009) and the Police History Society (**www.policehistorysociety.co.uk**).

Prisons

As Birmingham grew in importance during the Victorian era, more and more criminals were being tried and, following conviction, transported to Warwick to serve their sentence or face execution. It was a costly arrangement and in 1845 the Borough Council decided it was time to build a new gaol to replace the inadequate one currently in use.

Application for admission of Emma Heppingstall to Norton Girls Reformatory, Birmingham, 1855. (Courtesy of Library of Birmingham)

Birmingham's first gaol had been situated on Peck Lane, on what is now the site of New Street station. When that closed in 1806, prisoners were transferred to a new prison attached to the public offices in Moor Street. When this gaol was also unable to cope with the demands imposed on it, councillors searched for a new site, finally settling on a seven-acre piece of land at Winson Green Road, on the 'Birmingham Heath'.

Designed by architect Daniel R. Hill, the new gaol was built in the 'panoptican' design with wings radiating away from a central tower [LoB: MS 681]. This modern design, pioneered by Russian factory bosses overseeing production lines, allowed a warder standing in the central area a clear view down each wing. Featuring a gothic-style gatehouse that gave the building the appearance of a medieval castle, it became known as the Borough Gaol, and work was finally completed in 1849. The first governor at Winson Green was Edinburgh-born Captain Alexander Maconochic, a former naval officer and pioneer in penal reform.

Now known as HMP Birmingham, Winson Green remains one of the largest gaols in the country, serving magistrate and Crown Courts in Birmingham, Stafford and Wolverhampton, as well as smaller courts across the Midlands.

Debtors were catered for in a separate prison, known as the Court of Requests. Under an Act of 1752, the court dealt with small debts of no more than forty shillings for the Birmingham and Aston area; larger debts were still dealt with at the Quarter Sessions. It was held initially in a room above the Old Cross and moved to new premises in High Street in 1784. Seventy-two commissioners were chosen from the local area to pass judgement, only three sitting for each hearing, and always on Fridays. The Court of Requests also shared the building with the town's magistrates, but in 1807 they moved to new public offices in Moor Street, and the building became synonymous with the 'poor debtors' that it incarcerated. In that same year the building was also extended and another Act was passed allowing the court to deal with those with debts up to five pounds.

Calendars of prisoners, including debtors, are listed in Table 6.1 above. Online collections include:

- Warwickshire Calendar of Prisoners, 1800–1900: index at the WCRO site listing prisoners from Warwick, Birmingham and Coventry gaols tried at the Warwick Assizes and Quarter Sessions (**http://tinyurl.com/pzdjahk**).
- Birmingham Calendar of Prisoners, 1880–1891 and 1906–1913: on Ancestry, listing prisoners at Birmingham Assizes and Quarter Sessions. A subset of the main series, 1880–1971 [LoB: QS/B/20 and MS 1844].
- Calendar of Prisoners at Staffordshire Quarter Sessions, 1779–1900: on Staffordshire Name Indexes.
- Stafford Gaol Photograph Albums Index, 1877–1916: on Staffordshire Name Indexes, around 6,300 entries of prisoners compiled from surviving photograph albums.
- Calendar of Prisoners at Worcestershire Quarter Sessions, 1839–1849: downloadable index at WAAS site (**http://tinyurl.com/lpu2js9**).

Capital Punishment

Capital punishment would have been an aspect of justice that our ancestors, if not familiar with, would at least have been aware of. In the eighteenth century every county had a place of execution, normally at or near the county (Assize) town and often just outside the town on the west side. In some cases there were two places of execution within a county. At Warwick, the traditional site was at the appropriately named Gallows Hill; in Worcester, Red Hill was used; and in Stafford, Sandyford was the relevant location. Executions could also be carried out at or near the crime scene if ordered by the judge in particular cases.

After executions in London were moved from Tyburn to Newgate prison, other cities and towns followed suit and it became general policy to move executions from an open area near to the Assize to a location at or near the relevant gaol. Coventry was one of the last to comply, the execution of Mary Ball taking place in Cuckoo Lane, outside County Hall in 1849. With the ending of public hangings in 1868 most prisons continued to use the existing gallows, set up in one of the yards or within a purpose-built execution shed, as was the case at Warwick Gaol. Later executions were restricted to a few larger prisons with execution suites, of which Winson Green was one.

During the twentieth century thirty-three men and one woman were executed at Winson Green; taking other gaols into account, fifty people with strong connections to the city were executed. The last Birmingham execution was that of Oswald Augustus Grey on 20 November 1962. The Capital Punishment website (**www.capitalpunishmentuk.org**) lists all known British executions back to 1735, together with information on the methods used. Eddleston (1997) and Fielding (2009) tell the stories of those executed in Birmingham during the twentieth century.

Other Judicial Records

Every year parish officers drew up new lists of those qualified for jury service at the Quarter Sessions. The list was then displayed in the parish so that objections could be made. Under the Act for Better Regulation of Juries, 1730, jury panels were selected from the jury lists by lot, with the intention of preventing eligible jurors of higher social status from evading their responsibilities through undue influence with local officials.

Jury lists are found in the Quarter Sessions records. They generally show: surname and forename(s), place of residence, parish and hundred, and title/nature of qualification. Warwickshire jurors' lists, 1696–1848 are on Ancestry; these may include occupation and address. Staffordshire jurors' lists, 1811–1831 are on Staffordshire Name Indexes; survival is patchy but is good for South Offlow hundred, the area covering Great Barr, Handsworth and Harborne.

Although an ancient office dating back to Norman times, the Coroner's system as we know it today stems from the Victorian era. There was growing concern that, given the easy and uncontrolled access to numerous poisons and inadequate medical investigation of the actual cause of death, many homicides were going

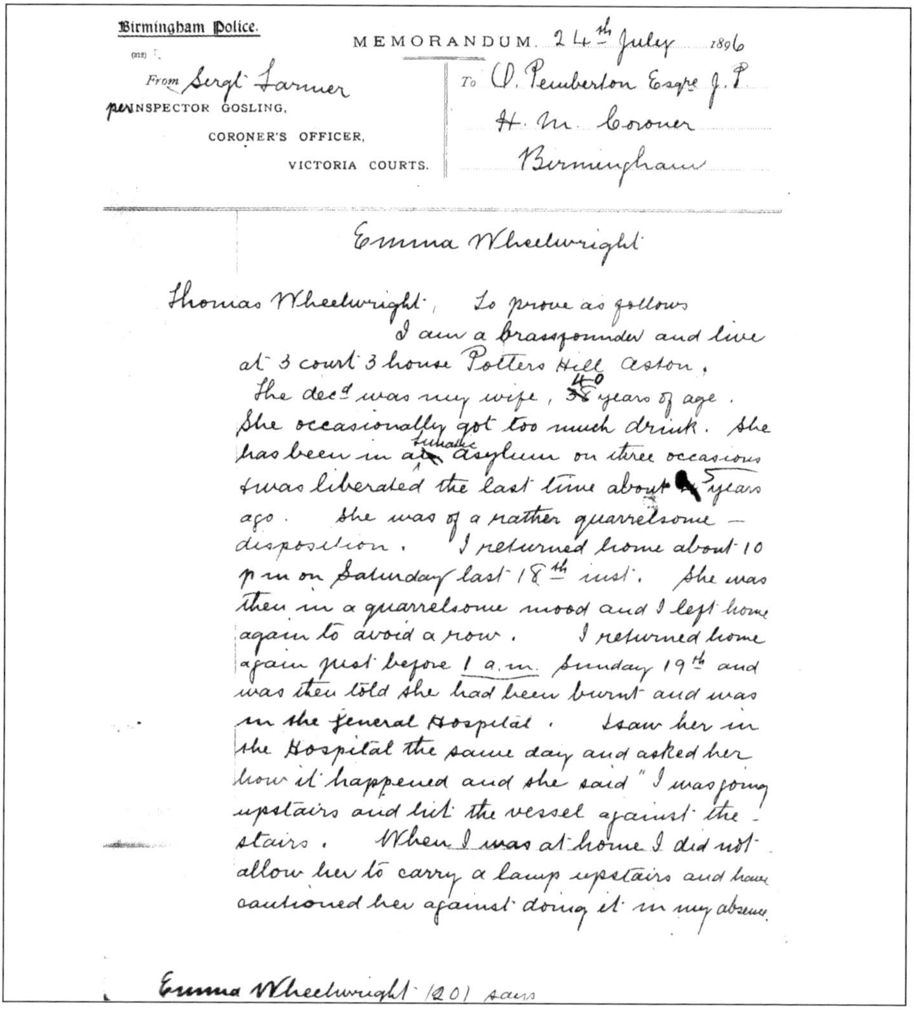

Birmingham Police.

MEMORANDUM. 24th July 1896

From Sergt. Farmer
per INSPECTOR GOSLING,
CORONER'S OFFICER,
VICTORIA COURTS.

To C. Pemberton Esqre J.P.
H. M. Coroner
Birmingham

Emma Wheelwright

Thomas Wheelwright, To prove as follows
I am a brassfounder and live
at 3 court 3 house Potters Hill Aston.
The decd was my wife, 40 years of age.
She occasionally got too much drink. She
has been in an lunatic asylum on three occasions
& was liberated the last time about 5 years
ago. She was of a rather quarrelsome –
disposition. I returned home about 10
p m on Saturday last 18th inst. She was
then in a quarrelsome mood and I left home
again to avoid a row. I returned home
again just before 1 a.m. Sunday 19th and
was then told she had been burnt and was
in the general Hospital. I saw her in
the Hospital the same day and asked her
how it happened and she said "I was going
upstairs and hit the vessel against the
stairs. When I was at home I did not
allow her to carry a lamp upstairs and have
cautioned her against doing it in my absence.

Emma Wheelwright (20) saw

Coroner's inquest into the death of Emma Wheelwright, 1896. The author's relative died of burns after tripping on the stairs whilst carrying a lighted gas lamp. (Courtesy of Library of Birmingham)

undetected. Under the Coroners Act of 1887, coroners lost many of their earlier fiscal powers and became more concerned with determining the circumstances and the actual medical causes of sudden, violent and unnatural deaths.

The coroner's involvement in investigating a death will be shown on the death certificate. If a post-mortem were held (but no inquest), this will be indicated in the 'cause of death' section on the certificate as: 'Certified by [coroner's name] ...after post mortem without inquest'. If an inquest was deemed necessary, the certificate will give the date it was held and the verdict: 'accidental death', 'natural causes', 'murdered', 'took own life', etc.

Coroners' records are generally held in the Quarter Sessions archives (see Table 6.1). Prior to 1838, inquests for deaths in Birmingham were held in Warwick and will be reported in the Warwickshire Quarter Sessions. There are also some Warwickshire coroner's inquests at the Shakespeare Library [ER 10/5]. The Library of Birmingham has the Birmingham Coroner's Court Roll on microfilm, 1839–1875. Original inquest files from the Birmingham Coroner are held from July 1875 onwards [class CO]; those more than seventy-five years old can be consulted in the Wolfson Centre. To enquire about more recent inquests contact the Birmingham Coroner's Court (address in Annex). Individual cases will almost certainly be reported in the newspapers, especially where an inquest was held. The LoB has some scrapbooks of inquest news-cuttings from 1876 onwards which may be consulted by prior arrangement.

Further Information

Carl Chinn, *The Real Peaky Blinders: Billy Kimber, the Birmingham Gang and the Racecourse Wars of the 1920s* (Brewin Books, 2014).

John J Eddleston, *Murderous Birmingham: The Executed of the Twentieth Century* (Breedon Books, 1997).

Steve Fielding, *Hanged at Birmingham* (History Press, 2009).

Jeremy Gibson & Colin Rogers, *Coroners' Records in England and Wales,* Third Edition (Family History Partnership, 2009).

Jeremy Gibson, Else Churchill, Tony Foster & Richard Ratcliffe, *Quarter Sessions Records for Family Historians,* Fifth Edition (Family History Partnership, 2007).

Philip Gooderson, *The Gangs of Birmingham: From the Sloggers to the Peaky Blinders* (Milo Books, 2010).

John W Reilly, *Policing Birmingham: An Account of 150 Years of Police in Birmingham* (West Midlands Police, 1989).

Stephen Wade, *Tracing Your Police Ancestors* (Pen & Sword, 2009).

Chapter 7

MIGRATION AND HOUSING

Rural Migration

Birmingham's transformation from a small market town to the manufacturing capital of the British Empire was fuelled by migration. Over the centuries emigrants from both home and abroad have been drawn to this industrially innovative town by the promise of work and a better life for themselves and their families.

Even before the Industrial Revolution, tens of thousands of people from adjoining counties flooded into Birmingham to escape the squalor and poverty of rural life. Many experienced no improvement in the overcrowded slum conditions they found there but, significantly, few opted to return to whence they came. Research using settlement certificates (see below) for Birmingham between 1686 and 1757 indicates that initially the majority of migrants had moved only a short distance. By 1757, sixty per cent came from distances within a fifteen-mile radius of the town and twenty-one per cent had come from further afield. Yet, people often travelled much further than we think. In the period 1686 to 1726, for example, the Birmingham records show only one settlement certificate from Herefordshire, compared with seventeen from Cheshire and eleven from Lancashire.

Whilst escaping poverty and the search for work were the main factors, people were drawn into Birmingham for other reasons too. Young people (mainly boys) came to take up apprenticeships in skilled industries. Although some returned to their home towns having learned their trade, many stayed and became master craftsmen or set up businesses of their own. With its reputation for political and religious tolerance, the town also attracted those, such as Quakers and other non-conformists, fleeing religious persecution elsewhere.

In many cases it was single people who moved to the urbanizing area, often for domestic work, and often it was women who led the way. This was partly because jobs in domestic service were plentiful (eleven per cent of females over age ten were listed as servants in 1851), and partly because of changes in women's work and pay in agriculture. Some migrants travelled beyond the West Midlands area, to London and elsewhere, using Birmingham as a stopping off point along the way.

Table 7.1: Migrant and Pauper Sources in Quarter Sessions Records

Category	Staffordshire	Warwickshire	Worcestershire
Bastardy Orders, Certificates and Returns		QS0050	1/3/7/5
Hawkers, Stage Coach Drivers, etc (Penalties)	Q/RLb	QS0017	
Poor Relief	No single reference, see catalogue	QS0020	1/3/7
Vagrants	Catalogued by parish	1/10/2	

Notes: The references shown are for the catalogue of the relevant county archive: SSA for Staffordshire; WCRO for Warwickshire; WAAS for Worcestershire. For web addresses of online catalogues and other details see 'How To Use This Book' in the Introduction.

Settlement records are one way of tracking rural migration. Settlement laws required incomers to possess a certificate issued by the parish they had left, which undertook to support them if they needed help within forty days of arriving in their new parish. To assess whether or not a person or family was entitled to legal settlement, an examination (interview) was conducted and based on this, either a certificate or a removal order was issued. These records can provide a detailed account of how the person came to be in the parish.

Settlement and removal records are found in several sources, depending on the period in question. Before 1836 settlement was a parish matter, so the records will be in the parish overseers' papers (at the LoB or relevant CRO). After 1836, responsibility passed to the poor law unions (see Chapter 5). If a removal order was issued, the receiving parish may hold a copy of the original order. The parish overseers' records for Allesley, in Warwickshire, for example, include several orders for families removed from the Birmingham area. These include Thomas Chamberlain, his wife Sarah and their children Ann (aged 6) and John (aged 1), who were one of two families returned from Birmingham on 11 September 1816 (records at Coventry History Centre).

Decisions on removals had to be ratified at the Quarter Sessions, where appeals were also heard. The relevant records are included either in the courts' general proceedings or under a separate heading. Table 7.1 gives catalogue references for this and related categories.

Apprenticeship, religious and workhouse records can all be useful in establishing the vital link between Birmingham and an ancestor's parish of origin.

The Jewish Community

There has been a Jewish community in Birmingham since at least the early eighteenth century. *Sketchley's Directory* of 1767 lists eight Jewish tradesmen, including Mayer Oppenheim, a Hungarian who established a glassmaking business in Snow Hill in 1762. Many of these new arrivals were from Eastern Europe, where Jews faced increasing persecution. They sought refuge in the town

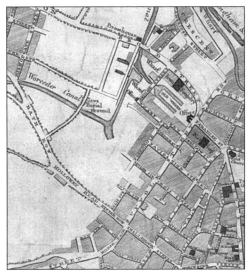

The Jewish Burial Ground, off Bath Row, on a map of 1810. (Public domain)

and a small Jewish quarter grew up around the Froggary. The first recorded synagogue was built here and was extended in 1791, and a second was erected in Severn Street in 1809.

After the Froggary was cleared to make way for New Street Station, the community relocated a short distance to the area around Hurst Street and Holloway Head where many historic Jewish buildings can still be seen. The Singers Hill Synagogue in Ellis Street opened in 1856 and is still in operation.

The Jewish community grew steadily and by 1851 numbered about 700. The majority were originally occupied in modest trades such as tailors, hawkers, glaziers, and also many pawnbrokers. The established families later became merchants, watch and clock makers and – most significantly – jewellers. Many achieved success in their respective trades and moved to more fashionable areas such as Edgbaston and Moseley. Some entered civic and public life, such as Sir David Davis, who became Birmingham's first Jewish Lord Mayor (1921–2). Jacob Jacobs was instrumental in setting up the Birmingham Jewellers and Silversmiths Association, which helped boost the jewellery trade.

In 1843 the Hebrew National School was established in Hurst Street. It later moved to premises adjacent to the Singers Hill Synagogue, before relocating to Moseley in the twentieth century, where it became the King David School. *The Criterion* public house in Hurst Street was a popular meeting place for Jewish working men until the official Jewish Working Men's Club opened in Hinckley Street around 1903.

A further influx of Jews from Central Europe and Russia in the late nineteenth century led to the creation of two further orthodox congregations: the Central Synagogue and the New Synagogue. They, in turn, were followed by the Liberal Synagogue formed in the late 1930s. Since the Second World War numbers have declined as people emigrated to Israel or moved to cities with larger Jewish communities. Although the old Jewish area has disappeared, new facilities have been set up in the suburbs including homes for the elderly and a synagogue in Solihull.

The archives of the Birmingham Hebrew Congregation, held at the Library of Birmingham [in series JA], contain a wealth of information about Jewish life in the city and the community's involvement with business, politics, social life, the arts and many other aspects. Most of the papers come from Singers Hill Synagogue and the Hebrew/King David School. They include: records of marriage registration [JA/2/C], death and burial registration [JA/2/D], and synagogue services [JA/2/E]. The papers of the Secretary of the Congregation also include correspondence about property and investment, publications and photographs. There is a separate index for Jewish burials at Brandwood End cemetery [MS 2635].

The archive contains collections of papers from charities and societies which were set up by the Congregation in the nineteenth and twentieth centuries. One of the earliest was the Hebrew Philanthropic Society, established in 1829 to distribute poor relief to the community. This was followed in 1840 by the Birmingham Hebrew School and the collection includes the school records [JA/1/C] and those of the Birmingham Hebrew Educational Aid Society [MS 2539]. Other nineteenth-century records include the Jewish Board of Guardians [MS 1678] and the Hebrew Ladies Benevolent Society.

In addition, the collection covers political, arts and social groups such as: the Birmingham Jewish Literary and Arts Society [MS 2520]; the Birmingham Jewish Youth Council [MS 2522]; and the Birmingham Young Israel Society [MS 2523]. Also preserved in the archive are personal and research papers of the historian Zoë Josephs [MS 2524], who has made an extensive study of Birmingham's Jewish community (Josephs, 1980 & 1988).

Catalogues for some of these series are available to download at the Connecting Histories portal.

The Irish Community

The Irish were the largest migrant community in Birmingham during the Victorian period. As early as 1828 there were around 5,000 Irish in the town; many of these were seasonal workers who drifted away to neighbouring rural counties during the summer months.

Following the Act of Union of 1800, Ireland was effectively ruled from Westminster. With the abolition of import duties, the country was flooded with cheap imports from the growing English industrial centres and the few commercial goods produced in Ireland soon disappeared. Poor harvests and attempts by Irish landlords to establish larger, more economical farms with fewer workers led to evictions and increased hardship for the peasants. Many headed to Dublin where it was possible to book a ship passage to Liverpool for threepence.

Whereas wealthier emigrants headed for New York and Canada, the England-bound passengers dispersed to developing industrial centres, like Manchester and Birmingham. Most of this first wave of settlers, including children, found work as poorly paid unskilled labourers building new housing and factories for the rapidly rising population.

The potato famine of 1845–48 brought another surge of settlers from the West of Ireland. They were escaping not just starvation but also tyrannical landowners who resented having to pay a poor rate for the impoverished peasants on their estates. Starving tenants were evicted *en masse* and forced to seek salvation elsewhere.

Urban housing in Summer Lane, around 1920. (Public domain)

The poor Irish settlers naturally congregated in some of the poorest areas of Birmingham, particularly in the slums around the Suffolk Street area. Having been displaced from a rural society to the worst kind of urban existence, they found themselves living on the edge. Language (many of the new wave were Gaelic speakers), religion (Catholicism predominated) and cultural ties drove the Irish into close-knit and inward-looking ghettoes, with the accompanying problems of disease, over-crowding and insanitary conditions. Visiting the Gullet in 1837, Thomas Finigan, who worked as a town missionary, wrote of finding 'dark passages and back courts'. He continued: 'In one of these I entered a house – I saw six females at card playing, and all of them almost in a state of nudity. Oh! How serious and how responsible is the work of the town missionary'.

Powerful evidence of the poor conditions facing the Irish community is found in the Birmingham Workhouse, which from the 1860s to 1900 accommodated a disproportionate number of Irish. The strain of providing relief led to many Irish being returned to the parish of their birth, despite the five-year residency qualification which legally gave them a claim to relief from the Birmingham authorities. Complaints relating to this practice were received from Cork, Galway and Dublin.

As the worst of the slums were swept away, later generations of Irish spread across the city, although were still concentrated within the poorer inner suburbs. In the 1940s and 50s the Republic became an important recruiting ground for the depleted council workforce. By the early 1950s around one-third of transport workers in the city were Irish; hospitals were another popular employment. To address the problems of accommodation and integration faced by this new generation of migrants, an Irish Community Centre was set up in Digbeth in 1968; this has since become the cultural focus for Birmingham's Irish community. Chinn (2003) and Moran (2010) give detailed accounts of the Irish community's experiences and contribution to the city.

Census records should be the first port of call where Irish origins are suspected. Unfortunately, birthplaces for settlers are often not recorded as precisely as those born in Great Britain. So while a county or village may be listed, an ancestor's entry may simply say 'Ireland'. As most (though by no means all) Irish settlers were Roman Catholic, church records at the Birmingham Archdiocesan Record Office should be consulted (see Chapter 2). Workhouse records (Chapter 5) and settlement records (see above) may also be useful. For research within Ireland see specialist guides such as Paton (2013).

The Charles Parker Collection at the Library of Birmingham has oral histories of twentieth-century Irish migrants as well as recordings of Irish folk music [MS 4000].

The Italian Community

Although never substantial, Birmingham had a well-established Italian community during the latter half of the nineteenth century. Their main businesses were music and ice cream. Brightly painted ice cream carts were pushed around the streets, whilst the music of barrel organs – known as hurdy-gurdies – attracted the crowds.

Most Italians settled in the St Bartholomew's district, close to the city centre. In this 'Little Italy', the markets and places of entertainment in the nearby Bull Ring provided both the ingredients for the manufacture of ice cream and ample sales opportunities. At first, ice cream was manufactured in the brew houses or other buildings in the back-to-back courts, but health scares meant that in time most of the businesses transferred to purpose-built premises. Each family's recipe was a closely guarded secret.

Redevelopment of the St Bartholomew's area in the 1930s led to the community being dispersed; by this time it was already becoming integrated into the local population.

Hopwood & Dilloway (1996) chronicle the history of the Italian community in the city. For specialist resources see the Anglo-Italian Family History Society (**www.anglo-italianfhs.org.uk**).

Travelling Communities: Romany and Gypsy Ancestors

Being a crossroads for transport links of all kinds, Birmingham has long been a meeting point for traveller communities. As early as 1705, the records of St John's, Deritend show 'travelling people' being baptized. A century later, Birmingham artist Joseph Barber sketched a scene he described as 'Gypsies near Bromford Forge' in 1807. His drawing shows a small community sheltered by bender tents who worked as 'hawkers'.

Many early travellers earned a living by mending shoes, making pegs or weaving baskets. Other itinerants took up trades in scrap metal, producing a sound that led them to be called 'tinkers'. Travellers' lives were deeply connected to struggles for jobs, land, accommodation and social rights. Whilst filling seasonal occupations and establishing their own routes and networks, travellers also became renowned for fortune-telling, story-telling and musicianship. Often Romany people continued to speak their own language and dialects. Prejudice made travellers frequent targets for physical attack, or for reformers who wanted itinerants to adopt a 'proper' religion and 'settled' ways of living.

Loss of open grounds for housing and factories became a source for conflict. At the turn of the twentieth century, for example, around 300 Romany people were living in Handsworth on land known as the Black Patch. They lived in tents and caravans under the leadership of 'King' Esau Smith. Despite their claim of a right to be on the land, the families on the patch faced constant harassment to leave the area and to make way for new owners. In July 1905 they were evicted without compensation. Their story was repeated many times over in the years that followed.

Rudge (2003) has a detailed account of the Romany, Gypsy and traveller communities within the West Midlands. The Charles Parker Collection at the Library of Birmingham contains substantial material collected during the 1950s and 60s [MS 4000]. A research guide to this and other LoB collections concerned with Gypsy and traveller communities is also available (**www.connecting histories.org.uk/birminghamstories.asp**). One specific resource is the fines imposed on hawkers, as recorded in the Quarter Sessions records (see Table 7.1 above).

Housing the Urban Poor

Back-to-back housing was seen as a solution to the urban overcrowding experienced in many towns from the late 1700s, and Birmingham was one of its main adopters. Under this design, the houses were laid out back to back, so that only the front had an entrance and windows. The houses were arranged around an open court. Sometimes they were built in the gardens of older dwellings, but new streets were also laid out all around the outskirts of the town.

In the early nineteenth century, at least, these houses could be a huge improvement over run-down rural cottages, and Birmingham's housing was generally thought to be better than other cities. In 1828, John Darwall, a doctor at the General Hospital, noted that in Birmingham: 'the streets are, for the most part, wide and spacious, and the courts have, generally, large yards. Unlike Liverpool and Manchester, excepting the part of the town which is occupied by the Irish, it is rare to find more than one family in one house, and I know not any situation where cellars are occupied by dwellings.'

Built in terraces two or three storeys high, most back-to-backs had two small bedrooms, a room downstairs, a scullery and a cellar. Access was often via an entry away from the street, where typically six or more houses were grouped around a courtyard. Construction standards were poor and infestation by bugs

The National Trust Back-to-Backs, Hurst Street. (Author's photograph, courtesy of The National Trust)

and cockroaches was the norm. External conditions added to the problems. Enquiring into the public health of Birmingham in 1849, inspector Robert Rawlinson found insanitary conditions. In many yards water was drawn from wells which were 'impregnated with offensive matter' flowing in from uncleansed streets, overfull cesspits, rubbish heaps and graveyards. Each court shared a few communal privies. Many courts were home not just to people but to animals as well: slaughterhouses, pig sties and heaps of manure added to the stench.

Little wonder, then, that back-to-back living led, more often than not, to poor health and an early grave. From the mid-nineteenth century through to the early 1900s, the issues were highlighted again and again in official reports, yet little was done. In 1875 Birmingham's Medical Officer drew attention to the difference in the annual death rate between wealthy Edgbaston, at 13.11 per thousand, and poor St Mary's ward (the Gun Quarter) at 26.82. A similar report in 1889 found that in St Bartholomew's ward (east of Digbeth), where over fifty per cent of houses were back-to-backs, the annual death rate was 32.7 per thousand. In areas with no such housing, the rate was dramatically lower at 17.1. And again in 1904, a report into the Floodgate Street area revealed a death rate sixty per cent higher than the city's average. Around two-thirds of houses in the street were back-to-backs and most of the men were unskilled labourers earning between 17s. and 21s. per week.

Dominated by politicians whose main concern was to keep the rates down, the town's authorities were slow to respond. The first major slum clearances were motivated by the need for economic expansion rather than concern for public health. The notorious labyrinth around Peck Lane, the Froggary and Old Meeting Street was cleared with the building of New Street Station (1846–53). This was followed in the 1860s and 1870s by the demolition of squalid property on the

---

Wash Day in Birmingham's Back-to-Backs

Day-to-day life for working-class families in Birmingham's back-to-backs was unforgiving, a relentless struggle against low pay, ill health, under nourishment and poor sanitation. Nothing illustrates these proud efforts more than the rituals of wash day.

First, dirty clothes had to be 'maided' with a dolly in a tub and then scrubbed in a smaller one. Then the clothes were boiled in the copper in the 'brew 'us'. It held about twenty gallons of water and was filled by the bucketful from the tap in the yard – whatever the weather. Next, washing was swilled in a tub of water and *Reckitt's Blue*, and then starched. This operation was followed by mangling, hanging out and ironing. Finally, water from the copper was used to scrub wooden toilet seats, stairs and floorboards.

Other heavy cleaning tasks for women included black-leading the grate, polishing brasses, whitening the hearth, and red ochreing the front step. Surrounded by factories belching out smoke and dirt, Brum's women waged their never-ending battle against dirt.

Colmore Estate to make way for new buildings around Edmund Street and Newhall Street. Those made homeless by these schemes were not rehoused, however, and so the displaced poor simply moved into adjoining slums around the central area.

An Act of 1875 gave corporations the power to acquire, demolish and redevelop slum areas. Birmingham Council used this law as the basis for the most ambitious of its nineteenth-century clearances. Known simply as 'the Improvement Scheme', it would take out many of the poorest streets in the town centre. Over a ten-year period from 1878 to 1887, a wide road was cut from New Street through to Lichfield Street and lined with fine new buildings. Joseph Chamberlain, who oversaw the project, likened it to 'a Parisian boulevard'. Corporation Street – as it was called – affirmed Birmingham's wealth and new civic status, but again little thought was given to those who had lost their homes.

By the early twentieth century it was clear that Birmingham was facing a major housing crisis. Soldiers returning from the First World War were promised 'Homes Fit for Heroes' by the Government. In Birmingham, the efforts of social reformer George Cadbury, who had successfully developed the Bournville Village Trust on land south of the city, offered a new model for working-class housing. And after the huge boundary expansion of 1911, the city itself now had no shortage of land on which to build.

Thus began the inter-war housing boom. Between 1919 and 1939, around 105,000 new homes were built in the city, just under half of which were council houses. Huge new housing estates sprang up in outlying areas such as Castle Bromwich, Sheldon and Perry Barr. The Kingstanding estate, the largest of the 1930s developments, had 5,000 municipal houses by 1939. Meanwhile, across the city private detached and semi-detached houses appeared for the new middle class. The Connecting Histories portal has oral histories of people's experiences of relocation and social housing schemes.

Housing Records

Rate books, held at the Library of Birmingham, may provide an insight into your ancestor's housing circumstances. Rates were collected in each parish for support of the sick and poor, and other local purposes such as highways, sewers, lighting, and gaols. These can be used to establish whether your ancestors were tenants or property owners whilst the rateable value of the property can be used to gauge the status of the occupant. The LoB's collection includes rate books from across Greater Birmingham (i.e. pre- and post-1911 authorities). BMSGH has produced an index to these holdings (**www.bmsgh.org/TYAIB/RateBooks.pdf**). Much of the collection, covering the period 1831–1913, is now available on Ancestry. Consequently, original records are now only produced in exceptional circumstances.

The National Trust has taken ownership of Birmingham's last three back-to-back houses, which after careful restoration are now open to the public in Hurst Street. Moving from the 1840s through to the 1970s, the properties explore the lives of some of the former residents who crammed into these small houses to

DISTRICT No. **2.**
Name or Situation of Property:— *New John Street West* ST. GEORGE'S RATE.

Number of assessment 1	No. of House 2 a Front / b Back	Arrears due or if Excused 3	Name of Occupier 4	Name of Occupier coming in after the making of the Rate, and the date when occupation commences 5	Name of Owner 6	Description of Property Rated 7
1_28	299 300	X ✓	Ernest Samuel Cole		W. Osborne	Retail Shop and House
9	and 301	X	Robert Halford		ditto	ditto
30	302	X	Richard Turpin		ditto	ditto
1	303	X	Henry Eaton		ditto	ditto
2	304	X	Joseph Pettit		ditto	ditto
3	305	X	Frederick Moss Garrett	Albert William Woodhouse July 14	William Kennedy	ditto
4	306	X	Albert Baughan		Francis Gilbert	Retail Shop, House and Bakehouse
5	307	X	Frederick Edwin Morden Josiah Wheelwright		Waddy	Retail Shop and House
6		W	Joseph Wheelwright		ditto	Stable
7	308	X	Josiah Wheelwright		ditto	Retail Shop and House
8	309	X	John Thomas Weaver		ditto	ditto
9	310	X	Josiah Donohaue		ditto	ditto
110	311	X ✓	Benjamin John Fawcett		ditto	ditto

Rate book for New John Street West, Hockley. The listing shows that Josiah Wheelwright, the author's great-great-grandfather, rented a stable yard, as well as a retail shop, a fact confirmed by family photographs. (Courtesy of Library of Birmingham).

live and work. Access is by guided tour only and pre-booking is required (**www.nationaltrust.org.uk/birmingham-back-to-backs**).

The UK Housing Wiki has details of all of Birmingham's pre- and post-war estates (**http://ukhousing.wikia.com/wiki/Birmingham**).

Child Emigration

Among the many institutions set up to tackle urban poverty during the late nineteenth century, the Middlemore Homes stand out. Founded in 1872 by John Throgmorton Middlemore as the 'Children's Emigration Homes', they aimed to offer local children a healthy upbringing and what was perceived as a better life through emigration to Canada.

In September 1872, Middlemore opened a home for boys on St Luke's Road, Birmingham, followed shortly afterwards by a similar home for girls in nearby Spring Street. Children were often placed into the care of the homes by the local magistrates or were transferred from the cottage homes of the local poor law unions (see Chapter 5). This extract from the annual report of the Children's Emigration Homes for 1896 gives an example of the circumstances under which children were admitted:

'March 3rd. – Cruelty. – Emma C., 8 years: first standard. Father in Stafford Jail, where he is committed for cruelty to this child, who has been sent to us by a magistrate's order and whose mother, we understand, is dead.'

Between 1873 and 1930 around five thousand children, mostly from the Birmingham area, were taken over to Canada for resettlement. They went first to a receiving home in Fairview, Halifax, Nova Scotia where the children were welcomed after their long sea voyage. From there, the children fanned out into communities across Canada, although many remained within the eastern provinces. These

Sir John Throgmorton Middlemore, founder of the Middlemore Children's Homes. (Public domain)

children experienced mixed fortunes once in their new land. Many child migrants, as John Middlemore had hoped, were better off than if they had remained in England. Others were ill-treated by their employers.

The Library of Birmingham holds the records relating to the Middlemore Emigration Homes, covering the period 1872–1955, together with related institutions such as the Sir John Middlemore Charitable Trust from 1955 onwards [MS 517]. Archives Canada has a copy of this catalogue (**www.archivescanada.ca**). In addition, a database of all children dispatched from the Middlemore Emigration Homes, compiled by Canadian volunteers, can be found at **www.bifhsgo.ca**. Further information on the project and a series of articles on the Middlemore scheme are available from the coordinator, Patricia Roberts-Pichette (pierpy@gmail.com). Other LoB papers detail the Birmingham Union's programme for the emigration of pauper children, 1898–1911, including case notes [GP B/11/2].

Although not relating specifically to child emigration, BMSGH has published records of immigrants to New Zealand who originated in the Birmingham area. The *'They Came to New Zealand'* database includes immigrant's name, date and place of birth and reference to original source documents, and is available as a download [D501D].

Caribbean and Asian Heritage

The post-war period opened a new chapter in Birmingham's immigration story. Just as Quakers, Jews, Irish, Welsh, Italian and rural English families had before them, migrants from the Caribbean and the Indian sub-continent added their particular cultures to the city's melting pot.

Before the War Birmingham had few non-white migrants, most of whom were skilled medical workers from India. By 1991 it had the largest ethnic percentage of the population in the UK, around twenty per cent of the total. As with the Irish a hundred years before, many of the newcomers originated from a few locations as news of those who had successfully made a new life spread between families and neighbours. With the economy growing and unemployment low, jobs – predominantly unskilled industrial – were plentiful.

Housing, however, was more difficult to come by. Applicants for council housing – which was concentrated in the inner suburbs and the outer estates – had to be resident in the city for five years. As the indigenous population moved into these new developments, the incomers became concentrated in the middle ring. Areas such as Handsworth, Aston, Sparkbrook, Balsall Heath, and Small Heath changed markedly as they took on distinct and distinctive African and Asian cultures.

In the 1980s, problems of racism, discrimination and deprivation briefly expressed themselves through riots and urban unrest. Whilst many issues still remain, earlier tensions have largely given way to the thriving multi-cultural city we see today.

The Solihull and Birmingham Caribbean History Group, based at Solihull Library, offers help and advice on research into Caribbean ancestors and has access to specialist resources (**www.solihull.gov.uk/caribbeanfamilyhistory**).

Although local repositories have few records relevant to tracing Caribbean or Asian ancestry, they hold a wealth of detail on the history and assimilation of these communities. The Connecting Histories portal has guides to the LoB's collections on racism, refugees and migration (**www.connectinghistories.org.uk**). Important aspects include: the African Heritage Initiative, a project to document the contributions of Africans in Birmingham since 1950 [MS 4180/B/1]; papers of the Indian Workers Association 1959–1998, an organization set up to help Asian workers resettle in Britain [MS 2141]; the work of leading Black photographers such as Vanley Burke [MS 2192], George Hallett [MS 2449], and Derek Bishton [MS 2478]; and the archive of the Banner Theatre, an amateur theatre group that promoted anti-racism [MS 1611]. Other aspects of the LoB's collections explore the early Black presence, migration, religion, art and politics.

Further Information

Carl Chinn, *Poverty Amidst Prosperity: the Urban Poor in England 1834–1914* (Manchester University Press, 1995).

Carl Chinn, *Homes for People: Council Housing and Urban Renewal in Birmingham, 1849–1999* (Brewin Books, 1999).

Carl Chinn, *Birmingham Irish: Making Our Mark* (Birmingham Library Services, 2003).

Peter L. Edmead, *The Divisive Decade: A History of Caribbean Immigration to Birmingham in the 1950s* (Birmingham Library Services, 1999).

Doreen Hopwood & Margaret Dilloway, *Bella Brum: A History of Birmingham's Italian Community* (Birmingham City Council, 1996). See also www.anglo-italianfhs.org.uk.

Zoë Josephs, *Birmingham Jewry, 1749–1914* (Birmingham Jewish History Research Group, 1980).

Zoë Josephs, *Survivors: Jewish Refugees in Birmingham 1933–1945* (Birmingham Jewish History Research Group, 1988).

James Moran, *Irish Birmingham: A History* (Liverpool University Press, 2010).

Chris Patton, *Tracing Your Irish History on the Internet* (Pen & Sword, 2013).

Ted Rudge, *Brumroamin: Birmingham and Midland Romany Gypsy and Traveller Culture* (Birmingham Library Services, 2003).

Chris Upton, *Living Back-to-Back* (Phillimore, 2005).

Rosemary Wenzerul, *Tracing Your Jewish Ancestors* (Pen & Sword, 2014).

Rachel Wilkins, *Turrets, Towels and Taps: Birmingham Public Baths* (Birmingham Museums and Art Gallery, 1984).

Moving Here – 200 Years of Migration in England (www.movinghere.org.uk). This excellent website is now closed but still accessible via The National Archives webarchiving service: http://webarchive.nationalarchives.gov.uk.

Chapter 8

ENTERTAINING THE TOWN: LEISURE TIME

Life in Birmingham was not all industry and hard work; people found time to enjoy themselves, too. In the precious hours not spent earning a living, Brummies engaged in various forms of entertainment, from theatres and variety halls, to cinemas and sports clubs, to libraries, galleries and museums. Birmingham has also contributed significantly to the cultural life of the nation. Figures as diverse as Ozzy Osbourne, Sir Edward Elgar, J.R.R. Tolkien, Edward Burne-Jones and Benjamin Zephaniah were either born in the city or have been closely associated with it.

Libraries, Galleries and Museums

Private subscription libraries set up during the eighteenth century were the first institutions with a cultural remit. The Birmingham Library was founded in 1779 by a group of non-conformists and numbered Dr Joseph Priestley as one of its earliest supporters. It moved to purpose-built premises in Union Street in 1797. At one guinea (twenty-one shillings) a year, its annual subscription was well beyond the reach of the working classes. A further venture, the New Library, was formed by religious Dissenters in the 1790s who were dissatisfied with the way the 'Old Library' was being managed. The original 180 subscribers are listed in a Tontine Deed of 1798 (**www.genuki.org.uk/big/eng/WAR/Birmingham/tontine.html**). The two libraries amalgamated in the 1860s and were eventually absorbed into the Birmingham and Midland Institute.

The Free Libraries Act of 1850 allowed councils to set up public libraries paid for through the rates. It was not until 1860 that Birmingham's ratepayers agreed to this and the Free Libraries Committee started to plan a civic library. The Central Lending Library opened in September 1865 and the Reference Library just over a year later. In his speech at the opening ceremony, social reformer and preacher George Dawson proclaimed that a library 'is one of the greatest results of man's civilisation'. 'It is, too,' he continued, 'a place for pastime; for man has no amusement more innocent, more sweet, more gracious, more elevating and more fortifying than he can find in a library.'

Galleries and museums took longer to become established. Exhibitions were staged initially in the Central Library and after the Corporation acquired Aston Hall, in 1864, it was made a temporary home for the growing collections. A purpose-built art gallery did not open until 1885, on a site behind the Council House that had originally been earmarked for the law courts. The scheme was financed in part by the Gas Committee, which used its extensive funds to build itself offices on the ground floor with galleries above. One of the Birmingham Museum and Art Gallery's display spaces is still called the Gas Hall (**www.bmag.org.uk**).

Subscription token for the Birmingham Library, 1796. (Wikimedia, Creative Commons)

Victorian manufacturers and industrialists felt the need for a different type of space in which to display and sell their wares. Thus began the concept of an 'industrial art gallery', or what today we would call an exhibition hall. In 1849 the grounds of Bingley House on Broad Street became the temporary home of 'An Exhibition of the Manufactures of Birmingham and the Midland Counties'. This early showcase of design and industrial art influenced Prince Albert, who visited the show, in planning the Great Exhibition of 1851. Bingley Hall, a permanent exhibition and concert hall, was later built on the site. This association with commercial exhibitions continues today in world-class venues such as the International Convention Centre and the National Exhibition Centre.

After the first Central Library was destroyed by fire in January 1879, the Council rebuilt on an even grander scale at Ratcliffe Place, off Paradise Street. The new building, constructed at the height of Birmingham's municipal building programme, was a cathedral of learning. The Reading Room, with its high vaulted ceiling and tall shelves stacked with books, rivalled any in the world. A report in the *Birmingham Daily Gazette* in 1904 noted the breadth of the clientele: 'One sees a quick-stepping messenger from a solicitor's office intent on unearthing a point of law, the next minute a mechanic searches the shelves, and reaches down a bulky tome on engineering, and there are students, both young and grey-headed, pencilling as they read as though life were at stake'.

By the 1960s it was clear that the building was no longer fit for purpose but it was several years before a replacement was built, partly to make way for new roads around the city centre. Prime Minister Harold Wilson opened the new Central Library in January 1974. Its stark architectural style and poor construction attracted controversy, however. In the 2000s it was decided that this building, too, should be demolished in favour of one more suited to the modern age. The Library of Birmingham, the city's fourth public library, opened in Centenary Square in September 2013.

The Birmingham and Midland Institute was founded in 1854 to promote arts, science and culture in the city. Charles Dickens gave readings in Birmingham

Town Hall to raise funds for its foundation and was its president in 1869. Now housed in Margaret Street, in one of the city's finest Victorian buildings, it continues to offer a wide-ranging programme of arts and science lectures, exhibitions and concerts. It is also home to several independent but affiliated societies, including the BMSGH. The Birmingham Civic Society, founded in 1918, began as a forum lobbying for better planning and facilities for residents and now embraces both the social and the physical environment.

The Library of Birmingham has records from numerous cultural and arts organizations, public and private, some of which include lists of members. Examples are: the Birmingham Amateur Opera Society, 1908 [MS 957]; the Birmingham Philosophical Society, 1800–1852 [MS 1237]; and the Birmingham Industrial Music Club, 1946–47 [MS 1235].

Artists, Painters and Photographers

The Midlands Enlightenment was not only concerned with science and industry; it found expression in the arts as well. From the late eighteenth century, the town began to establish itself as a centre for artists of all kinds – painters, sculptors, engravers – who met regularly and developed their own distinctive style. In 1809 a group that included Joseph Barber and Samuel Lines opened a life drawing academy in Peck Lane, now the site of New Street Station. From this group the Birmingham Academy of Arts was founded in 1814. A proposal to establish a museum led to the formation of the Birmingham Society of Artists in 1821. A

Greenfield House, Harborne, home of the artist David Cox, painted by his son, David Cox Jr. (Wikimedia, Creative Commons)

gallery and set of offices was built behind a neo-classical portico in New Street by architect Thomas Rickman. In 1868 the Society received its royal charter and became the Royal Birmingham Society of Artists (RBSA), which continues to the current day.

Early alumni of the Society included David Cox, one of the leading landscape painters of the early nineteenth century, Joseph Vincent Barber (son of Joseph Barber), Henry Lines and Frederick Lines (both sons of Samuel Lines), and Frederick Henshaw. The RBSA's golden years were in the late Victorian period when it became highly influential within the Pre-Raphaelite and Arts and Crafts movements. Its members included some of the most significant figures in English art, including Edward Burne-Jones (who was born in Bennetts Hill), William Morris, John Everett Millais, and Walter Langley (founder of the Newlyn School). Now based near St Paul's Square, the RBSA houses a permanent collection of over 400 works of art and has a substantial archive covering former members and their works (**www.rbsa.org.uk**). An earlier publication by the RBSA, *A Catalogue of Birmingham and West Midlands Painters of the Nineteenth Century*, draws on information from RBSA catalogues and other archives.

Birmingham was quick to embrace the new medium of photography. Local trade directories list professional photographers as early as 1842, barely three years after the daguerreotype process was introduced (although the origins of photography are disputed). Entrepreneurs soon recognized the business potential and within a few years photographic studios were being established across the town centre and its fast-growing suburbs.

The Library of Birmingham Photographic Collection contains work by many local photographers, including Sir Benjamin Stone and William Jerome Harrison (both founders of the Warwickshire Photographic Survey), William Smedley Aston and Harold Baker. The Birmingham Photographic Society Permanent Collection consists of work by local photographers from circa 1850 to 1980. The Library also holds a collection of the Society's annual reports, exhibition catalogues and journals; an index is available. The Midland Counties Photographic Federation Collection includes portfolios and exhibition prints by members of affiliated societies. These date from the 1930s to the 1980s, most notably work by Arnold Brookes and W.A.Watson.

Photographic historian Harry Wills spent more than fifty years researching Birmingham photographers and painstakingly seeking out examples of their work. Following his death in 2011, the Harry Wills Collection was donated to the Library of Birmingham [MS 4256]. The Library also has a handlist, *Birmingham's Professional Photographers, 1842–1914*, compiled from trade directories, magazines and newspapers. Further research based on this has been published as *Professional Photographers in Birmingham, 1842–1914* (Aston et al, 1987) [LP 25.69]. Photographic collections at the LoB and elsewhere are referenced in Chapter 1.

Other sources for information on photographers (often little more than lists) are: **www.cartedeviste.co.uk**; **www.earlyphotographers.org.uk**; and **www.victorian photographers.co.uk**. Midlands lists can be found at Warwickshire Pink Pages (**www.hunimex.com/warwick/photogs.html**) and GENUKI's Staffordshire site (**www.genuki.org.uk/big/eng/STS/Stsphots.html**).

Theatre, Cinema and Variety

The first theatrical entertainments in Birmingham were from travelling companies or performers. A theatre opened in Moor Street around 1740 but was short-lived. Detractors, particularly the town's strong Methodist community, saw theatres as a corrupting influence on the morals of society. They succeeded not only in getting the venue closed down, but had it converted into a Methodist chapel. A later venture in King Street met a similar fate.

A tide was turning, however, and the New Theatre, later the Theatre Royal, which opened in New Street in 1774, succeeded in establishing itself as part of the town's cultural life. Its position was aided in part by the support of leading intellectuals, like Boulton and Watt, who argued that having one licensed theatre of good reputation was preferable to two or three playhouses of dubious artistic merit. The building was restored on a number of occasions, including after a major fire in 1820. It finally closed in December 1956 and the former Woolworths building was erected on the site.

The nineteenth century was the highpoint of the theatre era, with a whole series of new venues opening within the city centre and the major suburbs. These included: the Prince of Wales in Broad Street (1856); the Grand Theatre in Corporation Street (1883); the New Star Theatre of Varieties in Snow Hill (1885); Birmingham Hippodrome in Hurst Street (1903); the Alexandra Theatre in John Bright Street (1901); and the Birmingham Repertory Theatre in Station Street (1913). These last three are still in existence today, although not all in their original locations.

When moving pictures arrived in the early 1900s public buildings and halls were used for screenings and in some cases converted to 'picture houses'. Curzon Hall, a large entertainment space in Suffolk Street, was one such venue. The first purpose-built cinema, the Electric, opened in Station Street in July 1910, the same month that the Aston Picture Palace opened in Lozells Road. Within a year there were seven cinemas in the city and by 1939 there were almost one hundred, with a total capacity of around 120,000. Their fall in the post-war

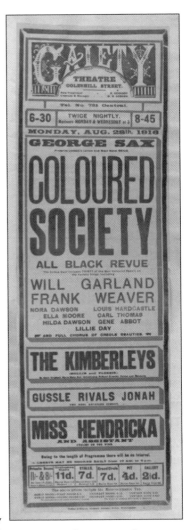

Playbill for the Gaiety Theatre, Coleshill Street, August 1916. George Sax's Coloured Society, an all black revue group, was top of the bill. (Public domain)

Birmingham Ballads: Mary Ashford's Tragedy

Early in the morning of 27 May 1817, the body of a young woman was found in a pool off Pen's Mill Lane, Erdington. Mary Ashford had been raped and strangled. She had attended a dance at Tyburn House the previous evening, Whit Monday, and had spent most of the time in the company of Abraham Thornton, a farmer's son from Castle Bromwich. He had accompanied her to Erdington after the dance, and footprints discovered near the fatal pool were found to match his.

Thornton was arrested and tried at Warwick but acquitted, largely on doubts over times. The jury took six minutes to reach their verdict. Thornton was nevertheless widely thought to be guilty, and public opinion forced him to emigrate to America, where he died about 1860. Mary Ashford's headstone can be seen in the churchyard at Sutton Coldfield.

The case captured the public imagination and a number of ballads were written, wherein Mary Ashford's ghost purports to give a true account of what happened. It includes the lines: 'I'm ravished and murdered she cried, Tho' it can't be denied, I for chastity died, Yet no friend will weep'.

This and other ballads of the period can be seen at Broadside Ballads Online, **http://ballads.bodleian.ox.ac.uk**.

period came just as quickly, with sites across the city being converted by disgruntled (and in some cases bankrupted) picture-house owners. A lasting legacy is the Odeon Cinema chain, launched by Oscar Deutsch in Perry Barr in 1930.

Price (1995) surveys the history of Birmingham's theatres, concert and music halls, and information on the main venues is presented at Matthew Lloyd's website, **www.arthurlloyd.co.uk**, dedicated to the music hall star. Local newspapers carried notices and reviews of performances. The Library of Birmingham has extensive information on the city's theatres, including major collections of theatre programmes. There is also a series of song sheets and silent movie scores (**www.libraryofbirmingham.com/collections**).

Sport and Parks

Sport as we know it today is essentially a Victorian construct. Before the mid-nineteenth century the term 'sport' generally referred to bloodsports or so-called 'cruel sports', such as cock-fighting and bear-baiting, and to gambling associated with these activities and with horse racing. One theory for the origins of the name 'the Bull Ring' is that in the Middle Ages a bull was tethered to a stake in the middle of a ring and dogs were let loose on the unfortunate animal.

The first evidence for competitive sport in the Birmingham area is a bowling green laid out by Sir Thomas Holte at Aston Hall around 1635. A similar green at the George Hotel, Solihull, dates from around 1693 and is still in use today. In the eighteenth century, cock-fighting and cricket were popular across all classes of society and were accompanied by widespread betting. Bare-knuckle prize fights also offered opportunities for betting, Birmingham's tough backstreets providing the ideal arena for young men to hone their pugilist tendencies. Fighters such as Isaac Perrins, who stood 6 feet, 3 inches tall and weighed seventeen stone, became the sporting pin-ups of their day. At the age of 39, Perrins had his last fight at Banbury on 22 October 1789 against a much younger opponent; it lasted sixty-two rounds and seventy-five minutes, at the end of which he had to be dragged from the ring.

With the Victorians' penchant for order, by the mid-nineteenth century sport became more codified and more organized. Clubs established during this period included: the Birmingham Amateur Swimming Club and Edgbaston Archery Society (both in 1860); Birmingham Athletic Club (1866); Moseley FC, the rugby club (1873); Aston Villa (1874); Small Heath Alliance, later Birmingham City (1875); The Priory Tennis Club (1875);

Sidney Mace of the Birmingham Athletic Club. He was athletics champion of South America and died at Rosario, Argentina in 1907, aged 33. (Courtesy of Roger Mace)

Aston Villa victory parade through the city centre after winning the FA Cup, 1957. (Public domain)

Birchfield Harriers (1877); West Bromwich Strollers, later Albion (1879); Warwickshire County Cricket Club (1882); and the Birmingham Anglers Association (1883). Several golf clubs followed during the 1890s, in Moseley, Harborne, Kings Norton, Olton, and Sutton Park, as well as the Midlands Sailing Club at Edgbaston Reservoir in 1894.

This new mania for regular spectating led, in turn, to the first major purpose-built sports venues: Edgbaston cricket ground (1886), Bromford Bridge racecourse (1895), Villa Park (1897), The Hawthorns (1900) and St Andrew's (1906).

It will be seen from these lists that Edgbaston holds a special place in Birmingham's sporting heritage. Its cricket ground is the home of Warwickshire County Cricket Club; Edgbaston Golf Club stands on the site of the parish's ancient manor house; and the Edgbaston Archery and Lawn Tennis Society claims to be the world's oldest tennis club still playing on its original grounds. The latter played a major role in the birth of modern tennis, thanks to Harry Gem, a well-known local solicitor (see **www.theharrygemproject.co.uk**).

Initially, Birmingham's green spaces were privately owned. They included Bridgman's Gardens in Aston, where Birmingham's first cricket match was played in 1751; Spring Gardens in Deritend; the elegant Apollo Hotel grounds in Moseley Street; and the exclusive Botanical Gardens in Edgbaston, opened in 1832. The best known, however, was Vauxhall Gardens in the grounds of Duddeston Hall, former home of the Holte family. A series of donations from the 1850s led to the setting up of municipally-owned public parks, the most generous of which was Cannon Hill Fields, gifted by wealthy landowner, Louisa Anne Ryland. Cannon Hill Park eventually had a pavilion, two boating lakes, a boat house and a bathing pool: it remains one of the city's most popular open spaces.

Played in Birmingham (Beauchampé and Inglis, 2006) is a comprehensive history of the development of competitive sport in Birmingham. It includes, for example, a list of the 677 companies that played in the Birmingham and District Works Amateur Football Association between 1905 and 1955 [LoB: MS 2658]. Although there are no team lists, one of the authors is willing to answer sports-related queries (sbeauchampe@waitrose.com).

Many clubs and associations published regular journals and some have produced their own histories. *First in the Field* (Davis, 1988) presents the history of the Birmingham and District Cricket League and is indexed with many names. *The Centenary Book of the Birmingham County Football Association, 1875–1975* (S.W. Clives, 1974) describes the county league; the names given relate mainly to council members. Original records from the latter are at the Library of Birmingham [MS 519], together with those of other sports clubs and associations.

The University of Birmingham has important collections relating to athletics: Midland Counties Amateur Athletics Association, 1900–82 [MCAAA]; the Midland Masters Athletic Club [ATH]; and the national Amateur Athletic Association, 1880–1992 [AAA]. Warwick MRC houses the National Cycle Archive including the archives of the National Cycle Museum Trust, the Cyclists' Touring Club (Birmingham and Midland District Association formed in 1899), and local cycling organizations such as the Midland Counties Cyclists' Association, 1908–1995, and the Midland Cycling & Athletic Club.

Newspapers, in particular the *Sports Argus* (see Chapter 1), carried sports reports. There are also many books depicting sports and recreations from old photographs and postcards.

Inns and Public Houses

Little remains of Birmingham's early pubs and inns. *The Old Crown* in Deritend, with its black and white timber frame, is claimed to date back to around 1368 but is more probably from the early sixteenth century. The earliest documentary evidence of its use as an inn is from 1626. *The Saracen's Head* in Kings Norton can claim to be Birmingham's oldest extant public house, although it was not converted to this function until the eighteenth century. It is now part of a group of late medieval buildings, known as St Nicolas Place, around The Green in Kings Norton.

Most of the town's pubs and inns were concentrated around the Bull Ring and High Street. A map of 1819 shows the *White Hart, George, Nelson, Swan, Castle, Saracen's Head, Stork*, and *Seven Stars* all within this area. Many of these had stage coaches running to and from them, a trade that died out in the late 1830s with the coming of the railway (see Chapter 4). The most up-market establishment was the Royal Hotel in Temple Row. Erected in 1772, it was the first building in the town to adopt the French styling of 'hotel'.

Victualling has always been a highly regulated trade. From 1522, a person wishing to sell alcoholic drinks had to apply for a licence from the Quarter or

Postcard of The Old Crown, Deritend, photographed in 1851. (Public domain)

Petty Sessions, and from 1617 licences were required for those running inns, hence the term 'licensed victualler'. A loosening of regulations during the 1820s and 30s led to a significant increase in the number of licensed premises, as a result of which drinking in public houses became much more popular.

The temperance movement was born in reaction to what many saw as 'the demon drink' affecting the working classes. The Birmingham Temperance Society, founded in 1830, was reinforced by later movements such as the Gospel Temperance Mission of 1882 and the Birmingham Coffee House Company, all of which aimed to offer alternative forms of recreation. Many of these initiatives were led by non-conformists who saw the fight against the evils of alcohol as part of their Christian mission. The creation of 'pub free zones', in areas such as the Calthorpe estate in Edgbaston and the Cadbury's (themselves Quakers) estate in Bournville, was another means of creating communities and a culture that was tee-total.

The Midlands Pubs and Breweries website records and preserves the histories of pubs, inns, taverns and breweries across the Midlands, with an emphasis on Birmingham and the Black Country (**www.midlandspubs.co.uk**). Pickard Trepess's site has a similar list extracted from trade directories (**www.hunimex.com/warwick/inns-indx.html**).

Victuallers' documentation is to be found in various categories of Quarter and Petty Sessions records (Table 8.1). Landlords had to declare that they would not operate a disorderly pub and to enter into certain obligations before the court could issue a licence; these oaths are generally catalogued as 'recognizances' or 'bonds'. Landlords that failed to adhere to these requirements would appear on charges of 'keeping a disorderly house' and so appear under the criminal headings of the court's records. Licensed victuallers' registers for Warwickshire, 1801–1828 can be searched online at the WCRO website. After Birmingham became a borough in 1838, licensing matters were dealt with by the new Birmingham Petty Sessions; however, no registers remain before 1899. LoB has many plans of public houses, theatres and cinemas submitted for licensing

Table 8.1: Victuallers' Sources in Quarter Sessions Records

Category	Birmingham	Staffordshire	Warwickshire	Worcestershire
Alehouse Keepers Recognizances		Q/RLv	QS0035, QS0036	1/3/15
Beer Licences, Applications for			QS0037	1/3/15
Licensing Act, 1872 & subsequent	PB 3/1 PB 3/2 PB 3/3		QS0038	1/3/15

Notes:

1. The references shown are for the catalogue of the relevant archive: SSA for Staffordshire; WCRO for Warwickshire; WAAS for Worcestershire. For web addresses of online catalogues and other details see 'How To Use This Book' in the Introduction.

purposes, with a card index. Gibson & Hunter (2009) has further details on all CRO holdings.

Ancestry has the Birmingham Pubs Blacklist, 1903–1906 listing around eighty persons convicted of drunkenness at the Birmingham City Police Court. The original list, compiled by the city's Watch Committee, is at the Library of Birmingham, entitled *Register of Portraits and Descriptions of Habitual Drunkards* [BCOL LF419].

Other sources for pub-related records include newspapers (e.g. brawls, festivities), land records (deeds, tithes, enclosures), rate books, fire insurance records, and apprenticeship agreements. Information on tied pubs and their owners can be found in the records of brewery companies, and in photographic collections.

Markets, Shops and Fairs

The Bull Ring has long been Birmingham's commercial centre. A market has been held there since at least the twelfth century (see Chapter 9). By the Georgian era this market quarter was an overcrowded and muddled hodge-podge of buildings, many of which encroached over the roads and scarcely left room for pedestrians, let alone carts. At its heart was The Shambles, a group of butchers' shops leading to St Martin's church. Another landmark was the Old Cross, an arched open market hall that served as a general market.

William Hutton described the chaos of an eighteenth century market day: 'For the want of a convenient place where the sellers may be collected into one point,

The Bull Ring market, early 1960s. (Phyllis Nicklin collection)

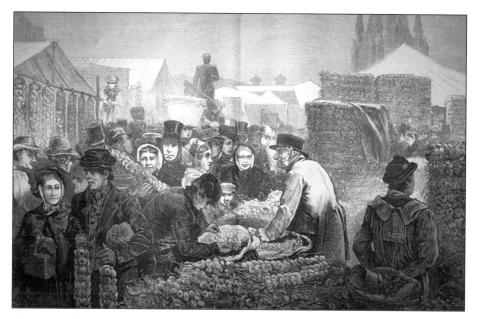

The Birmingham Onion Fair. (Author's collection)

they are scattered into various parts of the town'. After listing the staples on sale at various locations, he concludes: 'We may observe that if a man hath an article to sell which another wants to buy, they quickly find each other out'.

With the traditional marketplace becoming too small and crowded, from 1801 the Street Commissioners set about clearing the Bull Ring site so as to create a more useable open space. The scheme was completed by 1806, aided by the purchase of manorial lands adjacent to St Martin's. Market activities were now concentrated within a few designated locations rather than being spread throughout adjoining streets. In the 1830s the Market Hall was built and became the main site for the Birmingham markets through to the mid twentieth century; it continued to operate even after having its roof destroyed during the Blitz. The Library of Birmingham has records relating to the running of the markets, 1877–1977 [MS 619].

During the nineteenth century, the range of shopping facilities expanded significantly as retailers sought to cater for the town's growing population, and in particular for its growing middle class. Allins, at the corner of Ann Street and Congreve Street, was one emporium of note; a sort of *Old Curiosity Shop* that sold a whole range of goods, new and second hand. On the top floor was the *Cabinet of Curiosities*, a collection of ephemera amassed from travellers, such as stuffed birds and 'shells, medals and foreign coins from every nation'. Warwick House, Birmingham's first department store, opened in New Street in 1839.

In addition to the regular markets, fairs were held at set times of the year. The highlight was the Michaelmas Onion Fair, held in the Bull Ring in the last Thursday in September. As well as the local tradesmen and their wives, this brought in dealers and customers from rural Warwickshire and other counties. They were greeted by mountains of onions: piled in stacks, heaped in wooden crates or wicker baskets, spread upon wide stalls, or suspended in perpendicular ropes from cross-poles overhead. 'The air is fully charged with their pungent odour', reported the *Illustrated London News*, 'causing the unaccustomed eye, perhaps, to shed an involuntary tear'. As its importance as an agricultural gathering declined from the mid-1900s, the Onion Fair became more of a recreational event, offering all sorts of rides and fairground attractions (see Williams, 2001).

Key sources for shop owning ancestors include trade directories (look for advertisements as well as directory listings), rate books, and property records such as deeds. Commercial disputes may have ended up in court and be reported in the newspapers. Shop-owners frequently went bankrupt and so ended up in the civil courts or in debtors prison. Photobooks, such as *Old Birmingham Shops from Old Photographs* (Armstrong, 2011), serve to show not only the shops and their owners, but the diversity of products sold.

Midlands Film Archive

The Media Archive for Central England (MACE) preserves the 'moving image heritage' for both the East and West Midlands (**www.macearchive.org**). Its online catalogue comprises 50,000 titles, including over 4000 video clips for use by researchers and filmmakers. It also offers a range of high-quality DVDs and films on the Midlands for sale and/or download.

The West Midlands History portal is associated with the magazine of the same name (**www.historywm.com**). It regularly produces short films, which are free to view on its website, uncovering the stories of the people and events that shaped the region and the world beyond.

Birmingham Memories, a commercial DVD, contains recordings made between the 1930s and the 1970s, many of which have not been published before (**www.ukhistorystore.com**).

Oral and Community History

In recent years, historians and archives have placed increasing emphasis on so-called 'community history', collecting and documenting ordinary people's recollections and experiences of their communities. Digital Handsworth (**www.digitalhandsworth.org.uk**), Digital Ladywood (**www.digital-ladywood. org.uk**) and Digbeth Speaks (**www.connectinghistories.org.uk/digbethspeaks**) are three such projects. However, few of these efforts to collect oral histories provide access to actual audio recordings.

The Children's Lives project considers the life experiences of children in Birmingham and the West Midlands from the eighteenth century to the present day, drawing on the collections in regional archives (**www.connecting histories.org.uk/childrenslives**). *Fight for the Right: the Birmingham Suffragettes* is a project researching, interpreting and recording Birmingham women's history by young women living in the city today (**http://birminghamsuffragettes. wordpress.com**). *The Disability History Project* has collected stories from the lives of people with disabilities in Birmingham and the wider West Midlands during the twentieth century. These are accessible online and in a book, *Forward – The History of the Birmingham Disability Resource Centre* (**http://disabilityhistorydrc. blogspot.co.uk**). Research guides on the Connecting Histories portal look at issues such as urban childhoods, refugees, migration, and votes for women.

Brummies are noted, and sometimes castigated, for their distinctive way of speaking. *Proper Brummie: A Dictionary of Birmingham Words and Phrases* by Steve Thorne & Carl Chinn (Brewin Books, 2002) is an attempt to comprehensively document the Birmingham dialect.

Further Information

Eric Armstrong, *Old Birmingham Shops from Old Photographs* (Amberley Publishing, 2011).

C.E. John Aston, Michael Hallett & Joseph McKenna, *Professional Photographers in Birmingham, 1842–1914* (Royal Photographic Society, 1987).

Steve Beauchampé & Simon Inglis, *Played in Birmingham: Charting the Heritage of a City at Play* (English Heritage, 2006).

Carl Chinn, *Free Parks for the People: A History of Birmingham's Municipal Parks, 1844–1974* (Brewin Books, 2012).

Alex E. Davis, *First in the Field: The History of the World's First Cricket League – the Birmingham and District Cricket League* (Brewin Books, 1988).

Jeremy Gibson & Judith Hunter, *Victuallers Licences: Records for Family and Local Historians*, 3rd edition (Family History Partnership, 2009).

Joseph McKenna, *Birmingham Breweries* (Brewin Books, 2005).

Victor J. Price, *The Bull Ring Remembered: Heart of Birmingham and Its Market Areas* (Brewin Books, 1989).

Victor J Price, *Birmingham Cinemas: Their Films and Stars 1900–1960* (Brewin Books, 1995).

Victor J Price, *Birmingham Theatres, Concert and Music Halls, 1740–1988* (Brewin Books, 1995).

Chapter 9

BEFORE INDUSTRY

The Medieval Town

At the time of the Domesday Survey in 1086, Birmingham was a small manor worth 20 shillings (£1), one of the poorer manors in the area. Neighbouring Aston was worth four times as much. Other manors recorded in what is generally referred to as 'the Domesday Book' were Sutton, Erdington, Edgbaston, Selly, Northfield, Tessall and Rednal. Birmingham's manor house is believed to have been situated near a crossing of the River Rea, in what is now Moat Lane. It was initially a timber-framed building surrounded by a circular moat and was rebuilt in stone.

The town's fortunes changed decisively in 1166 when the lord of the manor, Peter de Bermingham was granted a royal charter by Henry II permitting him to hold a weekly market 'at his castle in Bermingham'. Under the charter, outsiders had to pay tolls to come into the market, which Birmingham townspeople did not. Thus, merchants and traders were encouraged to live in the town and so pay the lord a rate many times greater than agricultural rent would have produced. The market was the earliest to be established on the Birmingham Plateau and it would be almost a century before markets at Halesowen, Solihull and Sutton Coldfield provided any local competition. Even then the success of the town provided the model; the charter at Solihull, for example, was granted 'according to the liberties and customs merchant of the market of Birmingham'.

Birmingham's position at the hub of a network of medieval roads attracted traders from all around. Most likely, the main produce was agricultural at first

The manor of 'Bermingham' in the Domesday Survey, 1086. (Open Domesday, Creative Commons)

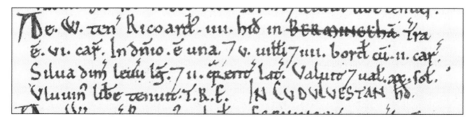

with some livestock, mainly cattle and sheep. The rise of a merchant class during the thirteenth century brought other traders to the town and by 1403 there is evidence of iron, linen, wool, brass and steel being traded; metal goods came from places such as Dudley, Wednesbury and Wolverhampton. The town seems to have been a particularly important centre of the wool trade, with Birmingham merchants trading across Britain and with continental Europe.

Medieval records, together with archaeological evidence, show the first industries being established during this period, primarily textiles, leather working and iron working. By the thirteenth century there were tanning pits in use in Edgbaston Street, and hemp and flax were being used to make rope, canvas and linen. The Borough Rentals of 1296 provide evidence of at least four forges in the town, four smiths are mentioned on a poll tax return of 1379 and seven more are documented in the following century. There is also evidence that Birmingham was already a specialized and widely recognized centre of the jewellery trade during the medieval period. An inventory of the personal possessions of a knight, made in 1308, refers to twenty-two 'Birmingham Pieces' – small, high-value items, possibly jewellery or metal ornaments. Other documents from 1384 and 1460 show the presence of goldsmiths, a trade that could not have been supported purely through local demand.

The prosperity of the twelfth and thirteenth centuries was interrupted briefly in the 1300s. Manorial records refer to a 'Great Fire of Birmingham' some time between 1281 and 1313 (fires in timber-framed houses in medieval towns were not uncommon). This setback would have been confounded by national calamities, such as the Black Death and a series of famines. Although still better off than the rural areas, the inhabitants of fourteenth- and fifteenth-century Birmingham appear to have endured a prolonged period of economic hardship.

The manor remained in the de Bermingham family until 1538 when, on the death of Edward de Bermingham, it reverted to the Crown.

Skipp (1980) and Upton (2011) describe the development of the town during this period. See also the fascinating blog, *Exploring Medieval Birmingham*, by freelance curator and writer, Sarah Hayes (**http://sarahhayes.org**).

Manorial Records

The Manorial Documents Register (MDR), administered by The National Archives, is a centralized index to manorial records for England and Wales. The index, which is gradually being computerized, provides brief descriptions of documents and details of their locations in both public and private hands. The process of revising and updating the existing paper-based register is proceeding on a county-by-county basis, working in collaboration with external partners. At present, Warwickshire has been fully computerized; Staffordshire and Worcestershire are in progress (see TNA Discovery Catalogue, **http://discovery. nationalarchives.gov.uk**).

Manorial records include court rolls, surveys, maps, terriers and other documents relating to the boundaries, franchises, wastes, customs or courts of a manor. Although manorial records do not record births, marriages or deaths as such, they may contain considerable information about individuals, including approximate dates of death. The key records here are those relating to changes in tenancy on the death of a tenant: presentments and admittances. Other records include: lists of jury members and manorial officials; presentments and orders giving the names of those who offended against local byelaws and committed minor crimes; and civil pleas brought against neighbours or others in the community in cases of debt or trespass.

As the ownership of manors changed frequently and did not necessarily remain within the local area, manorial documents can be spread far and wide. For the manor of 'Aston near Birmingham', for example, the MDR lists nineteen records split between the British Library, Library of Birmingham and Staffordshire & Stoke-on-Trent Archives. Those for the manor of Birmingham are held at The National Archives, Library of Birmingham, Warwickshire CRO, Derbyshire CRO and the Shakespeare Birthplace Trust.

Certain medieval records have been published by antiquarians or local societies. In particular, the Dugdale Society, named after esteemed Warwickshire antiquarian Sir William Dugdale, has produced much early Warwickshire material. This includes three volumes of the Warwickshire Feet of Fines (agreements confirming the legal freehold ownership of land or property) covering the period 1195–1509 (see **www.medievalgenealogy.org.uk/fines/ warwickshire.shtml**).

Other Dugdale Society (**www.dugdale-society.org.uk**) publications are: *The Lay Subsidy Roll for Warwickshire of 1327*; *Rolls of the Warwickshire and Coventry Sessions of the Peace, 1377–1397*, and *Ecclesiastical Terriers of Warwickshire Parishes* (two volumes). Commentaries on this period can be found in two publications in the Dugdale Society Occasional Papers series: *The Early History of the Town of Birmingham, 1166–1600* (Holt, 1985); and *Medieval Birmingham: the Borough Rentals of 1296 and 1344–5* (Demidowicz, 2008). The latter describes the relatively recent discovery of two borough rentals for Birmingham that has transformed scholars' understanding of the medieval town.

The Lay Subsidy Roll of 1327 was a tax imposed on those possessing goods to the value of 10 shillings and upwards levied by Edward III in order to fund his wars against the Scots. The list for Birmingham, Edgbaston and Aston was published by W.B. Bickley in *Warwickshire Tracts, Vol. 1.* (1885). Another early listing is Joshua Toulmin Smith's transcript of 'freeholders and indwellers from the 13th to the 16th century', published in his *Memorials of Old Birmingham* (1864).

Durie (2013) and Westcott (2014) provide further insights into interpreting and understanding early documents. The Medieval Genealogy website contains links to numerous sources, including public records, charters, manorial records, early church and probate records, funeral monuments, and heraldry (**www.medievalgenealogy.org.uk**). The heraldry of the three Midland counties has also been discussed in various articles in *The Midland Ancestor,* the journal of the BMSGH.

Tudor and Stuart Periods

The Tudor and Stuart eras saw continued growth and prosperity. By the 1520s Birmingham was the third largest town in Warwickshire, still well behind Coventry but now overtaking the county town of Warwick. The population was around 1000, roughly the same as in 1300; as the national population had decreased significantly, this actually represents an increase compared to elsewhere. At this time, the town comprised around 200 houses, squeezed into a small area around Digbeth and Deritend, Edgbaston Street, High Street, Moor Street and lower New Street, with many small side alleys. The *Survey of the Borough of Birmingham* of 1553, a study of land ownership, mentions eighteen streets by name, many of which still survive today.

Referring to an earlier visit, the antiquarian John Leland wrote in 1538 that:

> 'There be many smithes in the towne that use to make knives and all maner of cuttynge tooles, and many lorimers that make byts, and a great many naylors. So that a great parte of the towne is mayntayned by smithes. The smithes there have yren [iron] out of Staffordshire and Warwikeshire and see coale out of Staffordshire.'

Conjectural map of Birmingham in 1553, based on a survey of the manor, by Joseph Hill, 1890. (Public domain)

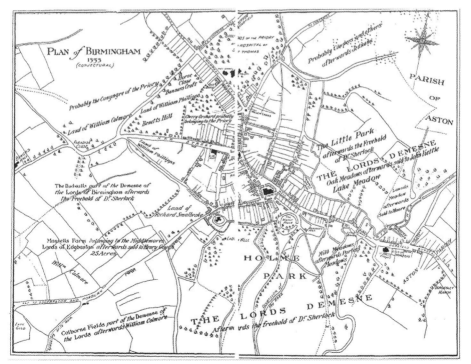

By this time Birmingham was not only a manufacturing centre but also operated as the commercial hub for manufacturing activity spread across the Birmingham Plateau. Sixteenth-century deeds record there being nailers in Moseley, Harborne, Handsworth and Kings Norton; bladesmiths in Witton, Erdington and Smethwick; and scythesmiths in Aston, Bordesley Erdington, and Yardley. But the ironmongers, the merchants who acted as middlemen between the smiths, their suppliers and their customers – organizing finance, supplying raw materials and selling finished products – were concentrated in the town of Birmingham itself.

The dissolution of monasteries and religious guilds brought a collapse in medieval Birmingham's principal institutions. In 1536, the Priory Hospital of St Thomas was suppressed and its property sold; in 1547 the same fate befell the Guild of the Holy Cross in New Street, the Guild of St John in Deritend and their associated charities. The former hall of the Guild of the Holy Cross, together with an endowment worth £21 per year, provided the basis for the establishment of King Edward's Free Grammar School in 1552. Following the end of the de Bermingham's tenure, the lordship of the manor passed briefly to the Crown and then to a series of absent lords and landowners. With local government remaining essentially manorial, this gave the townspeople a high degree of economic and social freedom that proved to be a significant factor in Birmingham's subsequent development.

The English Civil Wars saw Birmingham emerge as a symbol of Puritan and Parliamentarian radicalism. In August 1642, the town sent 400 armed men to reinforce Coventry, a move that proved decisive in establishing Warwickshire as a Parliamentarian stronghold. Later that year there were skirmishes at Kings Norton and the Birmingham townspeople attacked and looted the king's baggage train as it passed through the manor. Meanwhile, Birmingham's strategically important metal trades were put at the disposal of Parliamentary forces. Royalist revenge was exacted at Easter 1643 in the so-called 'Battle of Birmingham', when Prince Rupert sacked the town, burning eighty houses and killing around fifteen townspeople. This rampage through an unfortified town presented the Roundheads with a major propaganda coup that was eagerly exploited in a series of pamphlets.

Prince Rupert sacking Birmingham, depicted in a pamphlet, 'The Cruel Practices of Prince Rupert', 1643. (Public domain)

A number of buildings from this period remain, including Bells Farm (**www.bellsfarm.org.uk**), Blakesley

Hall (**www.bmag.org.uk**), Kings Norton Grammar School (**www.saintnicolas place.co.uk**), and Selly Manor (**www.sellymanormuseum.org.uk**).

Early Modern Records

In 1641–42, all males over the age of eighteen were required to swear an oath of protestant loyalty, as part of efforts to count and tax Roman Catholics. Each parish compiled protestation oath returns that were submitted to Parliament, effectively making this a census of all adult males. Regrettably, few records survive. In Warwickshire, the only extant records are for Coventry and vicinity, and a few areas in the south and east of the county; no records for Hemlingford hundred (comprising Birmingham, Aston and Edgbaston) survive. In Staffordshire, there are returns for the hundred of Offlow, including Handsworth, Harborne, Great Barr, Aldridge, Wednesbury and West Bromwich, some of which bear marks and signatures; these records are held at the House of Lords Record Office. In Worcestershire, only returns from the City of Worcester exist.

The National Archives has records from various taxes and assessments introduced by Parliament during the 1640s to fund its part in the Civil War [Class E179]. These include the Offlow hundred in Staffordshire, and the Halfshire hundred in Worcestershire, both of which adjoin Birmingham.

Following the Restoration, other taxes were introduced in order to rebuild the country's shattered economy. The hearth tax was a graduated tax based on the number of fireplaces within each household. Introduced in 1662 by Charles II, the hearth tax was collected twice a year, at Michaelmas and Lady Day. A person with only one hearth was relatively poor, whereas somebody with six or more

Wenceslas Hollar's 'Prospect of Birmingham from Ravenhurst (neere London Road)', 1640. The engraving was used in William Dugdale's *Antiquities of Warwickshire* in 1656. (Public domain)

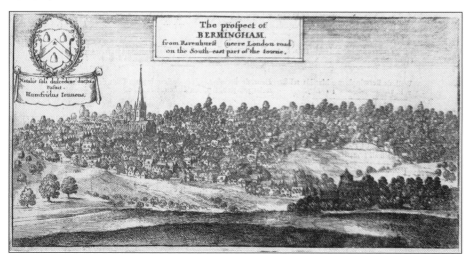

could be considered very affluent. Persons with houses worth less than twenty shillings per annum were exempt, as were those in receipt of poor relief, otherwise two shillings per hearth was payable. This unpopular legislation was repealed in 1689.

Warwickshire has the fullest set of surviving records of any county, listing nearly all the householders with their hearths, including those exempt from paying the tax. A transcript of the best of its eight returns, that for 1670, has been published by the Dugdale Society, together with Coventry's return for 1666 (**www.dugdale-society.org.uk**). Several hearth tax returns for the period 1662–1684 have been transcribed and indexed by the BMSGH and these are included in its Warwickshire Pre-1841 Censuses Index (see Annex for details).

The Staffordshire Record Society has published that county's hearth tax for 1666 (**www.s-h-c.org.uk**). This was released in stages between 1923 and 1927 and is denoted as part of the Society's 'Third Series'. Hearth Tax Online is an academic project providing data and analysis of the hearth tax records. Its collection includes the Worcestershire hearth tax for 1664–65 (**www.hearth tax.org.uk**).

Microfilms of most surviving hearth tax returns are also available via LDS Family History Centres. Original records are held at county record offices and The National Archives [Class E179].

The heralds visitations were enquiries by the College of Arms into those that claimed the right to bear arms (armigers) by investigating their pedigrees. Between 1530 and 1686, heralds travelled the country producing a vast amount of pedigrees and family trees – many of questionable accuracy – as well as notes and other comments. The visitations for Staffordshire (1583, 1614, 1663–64), Warwickshire (1618, 1682–83), and Worcestershire (1569, 1682–83) have been published by the Harleian Society and others; facsimiles are readily available online (see **www.medievalgenealogy.org.uk/sources/visitations.shtml**).

Great Houses and Estates

In the early eighteenth century, the town of Birmingham still had the country on its doorstep. Less than a mile from the beating workshops of the High Street and Digbeth lay fields where crops were grown. Areas that are now considered part of the inner suburbs – such as Moseley, Handsworth and Harborne – were still villages, separated from Birmingham by open countryside. Whilst some of this agricultural land was given over to small holdings, much of it was the property of wealthy landowners who had amassed substantial country estates.

As noted above, for historical reasons titled aristocracy was largely missing from the Birmingham area; there wasn't a duke, earl or marquis for miles around. Instead, these estates tended to be the seats of either minor aristocrats (barons and baronets) or the noveau riche; industrialists and bankers who were growing wealthy on the spoils of the Industrial Revolution. With Birmingham increasingly desperate for space, landowners had to decide whether to maintain their estates or to carve them up and profit from their land-hungry neighbour.

Aston Hall, around 1950. (Public domain)

Not surprisingly, it was the estate closest to the town that was the first to succumb. New Hall, the home of the Colmore family, lay on the far side of the new St Philip's churchyard. It was approached through iron gates, along a broad avenue of elms, roughly along the line of today's Newhall Street. In 1746 Ann Colmore obtained an Act of Parliament allowing her to develop the estate for a mixture of industrial and domestic use. The town's business sector seized on this opportunity to expand, moving away from its old base around Digbeth. The development of the Colmore estate thus laid the foundation for the specialized Jewellery Quarter that still dominates the area (see Chapter 3).

Other estates that grew up around the periphery of the town during this period included: the Pemberton estate around what is now Corporation Street; the Weaman estate around Whittall Street; the Jennens estate around Masshouse Lane and Bartholomew Street; the Gooch estate around Sherlock Street; and the Bradford estate around the street of the same name.

Many of the estates that existed prior to 1700 had grown up around the sites of ancient manor houses. Erdington Hall, for example, was originally a double-moated manor house that stood on a hill at what is now the junction of Wheelwright Road and Tyburn Road; it was rebuilt in the seventeenth century. Edgbaston Hall was the seat of the Middlemore family, who acquired the manor of Edgbaston in the fourteenth century. It remained in their possession until 1717, when the manor was sold to Sir Richard Gough, a director of the East India Company. He rebuilt the Hall, which is now the clubhouse of Edgbaston Golf Club. Perry Hall, in Perry Barr, was also owned by the Gough family; it was demolished in 1927 and is now the site of Perry Hall Park. Elmdon Hall, built on the site of the former Elmdon Manor, was the home of Abraham Spooner, a successful Birmingham ironmaster.

Other houses were built from scratch by wealthy merchants and gentry. Pype Hayes Hall, for example, was constructed around 1630 by Colonel Hervey Bagot, a Royalist supporter who was killed at the Battle of Naseby in 1645. Junior branches of the Bagot family continued to live at the Hall for over 250 years. Great Barr Hall, the home of the Scott family, was founded in the 1600s and rebuilt several times before the estate was eventually sold in 1911 and became St Margaret's Mental Hospital. Moseley Hall, an eighteenth century country house built by the Taylor banking family, was damaged by fire during the Priestley Riots of 1791. It was rebuilt and subsequently passed into the Cadbury family before being presented to the City of Birmingham as a children's convalescent home; it is now an NHS community hospital.

Only two of the great houses in the Birmingham area survive in anything like their original state. The gem is undoubtedly Aston Hall, a Grade I listed Jacobean house built in 1634 by Sir Thomas Holte, Lord of the Manor of Aston and a Royalist supporter during the Civil War. The Hall remained in the Holte family until 1817 when it was sold and leased by James Watt Jr., son of the industrial pioneer. In 1864 it was acquired by the Birmingham Corporation, becoming the first historic country house to pass into municipal ownership. It is now a community museum managed by the Birmingham Museums Trust (**www.bmag.org.uk**). Less well known is Castle Bromwich Hall, a Jacobean mansion built by the Devereaux family and noted for its fine eighteenth-century English formal garden (**www.cbhgt.org.uk**).

The number of English country houses and estates lost since the late nineteenth century is staggering. Matthew Beckett's Lost Heritage website claims to have a complete list, many entries include photographs (**http://lh.matthewbeckett.com**). For buildings that are still standing see English Heritage (**www.english-heritage.org.uk**) and the Historic Houses Association (**www.hha.org.uk**).

Land and Estate Records

The most important source for studying land and property during the eighteenth century is land tax. Introduced in the early 1700s, this was an annual tax levied on all landowners holding land with a value of more than 20 shillings per year. The surviving documents consist of assessments and returns and show the owners of real estate in each parish. From 1772, the returns were altered to include not just the owners but all occupiers/tenants of land and property in the parish with the exception of paupers. Most documents survive from 1780 to 1832, a period when the returns were used to establish a person's entitlement to vote and were in effect electoral registers. From 1780, duplicate copies were lodged with the Clerk of the Peace and are now found amongst Quarter Sessions records (see Table 9.1). Land tax records for Warwickshire, 1773–1830 are on Ancestry.

From 1788 land owners were able to commute their tax payments into a one-off payment but their names were still recorded each year. As part of the process a near complete listing of all occupiers and owners for the whole country was compiled in 1798 and can be found at The National Archives [Class IR 23, with related records in IR 22 and IR 24]; these are online at Ancestry.

Table 9.1: Land-related Sources in Quarter Sessions Records

Category	Staffordshire	Warwickshire	Worcestershire
Enrolments (Deeds, Wills and Papists' Estates)	Q/RD	QS0009	
Inclosure (Awards, plans, tithe agreements and exchanges)	Q/RDc	QS0075	1/5/2, 3
Land Tax Assessments	Q/RPl	QS0077	1/7/2

Notes: 1. The references shown are for the catalogue of the relevant county archive: SSA for Staffordshire; WCRO for Warwickshire; WAAS for Worcestershire. For web addresses of on-line catalogues and other details see 'How To Use This Book' in the Introduction.

The enclosure of agricultural land effectively broke up the smallholding system of farming and consolidated vast open shared tracts of land in the hands of wealthy landowners. The process began in the twelfth century but became widespread from 1750. Under a legal process known as Inclosure, open land was allotted to landowners by private Acts of Parliament and later by the Inclosure Acts between 1801 and 1845. These Acts list the landowner who brought the case to Parliament, while the enclosure award details how the land was to be divided up between the landowner and others, together with the amounts of land. In addition, a map of the land under investigation as part of the enclosure process might survive with the names of the landowners written on them. An academic project has produced an electronic catalogue and directory of enclosure maps for England and Wales (**http://hds.essex.ac.uk/em/**).

The Tithe Commutation Act of 1836 reformed the system of tithes that had been levied on farmers and landowners since the Middle Ages, whereby they paid one-tenth of their annual produce to the church. The Act allowed tithes to be converted into cash payments, called tithe awards. New maps were drawn up to show who owned each field and property, along with a schedule (known as an apportionment), listing all the owners and tenants, and what each plot of land was worth. Tithe Commissioners administered and collected the annual payments, which were based on land values and the price of corn. Records were made in triplicate: one for the parish, one for the diocese and one for the Tithe Commission. Parish and diocese copies, often including pre-1836 parish tithe lists, are at CROs. Warwickshire has an online index [**http://apps.warwickshire.gov.uk/TitheApp/ tithes/indexes**] with maps for sale through BMSGH. The Tithe Commission's returns are at TNA [series IR29 & 30] and are available online at The Genealogist as the 'National Collection of Tithe Records'. LoB holds various tithe indexes and maps for the Birmingham area.

Glebe terriers were surveys of the church possessions in the parish, listing houses, fields and sums due in tithes. Most date from the sixteenth and seventeenth centuries; surviving records for parishes within the Lichfield Diocese are at the LRO.

Mills were a key part of many rural communities. The Mills Archive holds a wealth of information about people connected with mills and milling, together with a separate database of mills across the country (**www.millsarchivetrust.org**). The area's two remaining water mills, New Hall Mill, Sutton Coldfield (**www.newhallmill.org.uk**) and Sarehole Mill, Hall Green (**www.bmag.org.uk/ sarehole-mill**) are both museums.

Numerous other sources are available that document the great estates and the lives of those who lived there. County record offices may hold deeds, estate papers, or the papers and archives of landed families. Auctioneers catalogues and sale notices in newspapers can provide a snapshot of an estate, or part of an estate, at the point when it was sold. The LoB has a large collection of sales catalogues of properties and businesses from around 1880 to the present day, with a card index.

Solicitors records are much under-rated but can contain a wealth of information, not just on large estates but also on town properties and tenants. Mortgages, conveyances, wills, deeds, tenancies and leases, marriage settlements: all of these can end up in solicitors' records. However, as the family may have used a solicitor some distance away (or firms may have moved), a broad search needs to be made (see box).

Those in the upper echelons of society will have been listed in the many directories of the peerage, baronetage and landed gentry published from the eighteenth century onwards by publishers such as Burke and Debrett; the LoB has an extensive collection.

Searching for Deeds

Property deeds and leasehold agreements can reveal much about our ancestors. But, as with other legal agreements, we may have to cast our net wide to find them. Consider this example from Dudley Archives in 1831 [DSCAM/2/11/3/10]:

> Lease (1 Sept. 1831) by Henry Beaumont of Meriden, Warwickshire, gentleman and Elizabeth his wife, to Joshua Horton of Great Bridge, Staffs., boiler maker, of a boat dock, messuage and 1a(cre). 0r(ods). 4p(erches). of land adjoining the Birmingham Canal and the Dudley-Birmingham turnpike, at Birmingham Heath, parish of Birmingham, for a term of 21 years from 24 June 1831, at a rent of £50 p.a.

Here we have a family from the rural parish of Meriden, east of Birmingham (the Beaumonts), leasing land within the parish of Birmingham to a businessman (Joshua Horton) from Great Bridge in Staffordshire. The deed itself was not deposited in either the Beaumont or Horton family papers, nor at Birmingham Archives, but at Dudley Archives in the records of Messrs Slater & Camm, solicitors, of Wolverhampton Street, Dudley. Its location bears no relation to either of the contracting parties, nor to the site of the property itself, but was entirely dependent on the firm of solicitors involved.

Georgian Birmingham

In 1700, Birmingham had a population of around 15,000 and was constrained within a street pattern that had changed little since medieval times. A century later, the population had grown five-fold and new building was underway in all directions, rapidly expanding the built-up area. By 1800, the town had five new Anglican churches, a Catholic church, numerous non-conformist chapels, two theatres, two libraries, a purpose-built prison, an Assay Office, a General Hospital, networks of turnpikes and canals, and several newspapers. Most importantly, in Matthew Boulton and James Watt's Soho Works it had the world's first factory arranged on modern principles, as well as a myriad of innovators and craftsmen who plied their trades in many smaller workshops. The scene was set for unprecedented growth and prosperity.

William Hutton (1723–1815), historian of Birmingham. (Public domain)

Arriving in the town in 1740, at the age of 17, William Hutton noted that the people 'possessed a veracity I had never beheld'. He continued: 'Every man seemed to know what he was about. The town was large, and full of inhabitants, and these inhabitants full of industry'. Hutton himself is a prime example of the sort of confident, industrious and enterprising individual who, though lacking a formal education, transformed Birmingham during the eighteenth century. Having walked to and from London to buy tools, in 1750 he set himself up as a bookseller in a small shop in Bull Street. Within two years he was binding, selling, and lending books from his own circulating library and went on to become a respected publisher and historian.

The developments seen during this period – generally referred to as the Midlands Enlightenment – in fields such as housing, transportation, industry and commerce, literature and the arts, institutions and local administration, all influenced by non-conformism, are described in other chapters within this book. In addition, Jenni Coles-Harris's excellent blog, Birmingham's Georgian and Regency Streets, chronicles this period of the town's development through the eyes of its Georgian and Regency inhabitants (**http://mappingbirmingham. blogspot.co.uk**). As well as informative articles, it contains many historical and contemporary images, and detailed maps.

From the mid-eighteenth century, many administrative and clerical matters began to be recorded in the Quarter Sessions records. These records were often related to the licensing or registration of particular activities, or to the collection of levies or taxes. Under an Act of 1799, for example, anyone operating a printing press had to obtain a licence; registration remained in place until 1866 when the Act was repealed [QS/73]. The Flax Bounty [QS/85] contains claims for reimbursement from flax growers made during the 1780s and 1790s. The Corn Returns for Warwickshire have details of the weekly prices of cereals and other

Table 9.2: Georgian Sources in Quarter Sessions Records

Category	Staffordshire	Warwickshire	Worcestershire	Comments
Corn Returns		QS0106		
Cotton Mills, Factories and Printing Presses	Q/SB	QS0073	1/10/7	Registration of cotton and other mills and factories, c.1800 Registration of printing presses, 1799–1866
Flax and Hemp Bounties		QS0085	1/3/8	
Game Certificates & Gamekeepers' Deputations	Q/RTg	QS0012-15	1/10/1	Under Acts of 1710, 1784 and 1785. Generally long series.
Hair Powder Certificates	D3377/72 (partial)	QS0016		Under an Act of 1795, short-lived
Weights, Measures and Balances, Returns of persons using	Q/AMw	QS0089	1/3/9	Law applied briefly in 1797

Notes: 1. The references shown are for the catalogue of the relevant county archive: SSA for Staffordshire; WCRO for Warwickshire; WAAS for Worcestershire. For web addresses of on-line catalogues and other details see 'How To Use This Book' in the Introduction.

agricultural produce for 1771–1777, together with a list of candidates for the post of Inspector of Corn Returns for Birmingham in 1840 [QS/106].

Quarter Sessions records relating specifically to the Georgian period, and not referenced elsewhere in this volume, are summarized below. Most of the Warwickshire series is also on Ancestry [indexed as 'Occupational and Quarter Session Records, 1662–1866'].

The window tax was one of many obscure taxes levied during the eighteenth century. Introduced by William III as a replacement for the much despised hearth tax, it imposed a flat rate tax per dwelling, initially at two shillings per house. Houses with between ten and twenty windows paid an additional four shillings and those with more than twenty paid another eight shillings. Some householders blocked up windows so as to reduce their tax liability. The tax was payable by the occupier of a property rather than the owner and those not paying the church or poor rate were exempt. From 1784 it was combined with the house tax. Few returns for the window tax survive as there was no requirement for the returns to be enrolled in the Quarter Sessions. Among these, LoB has returns for Harborne, 1763 and 1784 [DRO 61], and Sheldon, 1790 [DRO 42]. Ted Vallance's site has a finding aid for 1723 oaths of allegiance to George I (**http://1723oaths.org**); coverage of the Midland counties is extremely limited however.

Further Information

Simon Buteux, *Beneath the Bull Ring: The Archaeology of Life and Death in Early Birmingham* (Brewin Books, 2003).

George Demidowicz, *Medieval Birmingham: the Borough Rentals of 1296 and 1344–5,* Dugdale Society Occasional Paper No.48 (Dugdale Society, 2008).

Bruce Durie, *Understanding Documents for Genealogy and Local History* (History Press, 2013).

Michael Hodder, *Birmingham: The Hidden History* (History Press, 2004).

Richard Holt, *The Early History of the Town of Birmingham, 1166–1600,* Dugdale Society Occasional Paper No.30 (Dugdale Society, 1985).

Victor Skipp, *A History of Greater Birmingham Down to 1830* (Brewin Books, 1997).

Chris Upton, *A History of Birmingham* (History Press, 1993 & 2011).

Brooke Westcott, *Making Sense of Latin Documents for Local and Family Historians* (Family History Partnership, 2014).

Chapter 10

BIRMINGHAM AT WAR

Local Regiments

Since the modern army began to take shape in the mid-eighteenth century, Birmingham has been associated especially with three regiments linked to Warwickshire and the neighbouring counties.

The Royal Warwickshire Regiment

The Royal Warwickshire Regiment originated as Sir Walter Vane's Regiment of Foot, part of the British troops used by the Dutch Republic in its war against France in the 1670s. That regiment was brought over to Britain by William of Orange in his 1688 invasion and gained the nickname 'The Dutch Guards'. When line infantry regiments were ordered and numbered by seniority in 1743, this regiment became the 6th Regiment of Foot. In 1745 it helped put down the Jacobite rebellion.

Birmingham's first links with the 6th Foot began during the American War of Independence. After several years in the West Indies and North America, the regiment returned to Britain and in March 1778 began recruiting in Warwickshire. Four of its twelve companies were stationed at Birmingham; the regiment reformed two months later with many new recruits. The town also raised by public subscription £2,000 towards their equipment. In 1782, when a territorial system was introduced to aid recruiting, the regiment opted for Warwickshire as its county designation and it became known as the 6th Foot (1st Warwickshire) Regiment.

During the nineteenth century, the regiment's links with Birmingham – and Warwickshire in general – decreased, only being re-established when the regimental depot was sited at Warwick in 1873. Following further reforms the regimental title became The Royal Warwickshire Regiment in 1881.

The regiment's officers during the First World War included Bernard Montgomery, later the victor of El Alamein and instigator of the D-Day Landings, and William Slim, who successfully commanded the army in Burma during the Second World War. During 1939–45, eleven battalions of The Royal Warwickshire Regiment served in Europe, the Middle East and Far East. In 1963 the regiment became The Royal Warwickshire Fusiliers. Five years later it was absorbed as one of the four battalions of The Royal Regiment of Fusiliers.

The regimental museum is at Warwick (**www.warwickfusiliers.co.uk**). A list of regimental histories for Warwickshire, including yeomanry and militia units, was published in the March 2000 edition of *The Midland Ancestor* (BMSGH).

The South Staffordshire Regiment

The South Staffordshire Regiment was formed in 1881 through the merger of the 38th Regiment of Foot and the 80th Regiment of Foot, both of which had affiliations to the county. The 38th Foot, the new unit's 1st Battalion, served in Malta and Sudan, while the 80th Foot, the new 2nd Battalion, spent time in Egypt and India. After deployment to South Africa during and after the Boer War, both battalions served in France for most of the First World War. The regiment also raised eleven Territorial and New Army battalions during the conflict.

During the Second World War the 1st Battalion saw action in Palestine and Burma, while the 2nd Battalion fought in Tunisia, Sicily, Italy and at Arnhem. After the war it was granted an arm badge showing a glider in recognition of its service in an air-landing role. In 1959, the regiment merged with The North Staffordshire Regiment (The Prince of Wales's) to form The Staffordshire Regiment (The Prince of Wales's). Following recent reorganizations, it became the 3rd Battalion, The Mercian Regiment (Staffords).

The regimental museum is at Lichfield (**www.staffordshireregiment museum.com**). A list of regimental histories for Staffordshire, including yeomanry and militia units, was published in the June 2000 edition of *The Midland Ancestor* (BMSGH). GENUKI's Staffordshire page has a military bibliography (**www.genuki.org.uk/big/eng/STS**).

The Worcestershire Regiment

The Worcestershire Regiment was formed in 1881 through the amalgamation of the 29th (Worcestershire) Regiment of Foot and the 36th (Herefordshire) Regiment of Foot, which had already been recruiting from a single depot at Worcester since 1873. At one time the 29th Regiment drew so heavily on Birmingham for its recruiting that it was nicknamed 'The Brummagem Guards'. As the new regiment's 1st Battalion, the 29th deployed to India for 14 years, while the 36th, as its 2nd Battalion, spent time in Ireland, Bermuda and Canada. Both battalions then deployed to the Boer War. They both fought on the Western Front in the First World War, along with Gallipoli and Macedonia. The regiment contributed four regular and fifteen reserve, territorial and service battalions, whose members won nine Victoria Crosses during the conflict.

Two of the regiment's territorial battalions were part of the initial British Expeditionary Force (BEF) rescued from Dunkirk in 1940, while its two regular battalions served in several different theatres of the Second World War. The regular battalions merged in 1948 and in 1970 the regiment was amalgamated with The Sherwood Foresters to form The Worcestershire and Sherwood Foresters Regiment (29th/45th Foot). It is now designated as the 2nd Battalion, The Mercian Regiment (Worcesters and Foresters).

The regimental museum is at Worcester (**www.worcestershireregiment.com** and **www.wfrmuseum.org.uk**). A list of regimental histories for Worcestershire, including yeomanry and militia units, was published in the September 2000 edition of *The Midland Ancestor* (BMSGH).

Militia and Territorials

English militia were part-time military units established at county level for home defence. After a dormant period following the Civil War, they were reinstated by the 1757 Militia Act. The men would receive basic training at annual camps and be available to be called up in times of national emergency. When volunteers proved insufficient, a parish selected men by ballot. These men then either served or found a substitute to take their place.

The Warwickshire Militia served initially from June 1759 until December 1762, part of its time being spent guarding French prisoners on the south coast. In the ensuing years militias were raised in the county on several occasions, including during the Napoleonic Wars of 1803 to 1815. Warwickshire militia records covering the period 1776–1825 are in the Quarter Sessions records [QS0102]. These are available on Ancestry and comprise primarily certificates of service, reimbursements, notices of commissions, and general correspondence.

The Birmingham Independent Volunteer corps was established in 1782 as a territorial army unit, possibly associated with the 6th Foot. In 1797 the Birmingham Loyal Association of Volunteer corps was established; it comprised two companies, one mounted, the other on foot, each of 500 men. A parade on Birmingham Heath on 4 June 1798 was reported to be: 'to the delight of the local belles, who knew not which the most to admire, the scarlet horse or the blue foot.' A further corp, the Loyal Birmingham Volunteers was formed in 1803. These units were the forerunner of the 1st Volunteer Battalion of the Royal Warwickshire Regiment.

Midlands Historical Data has histories for most of these militia and early territorial units (**www.midlandshistoricaldata.org**).

Several new territorial units were raised in Birmingham and the surrounding area around 1908 as part of reforms introduced by Richard Haldane, Secretary of State for War, to improve the effectiveness of British forces in the wake of the Boer War. Carter (2011) has a full account.

First World War

Answering the Call

When the First World War broke out, in August 1914, Birmingham, like many towns and cities, answered Lord Kitchener's call for volunteers to enlist. The Lord Mayor of Birmingham, Colonel Ernest Martineau, C.M.G., was the Commanding Officer of the 6th Battalion of the Royal Warwickshire Regiment and left the city with his battalion. Thus, it fell to the Deputy Lord Mayor, Alderman William Bowater, to organize the recruitment effort.

Members of the Knowle and Dorridge Volunteers, Stoneleigh, September 1918. (Courtesy of Chris Myers)

The regular recruiting office in James Watt Street was soon overrun and so Bowater arranged for the Town Hall, the Municipal Technical School (in Suffolk Street), and Curzon Hall to be placed at the disposal of the military authorities. The Royal Warwickshire Regiment was the most popular choice for those Birmingham men wishing to join an infantry regiment. With the city having recently enlarged into parts of Worcestershire and Staffordshire, these regiments too attracted the loyalties of those enlisting. The Kings Royal Rifle Corp, the Oxford and Bucks Light Infantry and the Duke of Cornwall's Light Infantry were also popular regiments for Birmingham volunteers.

Regular and Territorial battalions were supplemented by special 'Service' battalions comprised of volunteers with no previous association with the military. By the end of August 8,000 men of all classes had enlisted in the city.

The Birmingham Pals

Mirroring moves in other towns and cities, it was suggested that special battalions should be formed of non-manual workers in order to encourage men from the middle and upper classes to enlist. A proposal for City Battalions was sent to the War Office during the last week of August. Kitchener replied that the proposal 'would be most acceptable, and a valuable addition to His Majesty's forces.' The scheme was unveiled in a leading article in the *Birmingham Daily Post* on 28 August.

Three Birmingham City Battalions were raised during September 1914. Officially designated the 14th, 15th, and 16th (Service) Battalions of the Royal Warwickshire Regiment, these battalions soon became known as 'The

Birmingham Pals'. After training at Sutton Park, Malvern and Yorkshire, the Pals battalions deployed to France in November 1915. Among other battles, they saw action at the Somme (July to October 1916), Vimy Ridge (April 1917), and Passchendaele (or Third Battle of Ypres, July to November 1917). For unit histories see **www.birminghampals.co.uk** and **www.1914-1918.net**.

The Birmingham City Battalions Book of Honour, written in 1920 by Sir William Bowater, contains a history of the battalions, medals awarded and casualties, and photographs of each platoon. Information on the nearly 4,000 men who served with the Birmingham Pals, extracted from the book, is available at Findmypast. A CD-ROM version of this book is available from Midlands Historical Data, as is a history of the Birmingham Territorial Units of the Royal Army Medical Corps, 1914–19. *Birmingham Pals* (Carter, 2011) is an authoritative history of the Birmingham City Battalions.

The Birmingham Collection at LoB contains many books relating to the Birmingham Battalions and local regiments, as well as more general books about Birmingham in the First World War [BCOL 75–75.9]. See also records of the Royal Warwickshire Regiment (1st Volunteer Battalion), Non-Commissioned Officers' Association [LoB: MS 956].

The War at Home

The war was felt on the home front as well (see Letheridge, 2012). Factories, such as Herbert Austin's new works at Longbridge, changed from their peacetime manufacture to work for the war effort. With the men away at the front, many factories took on women workers for the first time. The city also played its part in caring for the wounded. Many thousands of men were taken into local hospitals and when these were full the authorities resorted to other measures. The asylums at Rubery Hill and Hollymoor were taken over (with the inmates being transferred elsewhere), Birmingham University was converted, and many large houses were donated by their owners. The city also welcomed almost 5,000 Belgian refugees.

Rationing and air raids – two aspects generally associated with the Second World War – were features of this conflict too. The latter were undertaken by Zeppelins, though they struggled to find their target and the damage was minimal.

People's experiences of war on the home front during the First World War are the subject of Voices of War and Peace, a new community history project led by the University of Birmingham (**www.voicesofwarandpeace.org**).

The LoB has records relating to the War Refugees Fund (Birmingham and District) [MS 652] and a variety of other sources are listed in its First World War Research Guide (**http://tinyurl.com/o43bmqx**).

Second World War: The Home Front

Air Raids and Evacuation

When the twentieth century's second great conflict came, Birmingham found itself very much in the front line. As the heartland of Britain's manufacturing industries, Birmingham – together with other areas of the West Midlands – was a key target for enemy bombers. Over 2,200 of the city's inhabitants were killed during the prolonged bombing known as The Blitz; another 3,000 were seriously injured and around 3,700 wounded.

Air raids on the city began on 8 August 1940 and lasted through to 23 April 1943, although the most destructive attacks occurred between the end of August 1940 and May 1941. Prolonged and powerful raids destroyed over twelve thousand homes, 300 factories, thirty-four churches, halls and cinemas, and 200 other buildings. Thousands of other properties were damaged. Government censors made attempts – largely successful – to cover up the damage for fear it would undermine morale.

The Birmingham Air Raids Remembrance Association (BARRA) collects the memories of those affected by the Blitz in Birmingham and organizes visits and reunions (**www.birminghamairraids.co.uk**). The Association has compiled a database of those who died (**www.swanshurst.org/barra**) and also published a

Birmingham air raids, November to December 1940. Note how the targets are clustered in the industial areas north and east of the city centre. (TNA, Creative Commons)

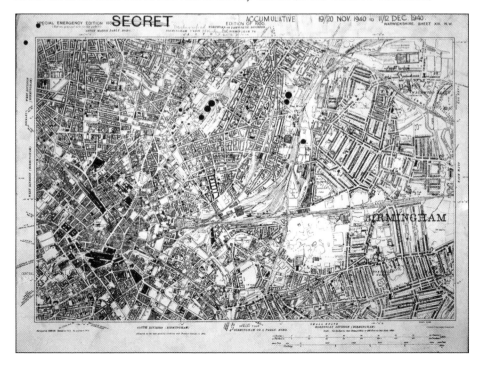

Evacuees at Birmingham Snow Hill Station. (Public domain)

book (Wright, 2014). LoB has maps [LS 8], logbooks [MS 984], reports and photographs [MS 794 & 1827] relating to air raids on the city, as well as Luftwaffe maps, aerial photographs and navigation charts [LS 443]. Minton (2002) gives a raid-by-raid summary of the Blitz and records notable stories of heroism. The National Archives flickr site has a map of bombs dropped on central Birmingham in 1940 (**http://tinyurl.com/kapoggb**). The Quinton At War site focuses on the effect of the war on that area of the city (**www.quintonatwar.org.uk**).

Evacuation was introduced in order to protect children. During the early days of the war around 30,000 children were evacuated from Birmingham and the immediate area, and schools closed until further notice. Most evacuees were put on trains to places such as Shropshire, Wales and the West Country. By the end of September 1940 the Education Committee extended the evacuation area in consequence of bombing raids. The experiences of the city's children are documented at the Birmingham Children's Lives website (**http://birmingham childrenslives.wordpress.com**). School files show how individual schools were affected and may contain lists of evacuees [LoB: class S]. Although rather dated, the LoB's Second World War Research Guide lists some further sources (**http://tinyurl.com/q4c3prp**).

At the beginning of the war all British citizens were required to register with the government, effectively creating a mini-census of the population. Records collected under the National Registration 1939 are administered by the Health and Social Care Information Centre (**www.hscic.gov.uk/register-service**). These are currently being digitized and a new service is planned (**www.1939register.co.uk**).

The Home Guard

In May 1940 the government broadcast a request for Local Defence Volunteers, the intention being to create a part-time civilian army to defend against any invasion. Within a few days 30,000 men had volunteered in Birmingham: they were organized into ten Home Guard Battalions covering all parts of the city. Although held together initially by little more than their own enthusiasm, organization was quickly tightened up and the Home Guard began to establish itself.

Towards the end of 1941 many factories began to form units drawn from their personnel, initially for the purpose of protecting their own factories. Ansells Brewery, the Birmingham Gazette, BSA, HP Sauce, and Norton Motors were among many factories that formed their own units. A Birmingham Battalion led the country in 1942 by creating the first Women Auxiliary. The idea was taken up by the War Office, which launched a national Women Auxiliary the following year. Birmingham Home Guard had its own 'Street Fighting School', known as GHQ Town Fighting Wing, located in Bristol Street.

At its peak, the Home Guard in Birmingham reached a total of 53,000. Its stand-down was finally announced when all danger of invasion had passed; the occasion was marked by a great parade through the city centre on Sunday, 3 December 1944.

The Staffs Home Guard site describes the British Home Guard and specific Home Guard units across the country and is particularly detailed for

Members of the Birmingham Home Guard, Street Fighting School outside their base at 130 Bristol Road, around 1944. (Courtesy of Chris Myers)

Birmingham and the West Midlands (**www.staffshomeguard.co.uk**). The LoB has the records of the 29th Warwickshire (Birmingham) Battalion Home Guard [MS 832]; as well as a list of prisoners of war from the Birmingham area held captive in Thailand [MS 1186]. The Don Wright Collection at Harborne Library comprises original documents relating to both the local Home Guard and the Air Raid Precautions (ARP) (**http://tinyurl.com/ouba3zq**).

The War Effort in Industry

The Luftwaffe's failure to knock out the Royal Air Force in the Battle of Britain owed much to the workers of the Spitfire factory in Castle Bromwich. By the end of the war, they were producing 320 Spitfires and twenty Lancasters a month, more aircraft than any other factory in the UK.

Although the most celebrated aspect, this is just a small part of the array of war work undertaken in Birmingham. The Longbridge factory turned out nearly three thousand Fairey Battles, Hurricanes, Stirlings and Lancasters; whilst at the nearby Austin works almost 500 army and other vehicles were made each week, as well as a multitude of other goods. Bristol Hercules engines were made at Rover; Lancaster wings, shell cases and bombs were manufactured at Fisher and Ludlow; Spitfire wings and light alloy tubing at Reynolds; and plastic components at the GEC. Other key sites were BSA, Dunlop, Kynoch (IMI), Lucas, Metropolitan-Cammell, Morris Commercial, Norton, and Wolseley. When BSA took a direct strike in November 1940, Churchill himself was alarmed at the consequent national fall in the making of rifles.

By 1944, 400,000 of the city's workers were involved in the war effort, a greater percentage of the population than anywhere else in Britain. WMRC has files relating to industrial production during this period [MSS. 180].

War Memorials and Rolls of Honour

Men and women who fell in various conflicts are commemorated in memorials and rolls of honour across the Birmingham area. These memorials and rolls cover many centuries in some cases, though concentrate mostly on the First World War and Second World War.

Following the First World War, an 'official' roll of honour was commissioned by the Lord Mayor and issued in 1925. This is available on Ancestry, as is the Birmingham section (Section VI) of the National Roll of Honour of the Great War, 1914–1918, which was compiled by subscription. Findmypast has the Birmingham Employers Roll of Honour, 1914–1918 commemorating around 1,100 soldiers from the city who died in the conflict.

The Roll of Honour website has transcripts from memorials and rolls of honour across Warwickshire, Worcestershire and Staffordshire (**www.roll-of-honour.com**). As well as later conflicts, it includes information about Birmingham's Boer War Memorial in Cannon Hill Park. Remember the Fallen contains transcripts from around 500 war memorials and rolls of honour in Worcestershire and neighbouring counties, including areas that are now within

Birmingham (**www.rememberthefallen.co.uk**). The Sutton Coldfield Great War Project aims to compile a similar index for memorials in the Sutton Coldfield area (**http://scgwp.blogspot.co.uk**). Birmingham City Council's memorials page has images and transcriptions of war memorials in council premises (**www.birmingham.gov.uk/memorials**).

Civilian cemeteries in the UK containing war graves and memorials (although not individual names) are listed at the WW1 Cemeteries site (**www.ww1cemeteries.com**). Witton and Yardley cemeteries are among those profiled. The National Railway Museum website has the roll of honour of railway employees from the conflict (**www.nrm.org.uk**). For those buried abroad see general sites, such as that of the Commonwealth War Graves Commission (**www.cwgc.org**).

Midlands Historical Data publishes many military books on CD, including rolls of honour and regimental histories (militia and territorials as well as regular units).

The Military Collection at Aldershot Public Library is a useful resource for those researching military ancestors. It comprises nearly 20,000 books, most available for loan, together with many specialist databases. The library staff will undertake searches for a nominal fee (**http://tinyurl.com/nau9c24**).

HMS *Birmingham*

Despite being virtually the furthest point in England from the sea, Birmingham has been associated with three Royal Navy vessels that have carried its name.

The first HMS *Birmingham* was a Town class light cruiser launched in 1913. On 9 August 1914, just five days after war broke out, the crew spotted the German submarine U-15 off Fair Isle. The U-boat's engines had failed and she was stuck on the surface in heavy fog. The ship opened fire but missed. As the U-boat began to dive, HMS *Birmingham* rammed her, cutting the submarine in two. U-15 went down with all hands, the first U-boat loss to an enemy warship. Later she saw action at the Battle of Jutland, where she sustained minor damage. She remained in service until 1931.

The second HMS *Birmingham* was a Town class light cruiser launched in 1936. During the Second World War she served in several theatres, including the Mediterranean, the Indian Ocean, and convoy escorts in the north Atlantic. She was broken up in 1960.

The third ship to carry the name HMS *Birmingham* was a Type 42 destroyer in service from 1976 to 1999. She spent much of her career as a Fleet Contingency Ship and following the Falklands conflict was deployed in south Atlantic waters in a patrol role.

From a much earlier period, the Warwick Quarter Sessions contains a series of orders and correspondence relating to 'the collecting of Straggling Seaman' across the county and their repatriation to 'His Majesty's fleet' during the period 1776–1782 [QS/96].

HMS *Birmingham*, 1913. (Wikimedia, Creative Commons)

The Fire Service

The Birmingham Fire Brigade was founded in 1875. At a time of national emergency, it merged with other fire brigades to form the National Fire Service in 1941, and then in 1948 reformed as the Birmingham Fire and Ambulance Service. It became part of West Midlands Fire Service in 1975.

The West Midlands Fire Service Community Heritage Group documents the history of West Midlands Fire Service and the previous fire brigades that served the West Midlands area. The group holds staff records for the Birmingham Fire Brigade from 1874–1941 and is able to offer assistance with enquiries. It also runs a small museum, which is open by appointment (contact: heritage.group@ wmfs.net).

A blog post by the Birmingham Conservation Trust describes the Birmingham Fire Office, the private initiative that pre-dated the municipal fire service (**http://tinyurl.com/o5jxd8l**).

Further Information

Terry Carter, *Birmingham Pals: A History of the Three City Battalions Raised in Birmingham in the Great War* (Pen & Sword, 2011).

Carl Chinn, *Brum Undaunted: Birmingham During the Blitz* (Brewin Books, 2005).

Jean Debney, *The Dangerfields: Munitions & Memories* (Brewin Books, 2011).

John Hartigan, 'Volunteering in the First World War: The Birmingham Experience' in *Midland History* 24/1 (1999) 167–186. Available at http://dx.doi.org/10.1179/ mdh.1999.24.1.167.

J P Lethbridge, *Birmingham in the First World War* (Newgate Press, 2012).

Michael Minton, *Heroes of The Birmingham Air Raids: A Tribute to Birmingham's Heroes 1940–1943* (Brewin Books, 2002).

Alan Tucker, *On the Trail of the Great War: Birmingham 1914–1918* (Brewin Books, 2014).

Brian Wright (ed.), *Birmingham Blitz....Our Stories* (Brewin Books, 2014).

TIMELINE OF BIRMINGHAM GENEALOGY

1715	St Philip's church consecrated
1741	*Aris's Birmingham Gazette*, Birmingham's first newspaper, launched
1749	St Bartholomew's church consecrated.
1774	St Mary's, Whittall Street consecrated
1779	St Paul's church consecrated
1786	St Peter's Catholic church, Broad Street opened
1836	General Cemetery, Key Hill opened
1837	Birmingham, Aston and Edgbaston moved from the Diocese of Lichfield & Coventry to the Diocese of Worcester
1837	Civil registration introduced. Birmingham area split across five main districts: Birmingham, Aston, Kings Norton, Solihull and West Bromwich.
1838	Birmingham receives a charter of incorporation making it a municipal borough. Includes the Aston townships of Duddeston & Nechells and Deritend & Bordesley.
1839	Birmingham Quarter Sessions and Petty Sessions courts opened; Birmingham Police founded
1848	Warstone Lane Cemetery opened
1849	Birmingham Borough Prison, Winson Green opened
1850	Birmingham Borough Lunatic Asylum, Winson Green (All Saints Hospital) opened
1850	Catholic Diocese of Birmingham established. St Chad becomes the cathedral church
1851	The Immaculate Conception, Edgbaston (The Oratory) opened
1852	Birmingham Borough Workhouse, Winson Green opened
1857	The *Birmingham Post* launched
1858	Birmingham District Probate Registry established
1889	Birmingham granted city status
1889	Birmingham Assize court opens at the Victoria Law Courts
1891	Harborne, Balsall Heath, Saltley, and Little Bromwich incorporated into the city
1897	*Sports Argus* launched

1905	Anglican Diocese of Birmingham founded. St Philip becomes the cathedral church
1909	Quinton incorporated into Birmingham
1911	Aston, Erdington, Handworth, Kings Norton, Northfield and Yardley incorporated into Birmingham
1911	Catholic Archdiocese of Birmingham created
1924	Reorganization of registration districts, creating Birmingham North and Birmingham South
1928	Perry Barr incorporated into Birmingham
1931	Castle Bromwich (west), Lyndon, Minworth (west) and North Sheldon incorporated into Birmingham
1932	Single Birmingham registration district introduced
1974	Sutton Coldfield incorporated into Birmingham. The Birmingham and Sutton Coldfield registration districts amalgamated
1974	Solihull Metropolitan Borough established

DIRECTORY OF ARCHIVES AND RESOURCES

Archives and Record Offices

Birmingham Archdiocesan Archives (BAA)

Cathedral House, St Chad's Queensway, Birmingham B4 6EU. tel: 0121 230 6252, archives@rc-birmingham.org; www.birminghamdiocese.org.uk
Holds the episcopal and administrative archives of the Catholic Archdiocese of Birmingham and its predecessors. Also houses the records of a number of Catholic charities, societies and organisations.

Black Country History

http://blackcountryhistory.org
A portal and search engine into the catalogues of eight archive and museum services within the Black Country. The partner sites are: Dudley Archives and Local History Service; Dudley Museums Service; Sandwell Community History and Archives Service; Sandwell Museums Service; Walsall Local History Centre; Walsall Museums Service; Wolverhampton Archives and Local Studies; Wolverhampton Arts and Museums Service.

Library of Birmingham, Archives, Heritage & Photography (LoB, AHP)

Centenary Square, Broad Street, Birmingham B1 2ND. tel: 0121 242 4242; archives.heritage@birmingham.gov.uk (general enquiries) and archives.appointments@ birmingham.gov.uk (appointments for the Wolfson Centre); www.libraryofbirmingham. com/archives
The Archives, Heritage & Photography (AHP) department is located on Level 4 of the new Library of Birmingham. It serves as the main archive service for the City of Birmingham and holds the official records of the Anglican Diocese of Birmingham. The Birmingham Collection is a major local history collection covering many aspects of the city's history and development.

The open research area provides access to many sources in hardcopy, microfiche and microfilm. Original documents are served in the Wolfson Centre for Archival Research for which an appointment is required; CARN tickets are accepted. Many of the archival catalogues are available to search online and include religious, official and public records. Important record sets are available on Ancestry, as the 'Library of Birmingham Collection' (see Web Resources section).

Related websites:
Library of Birmingham, Main Catalogue: http://library-opac.birmingham. gov.uk
Archives Online Catalogue: http://calmview.birmingham.gov.uk
Archives & Heritage Blog: http://theironroom.wordpress.com
Connecting Histories portal: www.connectinghistories.org.uk
Suburban Birmingham portal: www.suburbanbirmingham.org.uk

Lichfield Record Office (LRO)

The Friary, Lichfield, Staffordshire WS13 6QG. tel: 01543 510720; lichfield.record. office@staffordshire.gov.uk; www.staffordshire.gov.uk/archives
Formerly the diocesan record office for Lichfield and now part of the Staffordshire & Stoke-on-Trent Archives (see below). Its archives fall into two main categories: 1) records relating to the diocese of Lichfield and its predecessors, for which the LRO is the principal repository; 2) non-diocesan records relating to the Lichfield area, generally subsets of records held at the SSA or elsewhere. Under the first category, the LRO holds wills proved in the Consistory Court of Lichfield and in the peculiar courts, c.1520–1858; also applications for marriage licences filed in the consistory and peculiar courts, and bishops' transcripts for parishes in the historic diocese. General SSA conditions regarding access apply. *A Guide to the Contents of Lichfield Record Office* is available to purchase.

Shakespeare Birthplace Trust Record Office, The

The Shakespeare Centre, Henley Street, Stratford-upon-Avon, Warwickshire CV37 6QW. tel: 01789 204016; info@shakespeare.org.uk; www.shakespeare.org.uk/explore-shakespeare/ collections.html
The Trust is both a specialist repository for archives relating to William Shakespeare and the Royal Shakespeare Company and the local record office for Stratford-upon-Avon and the surrounding area. In the latter context, it holds materials that reference Birmingham places and inhabitants. These include: deeds, solicitors papers, family and estate papers, apprenticeship indentures, and settlements and removals.

Staffordshire & Stoke-on-Trent Archives (SSA)

Staffordshire Record Office, Eastgate Street, Stafford ST16 2LZ. tel: 01785 278379 (archive enquiries) and 01785 278373 (appointments); staffordshire.record.office@ staffordshire.gov.uk; www.staffordshire.gov.uk/archives
Gateway to the Past (online catalogue): www.archives.staffordshire.gov.uk
As the county archive service for Staffordshire, the SSA collects and preserves archives relating to Staffordshire and Stoke-on-Trent. The service currently operates across a number of sites, including the Lichfield Record Office (LRO, see above) and the William Salt Library (WSL), a specialist local history library covering Staffordshire (www.staffordshire.gov.uk/salt). Under centralization proposals currently being discussed, the WSL and LRO collections will be brought together under one roof at an extended Staffordshire Record Office (SRO) site. Appointments are necessary at all of the SSA's sites. The Service operates an independent reader registration system and CARN tickets are not accepted, although they may be used as proof of identity and address.

The National Archives (TNA)

Kew, Richmond, Surrey TW9 4DU. tel: 020 8876 3444; http://discovery. nationalarchives.gov.uk
The online search engine of The National Archives. Allows searches within many Midlands archives, as well as the TNA's own holdings.

University of Birmingham, Cadbury Research Library (UoB)

Special Collections, Cadbury Research Library, University of Birmingham, Edgbaston, Birmingham B15 2TT. tel: 0121 414 5839; special-collections@bham.ac.uk; www. birmingham.ac.uk/facilities/cadbury/index.aspx
The Cadbury Research Library holds the Special Collections and Archives of the University of Birmingham. The library is open to the public; users are required to register as a member on first visit. For family historians the main collections of interest are those for Birmingham and the wider West Midlands in relation to: charities, trade associations, hospitals and medical organizations, and sports associations. The Library also holds many personal and family papers from the Midlands, as well as the records of some local companies and political groups. The University's own archives are also held, including material relating to its forerunner, the Mason Science College.

University of Warwick, Modern Records Centre (WMRC)

University Library, University of Warwick, Coventry CV4 7AL. tel: 024 7652 4219; archives@warwick.ac.uk; www.warwick.ac.uk/services/library/mrc/
The Centre focuses on modern British social, political and economic history, in particular industrial relations and labour history. For family history purposes, the main collections of interest are those relating to UK trades unions, employers'

and trade association archives. Also records of the motor industry; radical British political groups; and pressure groups and other organizations. A series of research guides are available online, including sources by occupation. Appointments not necessary but advised; no readers ticket required.

Warwickshire County Record Office (WCRO)

Priory Park, Cape Road, Warwick CV34 4JS. tel: 01926 738959; recordoffice@ warwickshire.gov.uk; http://heritage.warwickshire.gov.uk/warwickshire-county-record-office/
Archives Unlocked (online catalogue): http://archivesunlocked.warwickshire.gov.uk/ CalmView/
As the county archive service for Warwickshire, WCRO collects, preserves and provides access to documents recording the history of the county, its people and places. The usual wide range of genealogical records is available: the collections relating to Warwick's role as the county town for Warwickshire (including Birmingham), such as the Quarter Sessions, are especially important. Appointments are not necessary but pre-ordering of original records is advised; CARN tickets are accepted. Now closed to the public for the first complete week in every calendar month - see website for details. The parish records collection and some other material are available on Ancestry.

Worcestershire Archive & Archaeology Service (WAAS)

The Hive, Sawmill Walk, The Butts, Worcester WR1 3PB. tel: 01905 822866; archive@ worcestershire.gov.uk; www.worcestershire.gov.uk/info/20019/archives_and_research
Online catalogue: http://e-services.worcestershire.gov.uk/CalmView/
Now co-located in The Hive alongside the Worcester City Library and the University of Worcester Library, the WAAS operates as the county archive and archaeology service for Worcestershire. Many family history sources are available in hardcopy, microfiche or microfilm in the self-service area which is open according to extended library hours (including Sundays). Original documents are served in the designated archives area according to a more restricted service. Appointments are not necessary for viewing original documents; CARN tickets are accepted. Several online indexes and databases, as well as downloadable research guides available via the website. Facilities also include the Historic Environment Record (HER), a database covering the county's archaeological sites, historic buildings, monuments and landscape features.

Libraries and Local Study Centres

BMSGH Reference Library

Birmingham & Midland Institute, Margaret Street, Birmingham, B3 3BS. www.bmsgh. org/library/libr1.html
Specialist library in central Birmingham operated by the Birmingham & Midland Society for Genealogy and Heraldry (see main entry below). Has all BMSGH

publications as well as other material for the area covered by the Society. The library catalogue can be downloaded at the website or contact: reference librarian@bmsgh.org.

Birmingham Community Libraries

www.libraryofbirmingham.com/article/libraries/communitylibraries
Community libraries across the city have their own local history collections and allow access to commercial family history websites. Some also have specialist family history materials for their area. See Library of Birmingham website for addresses and opening hours.

Family History Centres

Harborne: 38–42 Lordswood Road, Harborne, Birmingham B17 9QS. tel: 0121 427 6858; Sutton Coldfield: 187 Penns Lane, Sutton Coldfield B76 1JU. tel: 0121 386 4902
Access to a wide range of family history resources from the Family History Library of the LDS Church. Local centres as above (see also Solihull Library). Other centres throughout the UK, for addresses see: www.londonfhc.org/content/other-uk-centres.

Society of Genealogists

14 Charterhouse Buildings, Goswell Road, London EC1M 7BA. tel: 020 7251 8799; genealogy@sog.org.uk; www.sog.org.uk
The Society's genealogical library and education centre in Clerkenwell holds substantial material on Birmingham and the Midlands counties. See online catalogue for details.

Solihull Heritage and Local Studies, Solihull Central Library

Homer Road, Solihull B91 3RG. tel: 0121 704 6934; heritage@solihull.gov.uk; www.solihull.gov.uk/heritage
Specialist resources for tracing family history within Solihull. Also facilitates the Solihull and Birmingham Caribbean Family History Group (http://caribbean familyhistorygroup.wordpress.com/solihull_and_birmingham/) and an Irish Family History Group. The Library is an affiliate Family History Centre for the LDS Church.

Sutton Coldfield Local Studies, Sutton Coldfield Library

Lower Parade, Sutton Coldfield, Birmingham B72 1XX. tel: 0121 464 2274 (lending) or 0121 464 0165 (local studies); sutton.coldfield.reference.lib@birmingham.gov.uk; www.libraryofbirmingham.com/suttoncoldfieldlibrary
Specialist collection for local and family history in Sutton Coldfield. For catalogue see Birmingham Community Libraries entry above.

Family History Societies

Birmingham & Midland Society for Genealogy and Heraldry (BMSGH)

Jackie Cotterill, General Secretary, 5 Sanderling Court, Spennels, Kidderminster, Worcestershire DY10 4TS. gensec@bmsgh.org; www.bmsgh.org and www.bmsgh-shop.org.uk

Formed in 1963, the BMSGH covers Birmingham and the surrounding counties of Staffordshire, Warwickshire, and Worcestershire. The Society holds regular meetings in Birmingham and in eight branches across the Midlands and in London, several of which have their own websites. There is also a Heraldry Group. The Society organizes courses and coach trips to London archives. A Reference Library is located at the Birmingham & Midland Institute in central Birmingham (see above).

The BMSGH has compiled and operates a series of indexes, which are available for searches for members and non-members (see list overleaf). Costs and access conditions vary: for details see www.bmsgh.org/sea.html or contact gensec@bmsgh.org. Some datasets are available as downloads or on CD-ROM through the BMSGH Shop, which operates from a separate website (www.bmsgh-shop.org.uk or via email: bookshop@bmsgh.org).

There is also a series of parish-level directories to family history resources for Birmingham, Warwickshire and Worcestershire (see Web Resources section).

Midland Catholic History Society

Vincent Burke, Secretary, 16 Brandhall Court, Wolverhampton Road, Oldbury B68 8DE. tel: 0121 422 1573; www.midlandcatholichistory.org.uk

Promotes the study of Catholic history within the counties of Herefordshire, Shropshire, Staffordshire, Warwickshire, and Worcestershire. Publishes a regular journal, *Midland Catholic History*.

Nuneaton & North Warwickshire Family History Society

www.nnwfhs.org.uk

Family history society focusing on northern Warwickshire parishes. Publishes a quarterly journal and many publications in hardcopy and on CD-ROM.

Warwickshire Family History Society

Caroline Wetton, 31 Beaconsfield Road, Coventry CV2 4AS. chairman@wfhs.org.uk; www.wfhs.org.uk

Small family history society focusing on rural Warwickshire, offering various publications in hard copy and CD-ROM.

Table A2.1: BMSGH Indexes

Index Name	Coverage
Staffordshire	
Staffordshire Burial Index	Complete from the beginning of registers to 1837, containing all known recorded burials
Staffordshire Marriage Index	1500s to 1837 including some Roman Catholic registers
Staffordshire Monumental Inscriptions	As published by BMSGH (now available as a download)
Staffordshire Probate Index	Lists of Pre-1858 Staffordshire Probates and Administrations held at Lichfield Record Office
Warwickshire	
Aris's Birmingham Gazette	Obituaries, 1741–1861
Birmingham Index of Fines	1839–1851. Records of Petty Crimes – accused, victim, jurors, officials, crime & sentence.
Birmingham Non-Conformist Registers	1703–1858. Covers 14 chapels, births and baptisms, deaths and burials
Birmingham St Martin-in-the-Bullring, Parish Registers	Baptisms 1554–1929, marriages 1554–1903, burials 1554–1915 (with minor gaps)
Birmingham St Paul, Baptisms	1779–1897
Greater Birmingham and Black Country Burial Index	1838–c.1920 including Non-conformist, Roman Catholic, Society of Friends & cemeteries
Greater Birmingham Marriage Index	1776–1837. Includes the following parishes: All Saints, Aston, Edgbaston, Frankley, Handsworth, Harbome, Kings Norton, Northfield, Sheldon, St George, St Martin, St Philip, St Thomas and Yardley
Smith Surname Index (Birmingham)	Mid to late nineteenth century
Warwickshire Burial Index (excluding Birmingham)	1813–1837. Complete, plus about 70 parishes before 1813 with about 60 parishes after 1837
Warwickshire Marriage Index (excluding Birmingham)	1538–1837
Warwickshire Pre-1841 Census Index	About 70 pre-1841 indexes relating to 40 parishes, some only surname lists with size of household; others give ages and occupations
Warwickshire Poor Law Index	Dating from before 1834 for over 100 parishes. Including removals, settlements, apprenticeships and a few bastardy orders
Worcestershire	
Worcestershire Burial Index	Records from about 200 registers, much for the period 1660–1840, but many from a wider range
Worcestershire Marriage Index	1660–1837 (all parishes). Also many Non-conformists, Quaker, Roman Catholic and strays
Worcestershire Monumental Inscriptions	As published by BMSGH (now available as a download)

Index Name	Coverage
General	
Census and General Strays Index	Records from outside the area of people cited as coming from or having connections with Staffordshire, Warwickshire & Worcestershire.
Census Returns	1841: Solihull, Warwickshire; 1851: Full transcriptions for Staffordshire and Warwickshire
London Guildhall Apprentices	17 & 18c apprentices from Staffordshire, Warwickshire & Worcestershire
Unwanted Certificates Index	Birth, marriage & death certificates donated by family historians. Name index downloadable from the Society's online shop

Notes: For further details, including costs and enquiries, see **www.bmsgh.org/search/sea.html**

Publishers

Amberley Publishing

The Hill, Stroud, Gloucestershire GL5 4EP. tel: 01453 847800; www.amberleybooks.com
General histories, transport history, and the '*...Through Time*' and '*...From Old Photographs*' series on Midlands subjects and places.

Archive CD Books

Family History Research Ltd., Suite 14 Old Anglo House, Mitton Street, Stourport-on-Severn DY13 9AQ. tel: 01299 828374; www.familyhistoryresearch.org
Offers a range of genealogical and historical data on CD: trade directories, parish registers, census records, heralds visitations, with many Birmingham and Midlands titles.

Brewin Books

Doric House, 56 Alcester Road, Studley, Warwickshire B80 7LG. tel: 01527 854228; admin@brewinbooks.com; www.brewinbooks.com
Many local history titles for Birmingham and the Midlands, including books by local historians Carl Chinn and Alton Douglas. Also the '*...Remembered*' series for Birmingham suburbs.

Family History Indexes

14 Copper Leaf Close, Moulton, Northampton NN3 7HS. tel: 01604 495106; info@fhindexes.co.uk; www.fhindexes.co.uk
Offers a range of genealogical data on CD, notably the Criminal Registers and Criminal Lunatics Registers held at The National Archives, and militia musters and other military records.

History Press, The

*The Mill, Brimscombe Port, Stroud, Gloucestershire GL5 2QG. tel: 01453 883300;
web@thehistorypress.co.uk; www.thehistorypress.co.uk*
Birmingham-related publications are a mixture of thematic titles (e.g. pubs, shops
and shopping, canals) and histories of particular suburbs and localities.

Midlands Historical Data

enquiries@midlandshistoricaldata.org; www.midlandshistoricaldata.org
Digitized resources for local and family historians relating to Shropshire,
Staffordshire, Warwickshire (including Birmingham) and Worcestershire.
Includes directories, local history books, electoral rolls, regimental histories and
indexes.

Staffordshire Parish Registers Society

*Ian Wallbank, Secretary, 82 Hillport Avenue, Newcastle-under-Lyme, Staffordshire ST5
8QT. sec@sprs.org.uk; www.sprs.org.uk*
Formed in 1901, the Society publishes parish registers for the historic county of
Staffordshire.

Staffordshire Record Society

The Hon. Secretary, c/o The William Salt Library, Eastgate Street, Stafford, ST16 2LZ.
The Staffordshire Record Society originated in 1879 as the William Salt
Archaeological Society. It publishes books and transcriptions of records on the
history of the county under the title *Collections for a History of Staffordshire* (list at:
www.genuki.org.uk/big/eng/STS/Bibliography/CHS.html).

Web Resources

Only gateway resources, i.e. those mentioned multiple times in the main text, are
listed here.

Ancestry, www.ancestry.co.uk

http://collections.ancestry.co.uk/search/UK/LibraryofBirmingham
Hosts the official Library of Birmingham Collection, comprising digitized
original records from the Birmingham Archives, Heritage & Photography service.
The collection includes: Church of England parish registers; calendars of
prisoners from Birmingham Quarter Sessions; and an extensive series of rate
books. Ancestry also has substantial holdings sponsored by Warwickshire CRO,
including: parish registers for rural Warwickshire parishes; occupational and
Quarter Sessions records; land tax; and some coverage for the Warwickshire
militia and the poor law. Latest additions and updates to the collections are
accessible via the relevant county pages:

http://search.ancestry.co.uk/Places/UK/England/Staffordshire/Default.aspx
http://search.ancestry.co.uk/Places/UK/England/Warwickshire/Default.aspx
http://search.ancestry.co.uk/Places/UK/England/Worcestershire/Default.aspx

FamilySearch, www.familysearch.org

The massive family history website maintained by the Church of Jesus Christ of Latter Day Saints (Mormons). A key resource for parish register and census data. The FamilySearch Wiki, http://familysearch.org/learn/wiki/en/England, has articles on genealogical research within English counties written and maintained by volunteers.

FHS Online, www.fhs-online.co.uk

Portal, operated by S&N Genealogy Supplies Ltd, offering databases and other products produced by family history societies across the country. Within the West Midlands, offerings include censuses for several counties, Worcestershire boat records, and Worcestershire poll books.

Findmypast, www.findmypast.co.uk

Commercial website owned by DC Thomson Family History. Specialist Midlands offerings include: the Staffordshire Collection, the Shropshire Collection, indexes to Lichfield wills, registers from major Birmingham cemeteries, and strong regional coverage within the National Burial Index.

FreeBMD, www.freebmd.org.uk

Non-commercial site that aims to transcribe the Civil Registration indexes of births, marriages and deaths for England and Wales, and provide free online access to the transcribed records.

GENUKI, www.genuki.org.uk/big/eng/WAR/Birmingham

Non-commercial directory of genealogical resources across the UK and Ireland. Many useful links available via the Birmingham and individual county pages.

Origins.net, www.origins.net

Commercial website now owned by DC Thomson Family History. Includes the National Wills Index and good coverage of London apprenticeships. Data is gradually being integrated into Findmypast.

Staffordshire Name Indexes, www.staffsnameindexes.org.uk

A series of online indexes taken from the records held by the Staffordshire & Stoke on Trent Archives. Subjects include: apprentices, canal boats, jurors, police officers, prisoners, workhouses and wills.

Staffordshire Place Guide, www.staffordshire.gov.uk/leisure/archives/history/placeguide

A finding aid for information on Staffordshire parishes, maintained by Staffordshire & Stoke-on-Trent Archives. Information is summarized under various headings, with direct links to the online catalogue, Gateway to the Past. As yet, not all parishes are covered.

Staffordshire Places, www.places.staffspasttrack.org.uk

Also maintained by Staffordshire & Stoke-on-Trent Archives and rather confusingly named, this website showcases examples of archive sources for a variety of places in Staffordshire.

Tracing Your Ancestors in Birmingham, www.bmsgh.org/TYAIB/birmingham.html

An online directory of resources for Birmingham research, maintained by the BMSGH. Comprises inventories of parish registers (including non-conformist) and rate books at the Library of Birmingham; and lists of Birmingham cemeteries and burial grounds.

Tracing Your Ancestors in Warwickshire, www.bmsgh.org/parish/warw/tyaiw/index.htm

An online directory of resources for Warwickshire parishes, maintained by the BMSGH.

Worcestershire Parish Guide, www.worcesterbmsgh.co.uk/parishes

An online directory of resources for Worcestershire parishes, maintained by the Worcester Branch of the BMSGH. Has good coverage for those Worcestershire parishes subsequently incorporated into Birmingham.

Miscellaneous

Birmingham Coroner's Court

HM Coroner for the City of Birmingham and the Borough of Solihull
50 Newton Street, Birmingham B4 6NE
tel: 0121 303 3228; coroner@birmingham.gov.uk
Enquiries re inquests subject to the seventy-five year closure restriction.

Birmingham District Probate Registry

The Priory Courts, 33 Bull Street, Birmingham B4 6DU
tel: 0121 681 3400; birminghamdprenquiries@hmcts.gsi.gov.uk
Holds all original wills proved at Birmingham, as well as some proved at Lichfield and Worcester.

Birmingham Register Office

Holliday Wharf, Holliday Street, Birmingham B1 1TJ. tel: 0121 675 1000; register.office@birmingham.gov.uk; www.birmingham.gov.uk/registeroffice
Holds civil birth, marriage and death registers for historical registration districts in the Birmingham area. Facilities for ordering searches and certificates online.

Local History

The following is a list of local history societies, groups and general websites for Birmingham districts. Organized societies and groups are shown in **bold**, others appear to be personal sites.

Acocks Green History Society: http://aghs.jimdo.com
Allens Cross: http://allenscross.wordpress.com
Astonbrook Through Aston Manor: www.astonbrook-through-astonmanor.co.uk
Balsall Heath Local History Society: www.balsallheathhistory.co.uk
Barr and Aston Local History Society: http://myweb.tiscali.co.uk/greatbarrhall/balhs.htm
Bartley Green & District History Group: http://bgdhg.co.uk
Birmingham Canal Navigations Society: www.bcnsociety.co.uk
Cotteridge: www.cotteridge.com
Great Barr, Past & Present B43: www.b43.co.uk
Hall Green Local History Society: www.hallgreenlocalhistorysociety.org.uk
Handsworth Historical Society: www.handsworth-history.org
The Harborne Society: www.theharbornesociety.org.uk
Hay Mills & Tyseley: http://reynoldstechnology.biz
Jewellery Quarter Research Group: www.jqrg.org
Kings Heath Local History Society: www.kingsheathhistory.co.uk
Kings Heath & District History B14: www.bhamb14.co.uk
Kings Norton Local History Society: www.kingsnorton.info
Kingstanding Voices: http://kingstanding.wordpress.com
Ladywood Past & Present: www.oldladywood.co.uk
Marston Green: www.bickenhillparishcouncil.org.uk/History/history.html
Moseley Society: www.moseley-society.org.uk and www.moseleyhistory.co.uk
Perry Barr and Beyond: www.perrybarrbeyond.pwp.blueyonder.co.uk
Quinton Local History Society: www.qlhs.org.uk
Solihull Local History Circle: www.solihullarts.co.uk/local-history
Sutton Coldfield A-Z: www.suttoncoldfieldatoz.com
Ward End/ Washwood Heath: http://metcam.co.uk.nstempintl.com
Winson Green to Brookfields: www.ted.rudge.btinternet.co.uk
Yardley: http://aghs.jimdo.com/ (Acocks Green History Society)

The following are part of community history projects run by Birmingham City Council:
Digital Balsall Heath: www.digitalbalsallheath.org.uk
Digital Handsworth: www.digitalhandsworth.org.uk
Digital Ladywood: www.digital-ladywood.org.uk

INDEX